LET'S GET THIS STRAIGHT

Gerald P. Mallon

LET'S GET THIS STRAIGHT

A Gay- and Lesbian-Affirming Approach to Child Welfare

 COLUMBIA UNIVERSITY PRESS   NEW YORK

Columbia University Press
Publishers Since 1893
New York   Chichester, West Sussex

Library of Congress Cataloging-in-Publication Data
Mallon, Gerald P.
    Let's get this straight : a gay- and lesbian-affirming approach to child
welfare / Gerald P. Mallon
       p.   cm.
    Includes bibliographical references and index.
    ISBN 0-231-11136-3 cl
    ISBN 0-231-11137-1 pa
    1. Social work with gay youth. 2. Social work for lesbian youth.
    3. Gay youth—Services for. 4. Lesbian youth—Services for. I. Title.

    HV1426.M35 2000
    362.7′086′640973—dc21
                                                 99-054305

Casebound editions of Columbia University Press books are
printed on permanent and durable acid-free paper.
Printed in the United States of America
c 10 9 8 7 6 5 4 3 2 1
p 10 9 8 7 6 5 4 3 2 1

For Peg McCartt Hess

Contents

Preface   IX

Acknowledgments   XIII

Introduction: Reinventing Child Welfare Services   1

1   Competent Child Welfare Services for Gay/Lesbian Children, Youth, and Their Families   13

2   Keeping Families Together: Family-Centered Services and Issues of Sexual Orientation   35

3   Protecting Gay/Lesbian Children and Youth: Issues of Abuse, Neglect, and Familial Violence   57

4   Sexual Orientation and the Law: Legal Issues in Child Welfare   79

5   Gays and Lesbians as Adoptive and Foster Parenets   93

6   Meeting the Needs of Gay/Lesbian Children and Youth in Out-of-Home-Care Placements   109

7   Runaways and Homeless Gay and Lesbian Youth   127

8   Locked in the Child Welfare Closet–Who's Got the Key?   143

References   153

Index   183

Preface

Since 1990 I have spent a great deal of time traveling across the United States and internationally to lecture, train, and challenge child welfare policy makers and practitioners to broaden their vision of serving children, youth, and families to include the needs and experiences of *gay* and *lesbian* children, youth, and families. During these past nine years, I have been invited to speak in thirty-nine states, especially in the Deep South, I have participated in over fifty different conferences, most of which were hosted by mainstream child welfare organizations, and I have engaged in dialogue with thousands of colleagues in hundreds of child welfare agencies. Many colleagues were welcoming, open-minded about engaging in colloquy and, I believe, genuinely interested in beginning the process of creating more affirming environments for gay and lesbian children, youth, and families in their organizations.

I have come to have more understanding of my child welfare colleagues by listening to their accounts of their struggle about how to best develop a capacity for addressing the needs of this particular group. By visiting their agencies and meeting thousands of gay and lesbian children, youth, and families, I have also learned how much their lives are directly affected by the services the field does or does not provide.

My experiences at conferences were powerful preludes into the world of professionally appropriate public behavior versus the sometimes personally biased conduct that I was to encounter many times in the course of conducting these training sessions. In designing and framing training sessions for child welfare practitioners I intentionally claimed a morally neutral perspective of sexual orientation, offering gay and lesbian life as a *normal* variation of sexual orientation. My overarching goal was to replace the many myths and stereotypes about gay and lesbian persons with accurate, relevant, and professionally based information. I assumed, incorrectly I am afraid, that if consciousness could be raised about the real issues that affect gay and lesbian children, youth, and families, then professionals would stop acting on their heterocentrism and would understand bias as a civil rights issue and work against it, because certainly (I believed) all social workers are ethically opposed to violating an individual's civil rights.

Many times I realized this goal. At the conclusion of the training I was certain that it was effective in helping to transform a child welfare professional's notion of practice with gay and lesbian children, youths, and families, but with some groups, the goals of training fell short. In these cases, I was left feeling disheartened, exasperated, and distressed that despite my best efforts, the participants could not accept the information that was offered to them.

Teaching, writing, and advocating for the best interests of this special group within a child welfare context has been a very challenging experience. With very few exceptions (DeCrescenzo 1994; Faria 1994; Laird 1996; Stein 1996; Steinhorn 1979; Sullivan 1994; Ricketts 1991; Ricketts and Achtenberg 1990) I seldom, if ever, have encountered anyone else who was writing, researching, or lecturing about the needs of these particular individuals. Perhaps such an occurrence would normally be a scholar's dream, to be the only one, but I often found that this role to be a solitary one that left me feeling disconnected and isolated from many colleagues and peers in the field of children and family services. What was most distressing was my own awareness that every day thousands of gay and lesbian children, youth, and families come to child welfare agencies when they are in dire need of support and instead find, in many instances, an organization and its professionals thoroughly unprepared and, in some cases, unwilling to respond to their needs. This to me seemed an unethical violation requiring a prompt remedy.

From a philosophical perspective, I have also grappled with the twin roles of scholar and child welfare advocate. Complex as it has been to balance the two, I do not see scholarship and advocacy as mutually exclusive categories that must never intersect with one another. If we consider ourselves as social workers and child welfare professionals, I believe we are ethically bound, at various points in working with a client system, to be both advocate and objective party. As scholar, giving up one's cloak of academic objectivity to put on the role of advocate can be a frightening prospect, but it is sometimes a necessary responsibility.

My work has of course been tremendously colored by my personal emotions and my life experiences as a gay man and one who spent thirty-one years pretending to be heterosexual. It is also influenced by my experiences as a 24-year veteran child welfare professional and a parent. These experiences have deeply affected my teaching, my advocacy work, my clinical practice, and what I have chosen to study. Nonetheless, for me, the roles of scholar and advocate are complementary, inextricably intertwined, and evident in this book.

Let's Get This Straight: A Gay- and Lesbian-Affirming Approach to Child Welfare is my attempt to bring all of these experiences together. *Let's Get This Straight* is intended to enhance the reader's knowledge of gay and lesbian children, youth, and families within the traditionally defined domains of child welfare practice.

The book represents a first attempt to present a body of knowledge about and introduce a gay- and lesbian-affirming perspective for assessing the effects of traditional child welfare policies and services for gay and lesbian children, youths, and families. Trends in developing a broadened conceptualization of family, dealing with societal stigmatization, and abolishing myths and stereotypes about gays/lesbians are described throughout.

With the publication of this book, I hope to raise the importance of sexual orientation in the field of family and children's services. In future discourses on public policy and practice, as solutions to child and family troubles are sought, the critical variable of sexual orientation must be addressed with sensitivity and without bias.

Acknowledgments

In researching and writing *Let's Get This Straight* I have incurred debts of gratitude to many people. One of the most pleasant aspects in preparing the manuscript is the opportunity to thank them within its pages.

Several years ago, when no one else would even think of doing so because they thought that the topic was so controversial, Davis Tobis from the Family Policy Center at Hunter College gave me a generous grant through the Child Welfare Fund to work toward reforming the child welfare system for gay and lesbian young people in New York City. I was grateful to him and to the benefactor of the fund, who remains anonymous, for placing their faith in me with such an challenging task. One of the goals of that first grant was to organize a conference to educate New York City child welfare professionals about gay and lesbian children, youth, and families. This task had never been undertaken before and in November 1996 we held the first conference on Issues of Social Orientation in Child Welfare at the Hunter College School of Social Work; we have held two more since the first. That first conference provided me with the framework and the idea for writing this book, but without the support of David Tobis and the Child Welfare Fund, it would literally have never been possible. My gratitude to David and to the Fund is immense.

I have been blessed by having many child welfare colleagues in my twenty-four years in the field and I wanted to take this opportunity to thank some of them. My colleagues at Green Chimneys Children's Services in New York City and in Brewster, but especially the young people and staff at the Gramercy Residence, have always provided a safe haven for me to test my ideas and a place for me to call homebase after being on the road in the lecture circuit. I am always grateful to them for the care, understanding, and compassion that they have always shown me. I am also grateful to my

West Coast colleagues at G.L.A.S.S. (Gay and Lesbian Adolescent Social Services) in Los Angeles, particularly to Teresa De Crescenzo and Wendell Glenn and to my warm and wonderful friends down south at the Southern Christian Services for Children and Families in Jackson, Mississippi, especially to Sue and Chris Cherney, as they too have always provided me with a rich source of support, friendship, and information.

To be a member of the faculty of one of the best schools of Social Work at the City University of New York is a great privilege for me. At Hunter College I have the pleasure of having many good colleagues, and I would like to acknowledge two of them here—Dean Bogart Leashore, whose own book, *Child Welfare: An Africentric Perspective*, was a guide for my work in this book and my good colleague Irwin Epstein, who has always been a professional role model for me and a great supporter of me and my work. My appreciation is also extended to my other faculty associates at Hunter who have invited me into an environment that has nurtured and respected good teaching, sound practice, and honorable scholarship.

There have also been several people—good colleagues, good friends—who have also been closely connected with this book, and they deserve mention.

John Michel, my editor at Columbia University Press, is a man of exceptional good humor and is a genuine pleasure to work with. Alex Thorpe of Columbia University Press was also most helpful in bringing this book to print. The reviewers of my manuscript for the Press, who are anonymous, and my colleagues whom I impose upon to read and give me feedback, namely Sam Ross from Green Chimneys, Nina Aledort from the New Neutral Zone, and Marvin Peguese from the Lambda Legal Defense Fund, provided generous and thoughtful comments which I believe strengthened the work.

Mike Rendino, my partner, and our boys, Ian and Travis, provide the type of deep sustaining support that is almost impossible to express in words. My family is always so patient with me when I am traveling or immersed in writing and in doing so, they have taught me so much about the meaning of love and what it means to be part of a loving family.

Finally, I would like to acknowledge Peg McCartt Hess. Peg was my mainstay while I was on the faculty of the Columbia University School of Social Work. During my appointment there, and since I have left, Peg has read each word of every manuscript that I submitted for publication, including this one. She has consistently provided thoughtful, prompt, and generous feedback every time that I have asked her to read for me. Peg is a remarkable woman, a consummate professional, a social worker extraordinare, a university administrator of integrity and honor, and a bona fide model for me and others. More than anything else, however, Peg is a remarkably kind, compassionate, and a real human being. I am immensely grateful for her support and for her friendship. For these reasons and for others which are firmly placed in deep emotions and therefore not possible to put into words, I dedicate this book to her.

LET'S GET THIS STRAIGHT

Reinventing Child Welfare Services

Across the United States and Canada, gay and lesbian persons are challenging the social presumptions that have kept them marginalized and invisible. Current child welfare policies, however, continue to reflect the dominant heterocentric values of society as they relate to children, youth, and families in general and to the historic oppression of gay and lesbian persons in particular.

THE IMPACT OF HETEROCENTRISM

Despite the gains made by gays and lesbians in the last forty years, a significant number of Americans continue to believe that gays and lesbians get the treatment they deserve—as second-class citizens or even worse (Reiter 1991). Social scientists have called this phenomenon "homophobia" (fear of homosexuals or homosexuality) (De Crescenzo 1985; Gramick 1983; Hudson and Ricketts 1980); I prefer to label it *heterocentrism*.

Heterocentrism is understood as a result of heterosexual privilege or heterosexism and is analogous to racism, sexism, and other ideologies of oppression (Pharr 1988). Heterocentrism, which I feel most accurately describes the systemic display of gay and lesbian discrimination in major legal and social institutions—in this case the child welfare system—has as its primary assumption that the world is and should be forever heterosexual. This assumption, illustrated most clearly by heterosexual privilege, causes gay/lesbian children, youth, and families to engage in a constant search for a good fit between their individual natures, which are stigmatized by Western society (and usually by their biological families), and their environments, which are generally hostile and void of nutrients necessary for healthy growth. It is within this context that child welfare services are delivered to those in need. Other issues are best understood juxtaposed against a backdrop of heterocentrism (Raymond 1992). Gay/lesbian persons may experience systemic antigay and antilesbian discrimination from health care providers, from teachers and school administrators, from employers, and from those within the legal system (Hunter and Polikoff 1976).

Antigay and antilesbian sentiment, which is prevalent in Western society as well as the field of child and family services (Mallon 1998), acts as a social control mechanism, one purpose being to discourage gays/lesbians from becoming more visible. Although there has been a movement toward openness about one's sexual orientation,* many gays and lesbians (perhaps the majority) are painstakingly guarded not to disclose their orientation to others (Berger 1990; Cain 1991), especially to their own relatives. A major result is that gay/lesbian persons remain a largely unknown and invisible minority, this inspite of the persistent belief that lesbians and gays are easily identifiable by their appearance and behavior. There is no doubt that the invisibility of so many lesbians and gays contributes to the widespread stereotypes and myths. These exist precisely because nongays seldom notice those gays/lesbians who do not look or act according to their prejudicial patterns. The hostility that many heterosexuals hold toward gays/lesbians is justification for many gays/lesbians,especially children and adolescents, to remain hidden.

A related theory is that one of the primary social functions of antigay and lesbian sentiment is to preserve and promote power hierarchies that are traditionally based on conventional gender roles (Pharr 1988; Ricketts 1991). Evidence of this was present in a trio of appalling events in 1998: the bigotry of U.S. Senate Majority Leader Trent Lott, who equated homosexuality to kleptomania; the brutal murder of Matthew Sheppard at the hands of despicable thugs in Wyoming; and the Child Welfare Review Panel of the State of Arkansas as it moves to ban gay and lesbian persons from being foster parents in that state.

---

*Although sexual orientation denotes heterosexuality as well as homosexuality and bisexuality, sexual orientation becomes an issue only for those not in the majority. This chapter and the use of the term sexual orientation throughout this book concentrates on same-gendered sexual orientation.

As in the larger social systems, heterocentrism informs much of the child welfare practices and social policies concerning gays and lesbians. Heterosexual privilege underlies all of the statutes, regulations, and case laws that govern child welfare programs in the United States. In view of this concept, the need for a gay and lesbian perspective in child welfare issues is especially crucial. The fact that it has not been presented heretofore is directly linked to heterocentrism and the ubiquitous societal stigma which posits that lesbian and gay persons are sick, sinful, or deviant and which endures despite evidence to the contrary. It is for these reasons that I propose the need for viewing these child welfare policies, practices, and programs from the dual positions of heterocentrism and a gay- and lesbian-affirming perspective.

DISREGARDING SEXUAL ORIENTATION

The following case[*] illustrates the negative consequences of ignoring a child's sexual orientation as a factor in planning for that child in a residential treatment center (RTC). The family characteristics illustrated more or less resemble those of many families who have children placed in foster care.

LONNIE

Lonnie is an African-American 9-year-old with a full scale I.Q. of 105. He was referred at the request of the residential treatment center team members where he had been placed by his adoptive parents. Lonnie had lived at the RTC for two months after his adoptive par-

[*]Cases presented in this book are taken from interviews I conducted with gay and lesbian children, youth, and families whose lives have been affected by the child welfare system and the staff members and professionals who work with them, in the following 16 states: Arizona, California, Connecticut, Florida, Indiana, Illinois, Massachusetts, Minnesota, Missouri, Mississippi, New Jersey, New York, Oklahoma, Pennsylvania, Texas, and Utah between 1991 and 1999. The names of all those interviewed have been changed or omitted to insure confidentiality. The names of other individuals mentioned in these quotes or the names of most child welfare agencies have also been changed to protect the confidentiality of the informants.

ents voluntarily placed him to "change his negative behavior." The treatment staff asked for me to evaluate his Axis I Primary Diagnosis of Gender Identity Disorder, which his social worker misinterpreted to indicate that he was gay.

Lonnie presented as an average height, slightly built, dark-skinned African-American child. He was dressed appropriately in gender-typical male clothing (jeans, t-shirt, and sneakers). He was friendly, engaged, and polite throughout the interview. When I asked why he had been placed in the RTC he replied "because I do not behave the way they want me to in my adoptive family's home." When I asked him to elaborate, he first said, "I didn't act like the other boys, and then went on to tell me about physical and sexual abuse in prior foster homes. In one case he described the physical abuse that had resulted in the permanent loss of sight in one eye. It was clear to me at this point that this child's primary Axis I diagnosis, irrespective of his sexual orientation, which at this point I was unable to determine, should have been Post Traumatic Stress Disorder (PTSD), due to his physical abuse, not Gender Identity Disorder.

Lonnie appeared to be very comfortable in his identity as a male child and gave no indication that he desired to be a girl. There was some foreshadowing that, while comfortable within his gender identification as a male, Lonnie might later identify as gay. For example, when asked about his career goals he responded that he had artistic talent and wanted to be a dress designer (a rather stereotypical gay career choice, which might have been the only information that he had about gay people). He also volunteered rather strongly that "no matter what, I am not getting married to a woman." This assertion was unsolicited, and when probed further Lonnie replied, "if you get married to a lady, it will just end in divorce and then it's just bad for everybody"—an interesting but not an unusual connection for a child who has lived through multiple placements.

Lonnie denied sexual activity or interest in either girls or boys, but noted that sometimes the other boys teased him about not being active in sports and not being interested in rough-housing. Though he said that he did not like teasing, his responses indicated that it was manageable for him. Child welfare staff, who were met with prior to the interview, viewed his mannerisms as effeminate, but he himself did not see his mannerisms as atypical.

My recommendation to the team was to change his Axis I Primary Diagnosis from Gender Identity Disorder to Post-Traumatic Stress Disorder due to history of physical abuse. When the treatment team asked if he were gay, I replied that I did not have sufficient information to make a determination about his sexual identity status at this point, particularly because Lonnie himself did not identify as gay or even mention feeling "different," the term that most young people use at this time.

Three years later, when Lonnie was twelve and scheduled for discharge from the RTC to his adoptive family I was asked to meet again with him and his parents. Lonnie's family were convinced that he was, as they had been told, gender identity disordered. Fearful of what this meant, they were requesting that the agency or some health care facility conduct a chromosomal test to determine whether he was more of a girl or a boy. Since no such test existed, except to determine the genetic predisposition of hermaphrodites, the treatment team felt that his parents needed to meet with an expert. Mr. and Mrs. Johnson at this point were insisting that if Lonnie was going to "continue acting that way" he could not return to their home, but they were willing to meet with me.

Prior to meeting with the parents I met alone with Lonnie, who had grown significantly into a preadolescent since our last meeting. When I asked if he knew why we were meeting, he vaguely responded yes. Rather than talk in his social worker's office, we went for a walk around the grounds of the RTC where he lived. When we came to a bench outside of the maintenance department, we sat and talked. I used a narrative to tell him a story about a boy who grew up feeling "different." I asked if he knew anyone who felt like the boy in the story and he replied "that's how I feel." And then, pointing to another child who happened to be walking by, he said, "See that boy over there?" "Yes," I replied. "He's like me, too." When I asked what he meant, he said, "We talk, he feels like me and that boy you told me about in the story."

When questioned about his treatment at the RTC, he denied being verbally harassed by staff, but noted that sometimes the other kids' teasing got to him. It was at those times, he noted that he sought out the friendship of the other boy he had pointed out. When I asked if he had any questions, he said, "Yes, could you please tell me what 'gay' means." I defined it as boys who knew in their hearts that they liked other boys as more than just friends. He replied, "Oh, that's how I feel." I assured him that however he felt, even if he wasn't sure how he felt, it was all right and that there were other young people who also felt like him. I told him that he was not sick, or disturbed, or weird. I assured him that I supported him and asked for his permission to talk about this with his family. He said if it helped to stop his parents from trying to make him change, he was happy for me to talk with his parents.

Mr. and Mrs. Johnson were a Caucasian couple in their late 50's, married for over thirty-five years, and were devout Roman Catholics. They were the parents of four grown birth children and six adopted children, including Lonnie. All of their adopted children were African American with long histories of multiple placements and multiple problems. The Johnsons resided in an affluent suburb of a large northeastern city. Mrs. Johnson was a psychiatric nurse, her husband was a retired elementary school teacher. Their affection for Lonnie and their other children, all of whom accompanied them on this visit to the RTC to see Lonnie, was apparent. I met privately with them together.

I introduced myself and said that the agency had asked me to meet with them and to conduct an assessment of their son Lonnie. Mrs. Johnson, who was the more talkative of the couple, immediately began by saying that she was interested in having Lonnie tested. "Tested for what?" I asked. Tested to see if he had some sort of chromosomal abnormality. I asked why she thought this was necessary. She replied, "Well he has been diagnosed with gender identity disorder and we would like to ascertain to which gender he has a greater affinity." She went on: "He has been having problems on home visits and we just can't have him acting like he has been acting." When I asked how he was acting, she replied "like a girl." I asked her to describe what she meant and she said he was very effeminate and appeared to her and her husband to be more like a girl than like a boy.

At this point I interjected that based on my assessment of her son, whom I had met at age nine and then again at age twelve, was not gender identity disordered. Mrs. Johnson asked what I thought his true diagnosis was and I replied Post Traumatic Stress Disorder as a result of the physical abuse he had endured earlier. More directly she inquired, "I know that but, Dr. Mallon, do you think our son is gay?" I said, "Yes, based on our interview today and my observations from three years ago, I believe, and today Lonnie confirmed it for me, that your son is gay."

At this point, I was prepared for the worst possible response, but Mrs. Johnson surprised me by saying, "Thank you, you are the first person to ever answer us honestly." She then surprised me further by saying: "What can we do to help him?" Affected by her compassion, I replied, "Just let him know that you love him, just as he is. Help him to feel good about who he is. Continue to educate yourselves about what it means to rear a gay child."

They asked if I could be a resource, if there was information that they could read, and if there were any support groups that they could take part in. I supplied them with all of the information they requested and helped them to see that sexual orientation was not just sexual behavior, since they expressed concern about Lonnie's potential for engaging in sexual experimentation with his siblings. The strengths of this couple were without a doubt their openness to new information, and rather than being shocked by their child's differentness, they embraced it. I asked if we could then all meet together with Lonnie and they agreed.

When Lonnie entered he seemed apprehensive, but quickly relaxed when I said, "I met with your Mom and Dad and we talked about what it means for some people to feel different, to be gay." His mother immediately reassured him that his difference did not make her feel different toward him, in fact, she asserted, "your Dad and I have been seen by others as different all of our lives. Difference does not scare us." We spoke about continuing to meet and groups that might help the whole family. We also addressed Mrs. Johnson's concern about sexual experimentation and made it clear that this was an issue both Mr. and Mrs. Johnson felt strongly about. I reiterated that if his brothers tried to sexually experiment with Lonnie, he should feel free to discuss it with his parents as it might not always be at his initiation.

We stopped at this point and agreed to meet again in a week. We exchanged phone numbers and made an appointment. Later that summer, Lonnie was finally discharged to his family and they agreed to continue in therapy with the agency to work on family issues surrounding his sexual orientation.

In Lonnie's case, traditional assessments and intervention strategies had proven to be ineffectual for him and his family. Beginning with the psychiatrists' inappropriate diagnosis of gender identity disorder (since no diagnosis for homosexuality has existed since it was deleted in 1973, many clinicians erroneously use the gender identity disorder label if they detect an issue with sexual orientation) and given the clinicians' ostensible inability to diagnosis this child from a gay- or lesbian-affirming perspective, Lonnie and his family did not get the quality of child welfare services they deserved.

Had the agency not contracted with an expert in sexual orientation issues, Lonnie might have received treatment that continued to focus on changing him rather than affirming who he was. Lonnie's parents were frustrated by the clinicians who could not provide them with an answer about their child's identity. Many uninformed clinicians believe that it is not possible for a child to identity as gay or lesbian—when it is clear that some children are perfectly able to distinguish their sexual identity. I wrote about this anomaly in an earlier work (Mallon 1998:20):

> Why is it so difficult for child welfare professionals to detect and acknowledge the existence of gay and lesbian adolescents in their midst? There has always been a widespread assumption held by researchers and many practitioners that all children and adolescents are heterosexual. For children who identify as lesbian, gay, or bisexual, this assumption represents a major life stressor. The idea that a child or an adolescent could identify as a lesbian, gay, or bisexual individual is inconceivable to many.

While most professionals are convinced that it was "too soon" for an adolescent or a child to identify as lesbian, gay, or bisexual, the same professionals were equally convinced that every young person was heterosexual.

Lonnie needed information about his emerging sexual identity, as did his parents. Like most gay young people he had little accurate information about what it meant to be gay. His parents and his siblings also had limited insight into what it meant to have a gay-identified family member. Both parents and siblings were in need of support and information.

The treatment team also needed training and technical assistance in how to address issues of sexual orientation in their client population. The fact that Lonnie could identify another gay youngster as his peer but they could not suggests that professionals are looking only for children who conform to the stereotypical images of gay youngsters, which, as previously mentioned, is a narrow approach to practice.

A gay- and lesbian-affirming perspective is necessary to grasp the complexity and subtlety of any gay or lesbian client. A great deal of the available information about practice with gay/lesbian persons, especially in the child welfare context, has been at best sketchy. The limitations of traditional approaches that do not consider issues of sexual orientation lead to incomplete pictures of how to work with children, youth, and families whose lives are affected by issues of sexual orientation. These limitations can be minimized by 1) designing conceptual frameworks that provide a sound foundation for understanding the importance of issues of sexual orientation; 2) incorporating knowledge about gay and lesbian persons, including values, beliefs, attitudes, and behaviors into sound practice; and 3) designing appropriate and affirming service-delivery systems based on this knowledge and free from antigay/antilesbian bias.

PURPOSE AND GOALS

I had several reasons for writing this book. First, and most obvious, is that there is such a shortage of scholarship about this topic and there is a profound need for the experiences of gay/lesbian children, youth, and families to be heard. Second, there is a strong suggestion that the provision of child welfare services has failed these children, youth, and families. Third, the evolution of a gay- and lesbian-affirming perspective of gay- and lesbian-headed families and gay and lesbian childhood and adolescent development provides an alternative framework for training future generations of professionals to serve these human beings without further reliance on myths and stereotypes to guide their practice.

My first goal is to reframe the public discourse on child welfare issues in light of the experiences of gay and lesbian persons since the Adoption Assistance and Child Welfare Act of 1980 and more currently with respect to the new legislation of the Adoption and Safe Families Act of 1997. Despite all efforts since the passage of these landmark pieces of legislation, gay/lesbian children, youth, and families have received very little attention in the public sector. The reality of their existence rarely enters public debate. Gay/lesbian children are part of the population on which this nation's future depends. Presently the journey of most of them is discouraging. Most are socialized to hide or forced into silence because they have determined that it is unsafe to be open about their orientation within environments that they have found to be hostile to their existence. Something more than politically correct talk is necessary to meet their needs, especially those children in state custody. Through open and critical discourse about the policies and practices within the child welfare field, innovations that account for the unique qualities of young gays and lesbians can be engendered.

In this book, a gay- and lesbian-affirming perspective, firmly rooted in an ecological context, is used to describe the social context, value base, attitudes, and behaviors that shape the various belief systems, coping strategies, defensive styles, and social support systems these persons need. The gay- and lesbian-affirming perspective is the perspective that has been utilized by mental health practitioners since DSM II (APA 1974) declassified homosexuality as a psychiatric disorder. This approach affirms the gay/lesbian individual's identity at any point in time in his or her development, rather than trying to change it or view it in a pejorative frame. In using this approach professionals can evaluate their practice from a differing value base, while examining inconsistencies in their current practice with children, youth, and families. By using this approach I hope to elevate issues of sexual orientation in the practice of child welfare and in the development of policies that enhance and support diversity.

The Lack of a Gay-/Lesbian-Affirming Perspective in Child Welfare Literature

A content analysis of numerous textbooks on child welfare (Cohen 1995; Fraser, Pecora, and Haapala 1991; Gambrill and Stein 1995; Golden 1997; Gustavsson and Segal 1994; Laird and Hartman 1985; Lindsey 1994; Maluccio, Fein, and Olmstead 1986; McGowan and Meezan 1983; Pecora et al. 1992) indicates that virtually all, with very few exceptions (Crosson-Tower 1998: 28, 47, 382, 348; Laird and Green 1997; Kaplan and Girard 1994:132–137) completely omit the experiences of gay and lesbian children, youth, and families. Thus a second goal of writing this book is provide a single source for information germane to child welfare issues and gay/lesbian persons.

Contrary to past historical works which view homosexuality from a deficit perspective, this book illuminates the strengths in these persons.

No book can include every concern about this special population. I have not dealt with civil rights protections or with issues as they pertain to bisexual or transgendered individuals, nor do I address the important issue of gay and lesbian marriages. I operate from the assumption that the reader is familiar with basic child welfare terminology with respect to policy, practice, and programs with diverse service populations. In addition, I do not specifically address the developmental issues of coming out for the gay and lesbian child or adolescent as they have been previously discussed in detail elsewhere, by numerous practitioners and scholars (De Crescenzo 1994; D'Augelli and Hershberger 1993; Hetrick and Martin 1987; Hunter and Schaecher 1987; Mallon 1998a, 1998b; Malyon 1981; Martin 1982; Morrow 1993; Needham 1977; Remafedi 1987a, 1987b; Savin-Williams 1995, 1998; Schneider 1988, 1989, 1998; Schneider and Tremble 1985; Sullivan and Schneider 1987). Instead what I have done is to provide a broad ecologically based overview for understanding the complexity of the policies, programs, and practices that affect gay and lesbian children, youth, and families in the United States and Canada.

OVERVIEW

The eight chapters are organized around the primary domains of child welfare practice and provide a frame of reference for understanding issues of sexual orientation as they pertain to children, youth, and families, a knowledge base about these children and families, and a critique of the effects of current child welfare practices and policies. In an attempt to define the boundaries of practice competence with gay/lesbian children, youth, and families, the first chapter presents a model for developing a competent base of practice with gay and lesbian persons in a child welfare context. Family-centered policies, practices, and programs as they apply to gay/lesbian children, youth, and families are discussed in chapter 2. The third chapter addresses issues of child protection for these young people. Chapter 4 examines the impact of the law on gays and lesbians. Chapter 5 highlights the trend of those who are choosing to create families through foster parenting or adoption. The needs of gays and lesbians in out-of-home placements are reviewed in chapter 6. The unique circumstances of runaways and the homeless are featured in chapter 7. The book ends with chapter 8, which presents conclusions and suggests future directions for practice, programs, and policy development for all of these young people.

Case examples and actual quotations, taken from in-depth interviews collected from gay and lesbian children, families, and youth in sixteen states in the United States and in Toronto, Canada, have been woven in through the book to help the reader bear witness to the power of the persons behind the words.

This book makes an important contribution to the field by focusing attention on the situation of gay/lesbian children, youth, and families; summarizing in a single text what we already know about gay/lesbian families; presenting an affirming focus for understanding and practice with gay/lesbian children and youth; and making sound policy, program, and practice recommendations.

CHAPTER 1

Competent Child Welfare Services for Gay/Lesbian Children, Youth, and Their Families

And of course I am afraid, because the transformation of silence into language and action is an act of self-revelation, and that always seems fraught with danger. — Audre Lorde (1984: 42)

An examination about persons whose lives are affected by issues of sexual orientation in the child welfare system is in its genesis (Mallon 1992, 1997, 1998; Stein 1996; Steinhorn 1979; Sullivan 1993), nonetheless, issues of sexual orientation have been and will continue to be an area that child welfare practitioners and policy makers must face. The ostrich approach to child welfare practice and policy development with respect to this population has been heretofore the collective approach to addressing the issues, yet dispensing competent, relevant, and effective services to all children and families, while an enduring goal of child welfare, still remains elusive.

Historically, the treatment of minority children in the U.S. child welfare system has been marked by racism and cultural bias (Billingsley 1992; Billingsley and Giovannoni 1972; Hogan and Siu 1988; Siegal 1991). Differential treatment of minority children (Stehno 1982, 1990) by service delivery systems has also been identified as having a strong negative impact on the quality of care that these young people and their families may have received. The important child welfare criteria that relate to the treatment of minority children and their families (Chipungu 1991), namely, ensuring equal access to services, monitoring appropriateness of these services, ensuring equal treatment and protecting civil rights, are all issues that also clearly resonate with the experiences of gay and lesbian young people and their families as they interface with the child welfare system.

With respect to the provision of competent child welfare services, there are striking similarities between these marginalized communities, but there are important distinctions as well. Although the majority of child welfare systems have openly struggled to understand and adapt to racial, ethnic, religious, physical, and cultural diversity in providing competent child welfare services for children and families, most have been loath to add sexual orientation to that list (Mallon 1997). Social service and child welfare professionals who work with children, youth, and families have disregarded or have been inattentive to the issue of sexual orientation as a key factor.

Inasmuch as many child welfare professionals acknowledge that gay and lesbian young people have always been in the system, the issue of delivering comprehensive child welfare services to meet their needs and the broader needs of gay and lesbian children and family systems, has seldom been straightforwardly addressed by child welfare professionals. One child welfare program director, interviewed for this book, illuminates the point further:

> Most child welfare professionals and especially the administrators are scared to death to address this topic. Talking about gay and lesbian people (especially gay and lesbian kids) is still seen as taboo—it's impolite because it makes people uncomfortable. I mean if you can't even talk about a group of people how can you go about developing policies or programs for them. Most social workers still believe that if you say gay or lesbian—the next thing you'll be talking about is graphic descriptions of what gay men and lesbians do sexually. I know that it sounds silly, but even colleagues that I really admire get all bent out of shape when this topic comes up.
>
> There's another group of child welfare professionals who just dismiss the entire issue of services for gay and lesbian persons, proclaiming them to be a small and marginal group, unworthy of such attention. They minimize the needs of this population by focusing on the macro child welfare issues that never go away, saying things like—"I'm dealing with child abuse issues and not having enough foster homes for kids and you now want me to focus on gay and lesbian clients too?" Overall, I'd say, it's the one issue that most child welfare professionals avoid at all costs.

Despite family support and permanency planning mandates that aim to keep families together and to place children who need out-of-home care in the least restrictive settings, the needs of gay and lesbian children, youth, and families, as illustrated by the quotation above, are seldom considered. There are several reasons why this might be so, but I'd like to highlight two reasons. First, discussions about gays and lesbians continue to evoke a high level of personal discomfort, and second, many practitioners and policy makers in the field are traditionally biased against gay and lesbian persons (for personal, cultural, and religiously based reasons) and do not have adequate information about them. Also, most family systems are unprepared for dealing with a gay or lesbian family member, or with a gay or lesbian adult who wishes to be a foster or adoptive parent.

The reality is that most families lack competence in understanding and caring for gay and lesbian adolescents and most child welfare systems are equally inept. In line with the arguments of child welfare advocates in support of cultural competence (Cross et al. 1989; CASMT 1995; CWLA 1989; Diller 1999; Focal Point 1988; Siegel 1994; Sue, Arrendondo, and McDavis 1992; Sue and Sue 1990), this chapter calls for the development of child welfare competence in programming and developing policies that affect gay and lesbian children, youth, and families. It advances the conceptual understanding of what some child welfare practitioners have identified as a goal-competence in practice with these persons. A comprehensive model for achieving such competence is presented and implications of inept practice are also discussed. The underlying assumption of this model is that gay and lesbian children, youths, and families should be provided with health care and psychosocial services that are acceptable and that support the integrity and strengths of their sexual orientation, not their deficits. Child welfare practitioners have an obligation to provide appropriate interventions if they are to achieve, in actuality, the goal of preserving the best interest of children, families, and communities.

Before significant progress toward achieving these goals can be made, what constitutes competent practice with gay and lesbian persons must be elucidated. A Gay and Lesbian Affirming Competence Model of Practice, comprised of three components: Basic Knowledge, Illuminated Awareness, and Professional Amalgamation are described for use by child welfare practitioners. The effects of sexual orientation incompetence will also be discussed.

ADDRESSING ISSUES OF SEXUAL ORIENTATION

It is well-established that the professionals who provide health and social services to young gays and lesbians are themselves predominantly heterosexual (Mallon 1998a). During the past decade, a variety of efforts have been undertaken to enhance the ability of child welfare practitioners to respond to the needs of these vulnerable people in ways that are congruent and effective (CWA 1994; CWLA 1991; Mallon 1998a; O'Brien, Travers, and Bell 1993; Sullivan 1995). These efforts have been largely sporadic, with an emphasis on raising awareness and sensitivity. Additional efforts have sought to increase knowledge and understanding about the unique aspects of the history and culture of specific groups of lesbian and gay persons. These attempts, however, have not addressed the issue of effective practice in a comprehensive and sustained manner, and although a good beginning, are less than adequate. Competent practice with diverse populations (which has heretofore excluded issues pertaining to sexual orientation from its discussions) in child welfare practice has become a buzz phrase in dire need of clarification if we are to move beyond the splintered approaches that have characterized previous efforts.

Review of the Literature

Social work has a deep commitment to social justice for various oppressed groups, and a long tradition of concern and advocacy for lesbian and gay persons (Berger 1977; Gochros 1972, 1975, 1985; Hidalgo, Peterson, and Woodman 1985). In 1993, the National Association of Social Workers reaffirmed its landmark policy statement on Gay Issues (originally adopted by the Delegate Assembly in 1977) and updated its Code of Ethics (NASW 1994a, 1994b), emphasizing its ban on discrimination based on sexual orientation. Taking a similar position, the Council on Social Work Education (1992) revised its Accreditation Standards, requiring schools of social work to include foundation content related to lesbian and gay service needs and practice into the core course curriculum (see Humphreys 1983; Newman 1989). Such policies and accreditation mandates express the profession's commitment to social and economic justice as well as a respect for diversity. The resources needed to fulfill such commitments, especially in the area of child welfare, however, continue to be fully realized or developed.

Professional social work training emphasizes the dual focus of the person:environment (Germain 1991; Germain and Gitterman 1996). Helping individuals and families understand, adapt to, and cope with the stresses of their environments, while at the same time advocating for social change aimed at improving opportunities and enhancing the quality of life, child welfare professionals are uniquely positioned to address the service needs of lesbian and gay people. However, despite inclusive policies and accreditation mandates that call for nondiscriminatory professional practice, an inherent difficulty in separating personal attitudes from professional prerogatives with respect to homosexuality appears to have made service provision to this population a complex process. Homosexuality has been and continues to be a taboo subject for discussion even within most professional climates (Gochros 1995; Mallon 1992).

The elimination of homosexuality from the *Diagnostic and Statistical Manual of Mental Disorders* (3rd ed.) (D.S.M. III) in 1973 has not changed the opinions of many in the child welfare mental health communities. The work of several authors (De Crescenzo 1985; Gramick 1983; Gochros 1995; Hartman 1993) suggests ambivalence about gay and lesbian persons among social workers. A recent study of homophobia and heterosexism in social work (Berkman and Zinberg 1997) found that while 10 percent of those social workers interviewed were homophobic, which was considerably less than Wisniewski and Toomey (1987) found in a similar study over a decade ago, the majority of those interviewed were characterized as heterosexist. Although it is evident that antigay and antilesbian discrimination is present within the social work profession, its tangibility is difficult to detect because collegial norms inhibit disclosure of homophobic attitudes.

Despite these ongoing mandates, born of ethical obligation, there is reason to believe that the manifestation of competent practice with gay and lesbian persons has been substantially ineffective. Mallon (in press) concluded from a content analysis of recent social work literature that "while the social work profession has historically sought to bar discrimination on the basis of sexual orientation and encourages social workers to act to expand access, choices, and opportunities for oppressed people, the literature within the last thirty years does not adequately reflect such interest." Moreover, Mallon and many others (Lindsey and Kirk 1992; McMahon and Allen-Meares 1992; Meyer 1983, Minahan 1980) correctly assert that those who publish in the predominant social work literature have powerful influence on framing practice knowledge.

Similarly, Humphreys (1983) and Newman (1989) suggest in their study of graduate social work educators that 1) when schools did not make the inclusion of gay and lesbian content in the curriculum a priority and did not provide pertinent resources, the content rarely appeared; and 2) educators frequently described the lack of knowledge and competence to teach sexual diversity content as their most problematic teaching concern. These educators also described textbook content as inadequate and superficial. Many of the educators themselves were not generally knowledgeable about even time-honored works on diversity such as Gochros and Schultz's (1972) *Human Sexuality and Social Work*; or Schoenberg, Goldberg, and Shore's (1985) *With Compassion Towards Some: Homosexuality and Social Work in America*; or Hidalgo, Peterson, and Woodman's (1985) *Lesbian and Gay Issues: A Resource Manual for Social Workers*. Many of these same social work educators, while believing that practice with gay and lesbian persons required different skills, could not identify what the different skills were.

Another disturbing trend was the tendency of social work educators to repeatedly use the same content on gay and lesbian persons in each social work course (e.g., Lukes and Lands 1990), effectively thwarting the development of knowledge at an advanced or content-specific level. Many of these leaders of the profession's most fundamental education process openly admitted that they had not been educated and trained in their own social work preparation to deliver content that addressed the needs of gay and lesbian persons and did not feel confident or competent to do so in their courses. In 1996, the discussion about teaching content on lesbians/gays in religiously affiliated graduate and undergraduate schools of social work preparation included debates within the Council on Social Work Education (CSWE) that can best be described as moralistic in character (Parr and Jones 1996). Cain's (1996) heuristic study, which examined heterosexism and disclosure in the social work classroom, provides further evidence that some social work classroom closets are still quite shadowy.

Social work, however, is not alone in its inability to meet the complex challenge of sexual orientation competence despite its avowals to do so. Simoni (1996) has conducted similar research focusing on heterosexism in the teaching of psychology. Allen and Demo (1995) indicate that despite continued efforts by counseling professionals to press for a focus on practice with gay and lesbian families, they still always seem to be trying to justify the need.

All of these exhortations and descriptions are reminders of just how essential it is for practitioners in child welfare to move beyond the obvious identification of the need for sexual orientation competence. What is needed at this point demands an advanced level of activity, that is, critical discourse on what constitutes competence in dealing with sexual orientation and thoughtful delineation of the path one must traverse to achieve it. What follows is an effort to stimulate this critically needed initiative.

THE CHILD WELFARE CHALLENGE

There is a clear imperative in child welfare to provide services that deal effectively with the oftentimes life-threatening conditions that face gay and lesbian children, youth, and their families. Social work educators as well as child welfare practitioners often assume that competence with gay and lesbian groups can be achieved through short-term (and often "one-shot deal") workshops or gay and lesbian guest speakers in classes (Mallon 1998b). These assumptions reflect a short-sighted, simplistic view of a complex process. Restructuring one's worldview and developing a sound base of knowledge and skills are long-term professional endeavors (Diller 1999:25).

The first step toward achieving gay- and lesbian-affirming competence is understanding and accepting the reality that openness to long-term, ongoing, and persistent development is required. As in all professional development, there is no ideal completion. Mallon (1998c) describes the counselor skills in issues of sexual orientation as "a professional who begins with a well-developed sense of self-knowledge and then expands beyond his or her narrow worldviews to broadly include a diverse group of persons, including those diversities which pertain to issues of sexual orientation." Thus, any serious initiative to work effectively with gay and lesbian populations begins with this premise.

As firmly expressed by others (Berger 1977, 1982, 1983; Dulaney and Kelly 1982; Mallon 1998c) preparation for serving gay and lesbian populations effectively must be pursued on a multidimensional front. A unimodal focus on raising awareness or sensitivity is required but is inadequate by itself. Neither approach is acceptable to believe that increasing one's level of cognitive understanding of gays and lesbians is all one needs to do. Gordon Allport, a beacon in the movement to abolish prejudice of all types, noted this eloquently when he said: "It always has been thought that planting right ideas in the minds would engender right behavior . . . But one's readiness to learn facts, it is now pretty well agreed, depends upon the state of his attitudes. Information seldom sticks unless mixed it attitudinal glue" (Allport 1958:451).

The published literature gives much support to the idea that behavioral change does not automatically follow knowledge about social phenomena. For example, the perennial battle against racism has been debated for several decades now around the goal of bridging the gap between information about race and ethnicity, with only marginally positive results (West 1994:12). This could be, as Allport might describe it, because there has been little societal investment in attitudinal glue.

Over the course of more than twenty-four years of teaching and practice in the field of child welfare, it is clear to me that a comprehensive model for achieving sexual orientation competence is sorely needed. It is from my own work in child welfare that the following model, adapted from Anna McPhatter's work (1997) on cultural competence, evolved as a response. The discussion begins with definitions of several concepts critical to understanding the model.

A Gay- and Lesbian- Affirming Competence Perspective Defined

As used in this context, competence refers to a suitable skill or ability, that is, to achieve some purpose or goal (Diller 1999: 10–16). Further the competent practitioner is able to conduct her or his professional work in a way that is congruent with the behavior and expectations that members of a distinctive population recognizes as appropriate among themselves. Gay and lesbian competence denotes the ability to transform knowledge and practice awareness into health and/or psychosocial interventions that support and sustain healthy client-system functioning within the appropriate context for a gay- or lesbian-identified individual. McPhatter (1997) asserts: "this definition compels one to ask, What purpose is served by providing services in any other context?" Unfortunately, much of what occurs in child welfare practice falls far short of meeting the criteria as outlined here.

The Gay- and Lesbian-Affirming Competence Model

The proposed model assumes that (a) achieving competence in any sphere is development and (b) learning may take place in any or all of one's thinking, feeling, sensing, and behaving dimensions. In this regard, the model is holistic, circular, and interconnected. Again, the components of the model adapted from McPhatter's work are: Basic Knowledge, Illuminated Awareness, Professional Amalgamation.

Although each component represents a substantive goal unto itself, none is sufficient alone to produce competent practice with gay and lesbian children, youth, and families. Each dimension must be embraced as an essential part of a mutually influencing whole. This fact is precisely why earlier professional declarations of becoming "sexual orientation sensitive," brief overviews of gay and lesbian history communication techniques have not evolved into a level of competence that effectively encompasses the needs of culturally diverse child welfare clients (Faria 1996; Mallon 1998b). Focus in one area must not exclude substantive endeavor in the other areas. Each dimension of the model is discussed separately, but the reader is cautioned not to presume that mastery in one area takes precedence or priority over the others.

BASIC KNOWLEDGE We are all burdened with the heterocentric bias that is the foundation of our formal and informal education. The very nature of the education process, as well as the content that is selected and presented, is flawed in ways that make it extremely tedious to dissect and dismantle. The formal education process begins with the highly questionable if not false notion that science is neutral and lacks bias.

History, mythology, values, sexual orientation, practice wisdom, scientific methodology—all shape the basic essence of knowledge building. The bias is so deeply entrenched that it is often difficult for the most adept among us to engage the misinformation in a productive way. A basic knowledge base begins with the premise that everything must be exposed to a process of critical analysis. This is emphatically true because the selection of contents to which we are introduced has so thoroughly excluded perspectives that both challenge and broaden the homophobic worldview. The theory and practice wisdom that form the basis of social work practice demand considerable and ongoing critique, in addition to teaching future social workers how to develop this mode of inquiry.

Examples of major weaknesses and gaps in the knowledge base passed on to others in the social work profession are numerous. For example, the contributions made by gays and lesbians are rarely, if ever, included in the knowledge base. Further, most of us were introduced to mainstream developmental theorists—Freud, Erikson, Kohlberg, and their ilk—in human behavior courses, and completed this education exchange without knowing that these conceptualizations of normal life-course development described gay and lesbian people as deficient and abnormal. Theorists who define normal adult development as career attainment, heterosexual marriage, childrearing, and managing a household exclude the developmental experiences of a substantial number of human beings such as gays and lesbians. Even the historical recognition of social work as a profession forged by never-married women (Simon 1987) seldom if ever speaks to issues of sexual orientation. Unfortunately, in this educational scenario, alternative theoretical perspectives are either not available or seldom get presented.

The pursuit of a knowledge base demands creative use of a wide range of sources of information that includes other disciplines, related subject matter, and nonmainstream works. Communities of gay and lesbian persons, key informants, and traditional and nontraditional economic, religious, and social institutions are dynamic laboratories for relevant knowledge building and must be seen as valuable resources.

In the field of child welfare, developing an essential knowledge base is an expansive endeavor. A number of areas, however, are absolutely critical to enhancing competence with ethnically and culturally diverse people. Although it is beyond the scope of this chapter to review all of the literature delineating the knowledge requisite to achieve competent practice with gay and lesbian children, youth, and families, key components are highlighted in chart 1.

CHART 1   Literature on Gay Men and Lesbians

Key concepts and terms

Appleby and Anastas 1992, 1998; Gochros 1972; Hidalgo, Peterson, and Woodman 1985; Mallon 1998; Moses and Hawkins 1982; Schoenberg, Goldberg, and Shore 1985

Understanding heterocentrism and homophobia: Theory, manifestations, and implications for practice

Albro and Tully 1979; Berger and Kelly 1981; Berkman and Zinberg 1997; De Crescenzo 1985; Dulaney and Kelly 1982; Gramick 1983; Pharr 1988; Reiter 1991; Tievsky 1988; Wisniewski and Toomey 1987

Theories and models of gay and lesbian identity formation and the coming-out process

Cass 1979, 1983/1984, 1984; Chafetz et al. 1974; Chan 1993; Coleman 1981, 1987; Espin 1993; Folayan 1992; Gock 1992; Gutierrez 1992; Hidalgo 1995; Icard 1985/1986; Lewis 1984; Loiacano 1993; Lukes and Land 1990; Reiter 1989; Sullivan 1995; Troiden 1978, 1988, 1989; Tafoya 1992; Williams 1986, 1993

Bisexuality and transgendered issues

Blumstein and Schwartz 1977; Levine 1978; Wicks 1978

Social work with gay, lesbian, and bisexual children and adolescents
Cates 1987; De Crescenzo 1995; Hetrick and Martin 1987; Hunter and Schaecher 1987, 1994; Jacobsen 1988; Mallon 1994a; Malyon 1981; Morrow 1993; Needham 1977; Ryan and Futterman 1998; Savin-Williams 1989, 1998; Schneider 1988, 1989, 1998; Schneider and Tremble 1985; Sullivan and Schneider 1987

Gays, lesbians, bisexuals, and their families
Auerback and Moser 1987; de Vine 1983/1984; Gochros 1989; Laird 1983, 1996; Laird and Green 1996; Hall 1978; Lui and Chan 1996; Markowitz 1991a, 1991b; Slater 1995; Strommen 1989; Van Voorhis and McClain 1997; Wyers 1987

Lesbians, gay, and bisexual couples and their relationships
Berger 1990; Decker 1984; de Poy and Noble 1992; Kurdek 1994, 1995; Larson 1982; McCandlish 1985; McWhirter and Mattison 1984; Peplau 1993; Peplau and Amaro 1982; Shernoff 1995

Gays and lesbians raising children: Adoption/foster parenting, biological parenting
Benkov 1995; Bigner 1996; Mallon 1992, 1998; Martin 1993; Levy 1992; Lewis 1980; Patterson 1994, 1995; Ricketts and Achtenberg 1990; Shernoff 1996c

Lesbians and gays in midlife and old age
Berger 1982, 1983, 1996; Berger and Kelly 1981; Dorfman et al. 1995; Kehoe 1988; Kimmel and Sang 1995; Quam 1997; Sang 1993

Lesbian and gay health and mental health concerns for the social work practitioner
Baez 1996; Friend 1987; Huggins, Elman, Baker, Forrester, and Lyter 1991; Kus 1995; Lloyd 1992, 1995; Loewenstein 1980; Martin 1991; Peterson 1996; Renzetti and Miley 1996; Scott and Shernoff 1988; Shernoff 1984; Woodman 1992

Social service delivery: Programmatic and administrative issues
Anderson and Henderson 1985; Ball 1996; Beaton and Guild 1976; Bernstein 1977; Berger 1977; Dulaney and Kelly 1982; Gambe and Getzel 1989; Gochros 1975, 1985, 1992; Hartman 1993; Hartman and Laird 1998; Lopez and Getzel 1984; Icard and Traunstein 1987; Icard et al. 1992; MacEachron 1996; Morton 1982; Potter and Darty 1981; Rabin et al. 1986; Tully and Albro 1979

Literature as a guide is an important start but practitioners need further practice-based guidance about where to begin their journey toward competence. The following essentials, relying heavily on work previously presented by McPhatter (1997), are believed to be foundational components for every child welfare worker actively engaged in becoming competent in his or her practice with gay and lesbian persons.

1. Knowledge of the history, culture, traditions and customs, value orientation, religious and spiritual orientations, art, and music, of gay and lesbian communities is required. While it is frequently nec-

essary in cognitive processes to rely on generalizations, practitioners must discern important differences between and among gays
and lesbians who are typically, but erroneously, categorized as a
monolithic group. Further, the worker's exploration of her or his
own issues with respect to sexual orientation is essential because
the value and meaning others hold about gays and lesbians will likely emerge from it.

2. Child welfare workers need intimate familiarity about social prob-
    lems and issues that have different impacts on children, youth, and
    families whose lives are affected by a gay or lesbian sexual orienta-
    tion. These conditions are most especially sustained patterns of
    social stigmatization against gays and lesbians. Such conditions may
    lead to health and psychosocial risk factors such as substance abuse
    and feelings of isolation, depression, and anxiety. Incidence of suici-
    dal inclinations among gay and lesbian youth are also higher
    (Remafedi 1987). Increased rates of interpersonal and community
    violence (Rivers 1998) are also manifest. It is fundamentally impor-
    tant that workers understand the dynamics that sustain these prob-
    lems as well as their origin and etiology, so that interventions may be
    appropriately targeted.

3. Because children and families live in and relate to neighborhoods
    and communities in deeply interlocking ways, workers must include
    neighborhoods and communities as vital parts of their practice
    domain. Neighborhood and community profiles, including, for
    example, sociodemographic information and comprehensive knowl-
    edge of neighborhood needs and resources available for gay and les-
    bian children, youth, and families, are essential. Formal and informal
    civic resources are important. Although gay and lesbian communi-
    ties have had a history of developing their own services for their own
    people because needs were not addressed by mainstream agencies,
    workers should not overlook the valuable traditional community
    resources offered by religious institutions and other community-
    based programs that have a long history of helping those from
    oppressed populations. Workers should also be aware however that
    communities, churches, and neighborhoods are frequently viewed
    by gays and lesbians as hostile environments. As such, many have
    developed their own sense of community based on safety, accept-
    ance, and affirmation of one's identity.

4. Practitioners must demonstrate a firm understanding of the dynamics of oppression, heterocentrism, racism, sexism, classism, and other forms of discrimination that belittle gay and lesbian clients irreparably. In many child welfare programs gay/lesbian children, youth, and families of color deal with multiple oppressed statuses. It is also critical to understand the process by which clients internalize oppression, how that process is manifested, and how it compounds an already overburdened reality. Persons with an illuminated awareness no longer engage in the futile process of denying the historical and current existence of oppression for gay and lesbian persons; they no longer make excuses or try to justify the fear and hatred that fuel it. Instead, they acknowledge the need to develop strategic and persistent responses to thwart and eliminate individual and institutional mechanisms that maintain oppression, and busy themselves doing so. These efforts require knowledge of advocacy (McGowan 1988) and individual and community empowerment (Simon 1994; Gutierrez 1990; Mallon 1998d) as child welfare professionals form real collaborations with families and communities.

5. Child welfare workers who are heterosexually oriented must have a grasp of the daily effects of heterosexual privilege (Sutter 1995). Akin to the phenomenon of white skin privilege (McIntosh 1989), professionals who are part of the dominant sexual orientation seldom consider the privileges that are inherent in its status.

6. Child welfare workers should have knowledge of the formal child welfare system, its history, the contributions made by gay and lesbian persons to the development of services for children and families, the current issues confronting child welfare (including funding and policy shifts), and most especially, the historic obstacles to providing effective services to gay and lesbian persons (Sullivan 1993). Workers must clearly understand gay and lesbian group perception and feelings about the larger social welfare system generally, and specifically, their own perceptions and feelings concerning the child welfare system. Consumers of social and child welfare services have a long history of facing degrading and humiliating experiences within these systems and harbor great fear and distrust of the system. It is one of the main reasons why gay and lesbian social services providers have developed services for their own communities. Workers must be able to engage clients empathically and with sensitivity

concerning these very real perceptions, and most importantly, must stop citing the understandable resistance offered by clients as something inherently deficient in the client when inappropriate interventions fail.

7. Workers must be well versed regarding the diversity of family structure and the often overlooked functionality of diverse family forms among gay and lesbian families. Hare (1996), Hall (1978), Laird (1996), Levy (1992), and Mallon (1998d) all provide an exhaustive and informed description of the complexities of the ways in which gay and lesbian persons have created families.

8. Knowledge about family functioning is a broad and expansive area fraught with ambiguity concerning indicators of what constitutes optimal function or the inherent stress in daily living for families. Assessing family functioning is even more problematic when one lacks knowledge about gay or lesbian identity and development. Developing one's identity as gay or lesbian within the context of a family that views homosexuality through a lens of hostility; the needs of some gays and lesbians to parent and nurture children; responses to illness and health; and socialization within the context of hiding one's identity or at the very best managing one's identity are all areas here culturally competent practitioners must be adept. The imprecise nature of the ways in which the profession assesses risk for children and what genuinely constitutes neglect and abuse demands that we approach these areas solidly grounded in community and cultural norms. The incidence of intrafamilial violence in many gay and lesbian families, for example, is an area where great care and understanding must be exercised. Coping strategies and survival behaviors of gay and lesbian persons demonstrate great variance, and lacking knowledge that an immersion experience provides puts practitioners at an extreme disadvantage when seeking to discover "what works."

9. Knowledge of child welfare interventions is enhanced by incorporating alternative theoretical and practice perspectives that are gay and lesbian relevant. One must be constantly alert to the possibility of alternative explanations for behavior and events. For example, what is often described as manipulative or hiding behaviors may be reframed as problem-solving efforts in need of support and skill development. Chestang (1972), in a seminal work on character devel-

opment in hostile environment, describes effective dual responses wherein a balance is sought between a perennial belief in the goodness of people and the reality of threats posed by them. Workers who recognize and understand the dynamics of hostile environments for gay and lesbian persons do not ask them to give up a major survival and adaptive strategy before they are on firm footing with other more effective alternatives.

10. Child welfare practitioners must value and build on the gay and lesbian practice of creating kinship amongst nonrelated individuals. Because family preservation, family reunification, and family support interventions are pursued within a cultural milieu, they represent new challenges for practitioners.

11. Concepts related to strengths (Cowger 1994; De Jong and Miller 1995; Saleebey 1993, 1998); and resilience (Wolin and Wolin 1993) must be incorporated into explanations of behavior and approaches to intervention. The ability to identify assets in a family beset by overwhelming liabilities often produces the pivotal turning point toward successful interventions with diverse clients. Although a great deal of effort has been made by child welfare practitioners to incorporate a strengths perspective in work with families, many of the models that make up the backbone of practice continue to overemphasize deficits, making it difficult to help clients feel a sense of hope for positive change. This point is especially pertinent because of the unrelenting negative images of gays and lesbians portrayed in our society.

Such a knowledge base would significantly expand the social work and child welfare knowledge base as currently constructed. To become competent in practice with gay and lesbian persons, workers must engage in persistent and thoughtful analysis of the implications of the most basic and fundamental theoretical constructs and practice approaches. The search for relevance must be put to the test unapologetically and used in ways that continually enrich this critical knowledge base.

ILLUMINATED AWARENESS   Illuminated awareness involves a fundamental process of reorienting one's primary worldview. It often requires a radical restructuring of a well-entrenched belief system that perceives oneself and one's culture, including values and ways of behavior, as not preferred but clearly superior to another's. With specific respect to gay and lesbian persons its means that many myths and stereotypes must be corrected. The ultimate goal of this shift in mind-set is to create a belief in and acceptance of others on the basis of equality solely because of a sense of shared humanity. Much of what people have become through socialization, formal and information education, cultural transmission, and so on, contradicts the real embodiment of equality between and among us. This is particularly evident in century-old traditions and beliefs fueled by declarations of "unbiased scientific research" that support the superiority of heterosexuals over homosexuals. Altering one's worldview is often a frightening effort because it forces one to challenge the very foundation on which one's personhood stands, even when it is clear that this foundation is substantially out of line with reality.

This essential transformation begins with a shifting of consciousness and awareness of just how constricted and narrow one's socialization has been. Individuals who have been reared in social environments with persons like themselves have had an early heterocentric socialization. Most heterosexually oriented individuals will experience a great deal of personal and professional discomfort when interacting with people whose sexual orientation differ from theirs. In the real world of practice, such individuals often exhibit nervousness and insecurity with gay and lesbian clients and may resort to superficial small talk with these clients. It can be quite common in situations for such ill-at-ease professionals to declare that they "have nothing against gays or lesbians," or take great pains to assure their clients that they are "all right," that there is nothing wrong with being gay or lesbian.. The discomfort is often driven by a fear of offending, and a lack of understanding of the other's difference. Many professionals are uncomfortable even using the very word "gay," "lesbian," or "bisexual." Most professionals believe that "homosexual" is the appropriate and professional term, unaware that lesbians and gays almost never use that term to define their own experiences. In my experience, some professionals are so uncomfortable with the terms that gays and lesbians use to describe themselves that they either pause before saying any of those words or, in some severe cases, spell out the words, as if they were unacceptable in polite society.

Illuminated awareness also has attitudinal and affective dimensions. The restructuring of a worldview requires a critical review of what individuals believe is reality—in the case of gays and lesbians, this means smashing many myths. When our awareness, sensitivity, and genuine acceptance toward sexual diversity in others are internalized, our whole affective demeanor moves closer to one of openness to engagement. The reality of a diverse society is accepted, and the struggle to maintain the superiority/inferiority dichotomy eases. We acknowledge the shortcomings of our education and socialization, we express the need to expand our knowledge and understanding of others, and we make a staunch commitment to do the work necessary to move from the comfort of a monocultural existence to a bicultural one, and ultimately to a multisexual existence.

It should be apparent that this dynamic process cannot even begin in short-term or brief overtures into another's world. It must be a sustained effort motivated by a true desire to become accepting and comfortable in personal sexual diversity interactions and effective in providing services to clients whose sexual orientations differ markedly from one's own. This work requires immersion experiences through what Green (1995) refers to as "cultural guides." Genuine efforts to increase knowledge and awareness of others are often met with positive responses from professionals and clients alike, especially when attitudes of condescension and voyeurism are resolved. Professionals and clients of diverse sexual orientations must be willing to engage in a teaching/learning process that is approached from a position of equality and shared meaning. Gay and lesbian professionals often experience and admit to resentment when they are approached and expected by colleagues to be teachers or to "do their work for them" in unidirectional ways. Too often, they are requested to share content and material on diversity without accompanying offers to share resources or demonstrated effort to obtain information through normal pursuits. This failure is often viewed as a less than genuine commitment to expand one's knowledge base without clear and sustained previous work to do so.

Exploring the uniqueness of one's own sexual orientation, and identifying and embracing both positive and negatively perceived aspects, increases one's ability to approach these aspects in the sexual diversity of others. A state of Illuminated Awareness enables one to connect with others at a new level of excitement and job. Blockages and walls erected to separate can begin to crumble, making a way for a lifelong journey toward the attainment of competence.

PROFESSIONAL AMALGAMATION   Illuminated awareness and basic knowledge base are the bricks and cement that build professional amalgamation. Professional Amalgamation connotes the process nature of skill development and suggests that the practitioner who is committed to becoming effective recognizes the building and constructing nature of this effort. Professionalization is not a haphazard process; it is focussed, systematic, reflective, and evaluative. Continuing to use skills because we were trained that way or because we lack alternative skill proficiency is out of sync with the goal of achieving sexual orientation competence.

One of the most crucial skills for a competent practitioner is the ability to engage a client's reality in an accepting, genuine, nonoffensive manner. Practitioners who give equal value to others' worldviews are more able to engage clients in ways that put them at ease quickly and successfully. Gay and lesbian persons are adept at reading the slightest nuance or cue that carries even the most carefully concealed message of disapproval, discomfort, or nonacceptance. A description of a worker as "she's all right" by a gay or lesbian person in reference to a cross-orientation interaction is usually a response to an accurate reading of the worker's skill at entering a dissimilar milieu. Acquiring such a fundamentally important skill comes about only through consistent practice motivated by a genuine goal to be authentic with others.

Prevailing practice principles are clear about the importance of developing rapport and trust with clients. Sexual orientation differences, by their very existence, complicate the crossing of what often appear as unbridgeable gulfs. An inferior knowledge base, coupled with a skewed view of our societal reality, dooms the best efforts to connect with clients in productive work. In clinical practice, for example, it is futile to expect gays and lesbians, given their contravening history with the heterosexual world, to immediately trust the intentions of nongay workers or to honestly disclose deeply personal or threatening information about themselves or their families. Closing this cultural gap is the professional responsibility of the competent practitioner.

Assessment and intervention skills in a broad sense form the child welfare practitioner's armamentarium, and grow out of the critical knowledge base above. In assessment, the very questions we pursue are determined by worldview and practice theory. Our beliefs about why people experience unusual problems in living and how change occurs guide assessment and intervention processes. The areas we pursue in assessment must be informed by substantial understanding of the client's cultural reality or the result is often distorted, confused, and unhelpful.

Given the long-standing institutional and environmental structures that have a negative impact on persons who identify as gay or lesbian, the competent worker must be able to intervene skillfully at every level—organizational, community, social, economic, and political. Intervening swiftly and effectively to remove organizational or community obstacles to the benefit of clients sends powerful messages to gay and lesbian clients about the worker's skill and commitment, with invaluable outcome. This is especially true if nongay workers correctly identify and confront issues of heterocentrism and discrimination, a battle that gay and lesbian persons often feel they fight alone.

Practitioners who do not view macro issues as their domain, given their work with individual clients, function in a vacuum and will not achieve even minimal levels of effectiveness in their work with gays and lesbians. Knowledge of organizational and structural dynamics and related intervention skills are critical for effective work with these clients. Early and successful worker interventions in behalf of clients with court systems, social welfare agencies, and health care and other service providers often convince sexual minority clients of the worker's trustworthiness, thus easing the way for more intra/interpersonal interactions.

Cross-orientation communication skills are another must. Use of professional jargon is a frequent error made by child welfare workers. Incompetent workers more often than not walk away from interactions with clients with a distorted and incomplete view because the workers know so little about the language and cultural attributes of the clients. For example, how often do workers know to interpret a reference to "my T" as describing a confidence; "getting shady with me" as a disrespectful comment; or "ki-ki-ing" as having a gossipy talk with a friend. Take the fact that language and accompanying meaning change so frequently among some groups emphasizes the importance of frequent and ongoing connections within the environment of clients.

Proficiency in practice skills with diverse groups is an important component for measuring successful outcomes (MacEachron 1996). Effective cross-orientation communication results in increased accuracy in assessment of problem areas, leading to appropriate and strategically targeted interventions. If we clearly grasp expressed intrapsychic and behavioral dynamics, opportunities for effective resolution increase exponentially.

THE CONSEQUENCES OF INCOMPETENT PRACTICE

Persistence of the current level of incompetence regarding sexual orientation can only be a vast detriment to children, families, communities, the child welfare system itself, and society as a whole. Policy makers, administrators, planners, and organizers design irrelevant programs and services in sync with perceptions and agendas that are not only incongruent with the realities and needs of diverse populations, but also often exacerbate the very problems they aim to ease. The cost of this business-as-usual approach to child welfare concerns is incalculable. The socioeconomic, personal, familial, and community problems we now face are increasing in complexity each day. Burnout and worker turnover add to these complexities. Programs and practice interventions born outside of the appropriate cultural context pursue erroneous targets, squander scarce resources, and help few. Child welfare agencies continue in disarray and uncertainty about real visions and ways of reaching those who need them. Nongay professionals and gay or lesbian clients are estranged from one another; they are anxious, angry, and bitter as they seek targets for their confusion and sense of failure. Incompetence about sexual orientation does absolutely nothing to help the neediest of our children and families from the uncertain futures they face. Professionals cannot model or emulate what they do not understand and do not know how to practice.

What are the benefits of a genuine commitment to achieving a gay and lesbian affirming perspective? In the short run, efforts at illuminated awareness help free us from ignorance, and truth is aired. The effort helps us to regard, respect, and value each other. The real payoff is the realization that we are more effective in our efforts and more energized toward goal attainment when we are not constantly trying to protect our fears, trying to say or do the politically correct thing, and trying to avoid the most dreaded prospect—being thought of as a bigot. As Diller (1999: 21) so aptly pronounces, "moving toward competence is hard emotional work and there is almost always fear and pain associated with this action."

As we begin to develop a basis of trust at the core of which is equality, the result is more creative solutions to difficult problems. Competent child welfare practitioners provide relevant and sensitive services to children, youth, and families. We ask and listen to what diverse people say about their needs and we attend and respond to their views about how to approach resolution (McPhatter 1997).

The Challenge

The process of becoming competent in issues of sexual orientation begins with an honest assessment of one's level of functioning with "different" others. This challenge requires a level of honesty and forthrightness that eludes most of us. Practitioners and educators alike consistently perceive themselves to be considerably more effective in their cross-orientation work than, in fact, they are. It is these faulty perceptions that get in the way of the real work that must be done to achieve the level of effectiveness that children, youth, and families affected by issues of sexual orientation have every right to expect. The following questions, if honestly approached, are designed to assist the reader in the initiation of that personal and professional appraisal.

1. How much personal/social time do I spend with people who are gay or lesbian?

2. When I am with people of different sexual orientations from my own, do I reflect my own sexual orientation or do I spend the time openly learning about the unique aspects of another person's sexual orientation?

3. How comfortable am I in immersion experiences, especially when I am in a numerical minority? What feelings and behaviors do I experience or exhibit when I am a minority in the company of gay or lesbian persons? When this occurs do I finding myself needing to assure everyone present that I am heterosexual?

4. How much time do I spend engaged in cross-orientation professional exchanges? Is this time spent in superficial, cordial activity, or do I undertake the risk of engaging in serious discourse that may expose my fears and lack of knowledge?

5. How much work have I actually done to increase my knowledge and understanding of gay and lesbian children, youth, and families? Does this work include only an occasional workshop in which I am required to participate? What are my deficiencies and gaps in knowledge about important sexual orientation issues?

6. What is my commitment to becoming competent in practicing with gay and lesbian children, youth, and families? What personal and professional sacrifices am I willing to make in the short-term for the long-term benefit of all children, youth, and families?

7. To what extent have I nondefensively extended myself in approaching professional colleagues with the goal of bridging sexual diversity that I have not actually achieved?

8. Am I willing to discontinue representing myself as knowledgeable and as having expertise in areas of gay and lesbian diversity that I have not actually achieved?

9. If I am unwilling to commit to a path leading to practice competence, will I take the moral and ethical high ground and discontinue providing services to people I am unwilling to learn about?

Effecting changes in attitudes and beliefs in pursuit of competent practice with gay and lesbian adolescents and their families requires education, training, and self-exploration on both individual and institutional levels. The development of competence in this area holds promise for preserving and supporting families and for the establishment of appropriate gay/lesbian-affirming child welfare services for all persons whose lives are affected by issues of sexual orientation.

CHAPTER 2

Keeping Families Together: Family-Centered Services and Issues of Sexual Orientation

I begin with the premise that child welfare practice regards families as central systems in the lives of all people. It is within the context of family where individuals are nurtured, nourished, and sustained (Hartman and Laird 1983). Parents are expected to bring up their children according to the culturally sanctioned standards that society sets forth. Members of society assume that both parents and the children that they rear are heterosexually oriented. A sudden upset, such as the disclosure of a gay or lesbian sexual orientation within a family system, will assuredly send that family into a crisis mode as this violates one of the primary norms set by a heterocentric society—that the world is and should be heterosexual. Many families addressing issues of sexual orientation will find that it is bewildering to address these issues alone. Most families have not been prepared for the possibility that their family system might be confronted with addressing an issue of sexual orientation. Many families will conclude that they need professional assistance to emerge healthy and intact.

Like their heterosexual counterparts, all gay and lesbian individuals grow up within a family context, which in most cases is usually heterosexual and heterocentric. Viewed within an ecological framework, living as an openly gay or lesbian in a heterosexual family is by its very nature a transactional process where the individual correctly perceives that there is not a "good fit" (Mallon 1998b) unless the family is not heterocentric—which is not common. The difficulty of having to keep secret one's sexual identity and affectional preferences creates a serious emotional distress that is a result, not of the individual's gay or lesbian identity, but of society's and the family unit's heterocentrism. Living within a family where one cannot be or say who one truly is, places the individual in a position where he or she is in a constant state of having to negotiate life within a potentially hostile environment. As such, the individual is usually guarded and insulated as if to prepared for an emotional onslaught if he or she is "revealed" to family members.

Although some ideologues of Western society (see Bawer 1998; Helminiak 1997; Herman 1997) regard homosexuality as a threat to the family, as if it were intrinsically antithetic to the idea of family life, nothing could be further from the truth for most gays and lesbians. Many of them need to be and want to be part of their families as much as any heterosexual. Given the stigmatizing status that a gay or lesbian identity continues to hold for many in society, the family is one place where a gay or lesbian individual most needs to feel accepted. Although most are initially socialized to hide their sexual orientation from their families (Mallon 1998b), most hold onto the hope that if they come out or are found out, their families, those who know them best, will see that they're the same persons they've always been. For some, as we shall see, this goal is realized; for others, it is not.

Utilizing an ecological lens of practice (Laird 1979), I will set up a conceptual framework for understanding gay/lesbian individuals within the context of their family systems and describe the insights gained from actual interviews and clinical practice with gays and lesbians and their families. In presenting such a framework, I use case examples to address the issue of disclosure within the family system—first, when a child comes out or is found out by his or her family, and second, when a parent comes out or is found out by family members, including spouses and children. "Created" families, which for some gay/lesbian persons substitute for the lack of support from their families of origin, are extremely important social networks of sustenance for many of them, but these will not be discussed in this text as they are beyond the scope of this chapter and have been examined elsewhere in the literature (Dorrell 1990; Mallon 1998c; Weston 1991). Guidelines for child welfare practitioners and counselors concerned about how and in what ways they can work with families to keep them together and to support them while navigating the potentially tumultuous disclosure of gay or lesbian identity with lesbian and gay individuals and their families are presented within a family-centered framework at the chapter's conclusion.

FAMILY-CENTERED SERVICES

Family-centered services (Brown and Weil 1992; Hartman and Laird 1983, 1985; Savage 1998) are all-encompassing and represent an array of services delivered to children, youth, and families within a multidisciplinary, multi-service context. The term "family-centered services" is generally affiliated with any service that attempts to overcome threats to family stability (Cole and Duva 1990:1; Savage 1999:198). Family-centered services can be targeted for mandated client systems, such as for families with maltreated children or for healthy children as a prevention measure. Family-centered services have historically been identified as either family preservation services or family support services. Although there are similarities in these approaches, there are difference as well. Gay and lesbian children, youth, and families are affected by both.

Family *support* services are usually sought voluntarily and are generally categorized in the child welfare spectrum as preventative. Most of these services are community-based. Family counseling, peer-support groups, school-based programs, parenting training, community center programs, and in some cases recreational type programs are all part of this diverse array of family support services.

Family *preservation* services are mandated approaches, usually after a crisis of child maltreatment has been reported. Family preservation services are sometimes referred to as intensive family-centered crisis services (Nelson 1994; Wells and Biegal 1991; Whittaker 1991; Whittaker et al. 1990). The distinctive characteristics of the intensive family preservation models are short-term, intensive services, provided because of an imminent risk of child placement; 24-hour worker accessibility; and low worker/caseload ratios (Barthel 1992; Edna McConnell Clark Foundation 1990; McCroskey and Meezan 1997). The undergirding principle of all family-centered programs is threefold: 1) to keep the family safe; 2) to avoid unnecessary child placement in an out-of-home setting; and 3) to improve family functioning toward amelioration of the problems that threaten the stability of the family (Cole and Duva 1990:1)—all of which seem to resonate so clearly for a family that might be confronting issues of sexual orientation. Whether prevention-based or mandated, family preservation and family support programs share many common characteristics.

COUNSELING WHERE SEXUAL ORIENTATION IS AN ISSUE

Some gay/lesbian persons may need counseling because sexual orientation issues become a stressful condition; others will not need counseling. Some families will come to a family and children's agency for a variety of reasons and services that might not at initial assessment seem to pertain to issues of sexual orientation. The following case illustrates the relevance of these dimensions.

NICOLE AND JERRY

A young couple, Nicole and Jerry, sought help from a family service agency. Initially they identified concerns with the behavior of their 8-year-old son, David, who was attending an after-school program. The after-school center staff reported that he was hitting other children, unable to relax during quiet time, and had frequent temper tantrums. Nicole and Jerry were concerned that the center might refuse continued service, affecting their ability to maintain their employment. The social worker engaged with Nicole and Jerry to assess David's behavior, the tensions with the marital relationship, and both parents' satisfaction with their lives.

Jerry was struggling with a worsening depression that he attributed to a growing remoteness between himself and Nicole, a detachment he couldn't explain. Several times Nicole mentioned being unable to be herself in the relationship and alluded to a secret that she couldn't share. Through a skillful series of individual and joint discussions, the social worker was able to help Nicole acknowledge the reality of her lesbian sexual orientation and share this with Jerry. With the secret out, the social worker, Nicole, and Jerry began to identify and work together on the many decisions that each faced individually and together as parents to David. In reflecting upon their initial call to this particular family service agency, Nicole noted having seen a brochure in David's pediatrician's office describing the agency's service, including a group on parenting issues for lesbian and gay parents. Once connected to the agency, Nicole had experienced the social worker as open in her ongoing assessment of the range of possible sources of Nicole's expressed ability to "be herself" in her relationship with Jerry.

The following case example explores issues of sexual orientation from a different family-centered perspective.

Joshua

Joshua, a 15-year-old African-American male is sitting in his bedroom in the apartment which he shares with his mother, father, and three younger brothers, reading a very personal letter that a boy in school wrote to him. He has already read this letter several times, but like many adolescents venturing into the world of relationships, he is rereading it because it is a special letter to him. When his mother yells to him from the kitchen that he has a phone call he puts the letter down on his bed and leaves his room to get the phone. During the time that he is on the phone his 9-year-old brother enters his room and begins to read the letter Joshua has left on the bed. The younger sibling, realizing that its contents are racy, shows the letter to his mother.

When Joshua returns from his phone call, finding his letter missing, he begins to panic. Joshua knows that it will be obvious to anyone who reads the letter that he is gay. Up to this point, Joshua has been successful at keeping his identity a secret. But now his secret is out in the open— he is angry that he didn't have an opportunity to come out on his own terms—he has been found out—and there is a big difference! When he sees his mother's face, he knows that she has read the letter, but she says nothing to him. When he approaches her, she backs away and says, "We'll talk about this when your father gets home and when all of your brothers are asleep."

The next few hours are filled with dread and isolation for Joshua. What's going to happen? What is his father going to do? He's not prepared for this, he's terrified of the repercussions.

What Joshua doesn't know is that his mother and father feel the same way—this is not the way things are supposed to be —they are not prepared for this. No one ever told them about the possibility of having a son who was gay. Should they send him for therapy? Should they send him away to protect the other boys? Should they even tell anybody about this?

For the social worker experienced in working with family systems, the situation in the above vignette presents the ideal opportunity for an inter-vention. A crisis has occurred, the family is in turmoil, and everyone is poised for something to happen. Family members are confused, fright-ened, shame-filled, unprepared, and angry. They can act in a reckless man-ner, lashing out at the individual who has disclosed or they might fall into a conspiracy of silence and become completely paralyzed and numbed by the circumstances. Professionals who have spent years with families, or even those who have recently entered the field, know that what happens next is not always predictable. When the situation involves an issue of sex-ual orientation in the family, one can almost guarantee that there will be a great deal of ambivalence in this process. Coming out in the context of a family system can yield unpredictable outcomes.

THE COMING-OUT PROCESS WITHIN A FAMILY

Coming out, a distinctively homosexual phenomenon (see Coleman 1981, 1987; Cass 1979, 1983/1984, 1984; Troiden 1979, 1988, 1989), is defined as a developmental process through which gay and lesbian people recognize their sexual orientation and integrate this knowledge into their personal and social lives (De Monteflores and Schultz 1979:59). Although several theorists have written about coming out from a uniquely adolescent expe-rience (Hetrick and Martin 1987; Malyon 1981), developmentally, the com-ing-out process can eventuate at any stage of an individual's life. Therefore, it is important to consider the consequences of a person coming out in the context of his or her family, as a child, as an adolescent, as an unmarried young adult, as a married adult, as a parent, or as a grandparent.

The events which mark coming out and the pace of this process vary from person to person. Consequently, some people move through the process smoothly, accepting their sexuality, making social contacts, and finding a good fit within their environments. Others are unnerved by their sexuality, vacillating in their conviction, hiding in their uneasiness, and struggling to find the right fit.

Although the experience of a child coming out is qualitatively different from that of a parent who comes out, there are several conditions, broadly conceived, which both family members share. Earlier literature (Silverstein 1977) focused primarily on the negative consequences of disclosure, and indeed there can be many, but a range of responses to a family member's disclosure is perhaps a more appropriate characterization. Rothberg and Weinstein (1996:81), I believe, capture many of the salient aspects of this experience:

> When a family members comes out there are a multitude of responses. At one end of the spectrum is acceptance, . . . but rarely, if ever, is this announcement celebrated. Take for example, the announcement a heterosexual person makes to his or her family of origin of an engagement to marry. This is usually met with a joyous response, a ritual party and many gifts. The lesbian and gay man does not receive this response. Instead, the coming out announcement is often met with negative responses which can range from mild disapproval to complete non-acceptance and disassociation. These responses, though usually excepted, cause considerable stress and pain for the lesbian and gay person seeking approval.

Religious Factors

Some families, particularly families with strong religious convictions, may openly condemn homosexuality, unaware that one of their own family members is lesbian or gay. Blumenfeld and Raymond (1988) note that families with strong religious convictions often support their views of their religion even against a family member. Personal biases, particularly cultural or religious biases that view a gay or lesbian identity negatively, can make "coming out" to one's family a painful experience. Such distress is manifest by this young person's narrative:

> Everybody in the family knew that I was gay. The only person that could not deal with me being gay was my mother. Everyone else that I thought was going to have a hard time didn't. My mother is a devout Jehovah's Witness and she has a very hard time with my being gay. She has said that she hated me and to this very day she tells me that it is against God's will and it's against His proposition and when the day comes for Him to take over the world again I'm going to suffer. She always says that she doesn't want me to suffer because I am her son, but she doesn't realize that she is making me suffer because of the way that she acts toward me.

Social workers must be aware of the strong antigay/lesbian sentiment held by many religious groups and the impact that this has on family members for whom sexual orientation is an issue. The Bible has historically been erroneously used as a weapon against gay and lesbian persons causing a great deal of distress in many families of faith. Several excellent resources (Cooper 1994; Metropolitan 1990; Parents and Friends of Lesbians and Gays 1997) exists which provide practitioners with an alternative gay- and lesbian-affirming perspective.

Cultural Factors

Race and culture can also play important roles in the disclosure process. Persons of color, many of whom have experienced significant stress related to oppression and racism based on skin color may experience even greater difficulty coming out within the family context as some may view a gay or lesbian sexual orientation as one more oppressed status to add to one's plate (Greene 1994; Savin-Williams and Rodriguez 1993; Walters 1998).

People of color who are lesbian/gay/bisexual confront a tricultural experience. They experience membership in their ethnic or racial community and in the larger society. In addition, they are not born into the lesbian/gay community. Many become aware of their difference in adolescence and must deal not only with the stigma within their own cultural/racial community but must also find a supportive lesbian/gay community to which they can relate. The lesbian/gay community is often a microcosm of the larger society, and many may confront racism there, as in the larger society. To sustain oneself in three distinct communities requires an enormous effort and can also produce stress for the adolescent (Chan 1989; Hunter and Schaecher 1995; Morales 1989). The reality that gay and lesbian persons are part of every race, culture, ethnic grouping, class, and probably family, are other areas where child welfare practitioners must focus attention.

Emotional Factors

If the gay/lesbian-identified individual chooses to come out voluntarily, then he or she has had time to prepare for the event. Some individuals may have role-played their coming out process with a supportive friend or therapist, others may have written a letter or planned the event after experiencing positive disclosure events with several other trusted confidants. The truth is, however, that in most cases, even if the individual has had time to prepare for the event, the actual moment of disclosure catches most families off guard. Families have frequently not had this period of grace in which to prepare themselves and are often shocked by the disclosure. Jean Baker (1998), psychologist and mother of two gay sons, expresses these feelings perfectly when she writes:

> I still recall the night so vividly. Gary was helping me with dinner, which he occasionally did. He had just gotten a new haircut and immediately I hated it. I still don't know why, because it had never occurred to me that Gary might be gay, but for some reason I said to him, "With that haircut people will think you're gay." He hesitated for a moment and then, looking directly at me he said, "I think maybe I am."
>
> I stared at my son, totally speechless, stunned, momentarily unable to react. Then I started crying and found myself talking incoherently about the tragedy of being gay. . . . I rambled on senselessly about homosexuality as an adolescent phase, something people can grow out of, something that may be just a rebellion . . . Knowing what I know about homosexuality and having examined my own feelings and attitudes, I think my reactions that night were deplorable. My son deserved to hear immediately that I respected him for his honesty and his courage. What he heard instead was that his mother thought being homosexual was a tragedy.
>
> As I think about my reactions that first night and during subsequent days and nights, I am still ashamed of what I learned about myself as a mother dealing with a son's homosexuality. Instead of thinking first about how I could help my son cope with what he might have to face in a society so condemning of homosexuals, I focused on how I felt. Though I didn't want to admit it, I was concerned about the prejudice and stigma I myself might have to face. (Baker 1998:41–43).

Feelings surrounding the initial disclosure can range from shame to guilt, to embarrassment, or even to complete disassociation. Acceptance is also a possible reaction, but one that is seldom experienced by most gay and lesbian persons with whom I have worked.

Managing Disclosure to Others

Deciding how to manage the disclosure of a gay or lesbian sexual orientation to the family is an important consideration at this point. The family that reacts extremely negatively to the disclosure, i.e., parents ordering a child out of the house or a spouse who tells the one coming out to leave their home may require outside intervention to assist them in dealing with the disclosure which should be viewed as a crisis situation. Who to tell and who not to tell, and how to address the disclosure within the context of the family, are other issues that families must eventually discuss. Getting through the initial crisis of disclosure, however, should be the primary focus of the intervention.

Being "found out," as illustrated in Joshua's case, precipitates a somewhat different type of crisis that may also require immediate intervention. In the sections that follow, I will explore the possibilities of a child or adolescent's coming out in his or her family system.

COMING OUT OR BEING FOUND OUT WITHIN THE FAMILY SYSTEM

Child or Adolescent

Although disclosure can occur at any point in the developmental process, for the purposes of this section, I will specifically address the issues as they pertain to a child or adolescent who comes out or is found out by his or her family.

Although one of the primary goals of adolescents is to move away from their families toward independence, families are still extremely important economic and emotional systems for them. Lack of accurate information about gay/lesbian identity and fears about individuals who identify as gay or lesbian lead many families to panic about how to manage the disclosure of a family member.

The following cases illustrate several points with respect to the coming out process for adolescents.

ANDY

Andy Yang is a Chinese-American 17-year-old senior in a public high school in a large West Coast city. He resides with his parents who are Chinese-born in an apartment with an older brother, age 20, and two younger siblings, ages 12 and 10. Andy is the captain of the football team, well-liked by his peers and by teachers. He is a very handsome young man. Andy has dated a few girls, but is so into his football career that it leaves little time for anything else. Andy has been aware of his feelings for guys for some time and has been trying to repress these feelings. Recently, however, he met a guy named Paul, whom he really likes, and Andy's feelings have become more difficult to repress. Paul and Andy begin to see each other, first as friends, and then their friendship blossomed into a full-blown romance.

One evening, while talking to Paul on the phone, Mrs. Yang overhears their conversation. It seems to her that Andy is speaking to Paul like she would expect him to speak to a girl that he was dating. When Andy hangs up the phone his mother confronts him about what she heard. Andy blows it off and laughs, blaming her interpretation on her imperfect English, but he knows that this is not the case. He is in a panic because he knows that his mother will not let this go.

Mrs. Yang becomes hyper-vigilant about Andy and begins to search in his room for clues while he is at school. She finds letters that Paul has written to Andy and then when she finds a small card from a gay and lesbian youth group she takes it as confirmation that Andy is gay. Mrs. Yang shares this information with her husband, who chastises her for snooping in their son's room. But they are both upset and unprepared for how they should deal with this new information which changes their notion of their family.

When Andy arrives home from football practice, both Mr. and Mrs. Yang ask to speak with him. They tell him what they have found and ask him if he is gay. Andy, fearful and caught off guard, is unsure of how to respond, but it seems like there is no way out. Even though he is pretty sure that he is gay, Andy tells them, "I think I am bisexual." Rationalizing that being half gay is easier that being totally gay. Mr. and Mrs. Yang ask if he has ever been sexually abused by someone, they ask if he is just going through a phase, and insist that he is going to see their family doctor. Although they do not say it out loud, Mr. and Mrs. Yang are also concerned about how this will affect their two younger children. Andy has on occasion baby-sat when they went out and they wonder if Andy might molest the younger children. This family is obviously in a crisis state.

KARINA

Karina is a 15-year-old Caucasian who lives with her mother, father, and two younger sisters on a small family-run farm in the Midwest. Karina is an average student in the tenth grade in a public high school. She has a very close friend named Jane, who is a year older and attends the same school. After an initial period of confusion, Karina and Jane realize that they have strong feelings for one another that are "more than just a phase." Although neither of them identify as lesbian at first, in time they come to label their identity as lesbian.

Karina has always been close to her family and has always been helpful around the farm. Not wanting to lie to her parents, Karina decides that she should tell her parents how she feels about Jane. She plans the event, making sure that it is an evening when her sisters are already in bed and asks her parents to sit with her in her bedroom. She starts by telling her family that what she needs to tell them is not an easy thing to tell, but that she loves them and wants them to know her for who she really is. They seem puzzled thinking that they already know their daughter quite well. She explains that since she was little, about six or seven, she has always liked other girls, not boys. She tells that at first she thought the feelings would go away, but they didn't. At this point, her mother and father are completely aghast about what she is trying to tell them. Karina make it clear and says "Mom, Dad, I still like girls and I have come to understand lately that I am a lesbian."

Karina's parents are without words. They are completely unprepared for having a lesbian daughter. They suggest therapy, they ask if she is sure and suggest that it still might be a phase, they ask if it is her way of rebelling against them. She answers no to all of their queries. Karina's parents are in shock, confused, embarrassed, and unsure of what to do. Karina's disclosure has thrown this family into an imbroglio that nobody was prepared to deal with.

Like many families, these families had little accurate information about gay and lesbian persons and as a consequence relied mostly on myths as their primary source of information. At first both families believed that the gay/lesbian child's differentness might be an adolescent phase. Both families suggested that the gay/lesbian child should change sexual orientation via therapy. Additionally, although it was almost too frightening to mention, the families expressed fears about the possible molestation of younger siblings by the gay/lesbian child. These families, like most families who have had to deal with an unexpected disclosure, are in shock. Consequently, they are unprepared as their children are growing up gay or lesbian in a heterosexual world. Most parents never allow themselves to think that they might have a child who is gay or lesbian. Parents are also aware of the shame and secrecy surrounding homosexuality and as such are unsure of what the child's disclosure will mean for them and for the other family members.

In some cases, though not in Andy's or Karina's, the disclosure of a gay identity can lead to an array of abusive responses from family members (these issues will be addressed in chapter 3). In other instances, a gay/lesbian disclosure can lead to expulsion from the home, leading to out-of-home placement (which will be addressed in chapter 6). In some families the crisis of disclosure is resolved and the family moves forward. When a parent comes out in a family context, the issues are quite different

A Parent or Spouse

When a parent or a spouse comes out or is found out by family members there are unique and distinctive repercussions. As observed in the above examples, lack of accurate information about gay and lesbian identity and fears about individuals who identify as gay or lesbian lead many families to panic about how to manage the disclosure of a family member. The issues of shame and stigma serve to further complicate these issues. The following cases illustrate several points with respect to the coming out process for family members. A mother discloses her lesbian identity to her daughter in the first example, a husband is unexpectedly found out by his wife in the second.

PEG

Nancy, an African-American fourth-grade child attending a Catholic elementary school, resides in a large urban environment in a middle-income housing apartment with her Mom, Peg, aged 35, and Betty, her "aunt." Nancy was 10 when her Mom decided to tell her that Aunt

Betty, who had lived with the family for eight of Nancy's ten years, was really her mother's lover.

Peg decided to disclose her lesbian orientation to Nancy because she felt that she was getting older and she wanted her to know the truth about her Mom. She didn't want anyone to make fun of Nancy or for her to find out that Mom was lesbian before she had the opportunity to tell her. Peg planned the disclosure and sat with Nancy privately in their kitchen to tell her. Betty, although not initially involved in the disclosure, joined them after Peg had told Nancy.

At first Nancy was shocked and denied that her Mom or Aunt Betty, with whom she had an excellent relationship, were lesbians. Nancy said she didn't want to talk about it. Although she didn't say it at the time, she was embarrassed that her friends and teachers in school would find out and that she would be treated differently. After the initial disclosure Nancy began to distance herself from her mother and Aunt Betty. When Peg checked in to see how things were going with her, Nancy simply replied that things were "fine."

But things were not fine. Nancy began to have problems in school (prior to the disclosure Nancy was an A student) and on two occasions, Nancy's Mom received notices from school notifying her that Nancy had gotten into trouble in the classroom. Noting this marked change in behavior, the social worker at the school phoned Nancy's Mom and asked her to come into school for a conference.

MARCO AND LUZ

Marco, a 31-year-old Latino, has been married to Luz, a 29-year-old Latina for six years. They have two children, Jorge, age 3, and Myriam, age 1. They live in an apartment in a suburb of a large southern city, which is composed primarily of working-class Latinos like themselves. Although they have been married for six years, Marco has always known since he was a teenager that he is "different." When he married, he thought that his feelings for men would change, but they did not. He never discussed these feelings with Luz, but some part of him always thought that she knew.

One evening, while Marco was exiting a well-known gay bar near where they lived, he ran into Luz's sister, Yolanda. Yolanda immediately confronted him about being in the gay bar and he denied being gay, saying that he just met a friend from work who was gay. His sense of panic, however, was evident. Yolanda went to her sister's home, asked to speak with her privately, and told her about seeing Marco coming out of the gay bar. Luz was devastated by this information and asked Yolanda if she would watch the children so that she could talk to Marco privately.

When Marco arrived home, Luz met him at the door and asked for an explanation. Marco initially denied that he had been in the bar, but after a few minutes acknowledged that he had indeed been there and further noted that it was not his first time. Luz told Marco that he had to leave their home immediately. She screamed that he had exposed her and her children to all kinds of things and that he had lied to all of them. Marco did not know where to turn. His family lived in Argentina and he did not have a close support system. Marco pleaded with Luz to go with him to see someone—a marriage and family therapist. Luz refused and told him to leave their home immediately.

Marco was confused, now estranged from his partner and his children, and feeling completely dejected. He went to the home of a coworker to ask if he could stay over night. In the morning he went to visit his parish priest to ask for counsel. The priest referred him to a family center in the community.

Luz was devastated, ashamed, and told no one except her sister about her separation from Marco.

Although the issues of disclosure for a parent coming out to a child are far different from those for a wife who finds out that her husband is gay, both cases reflect the level of denial, shock, and confusion that some family members experience in this situation. In the first case, Peg has clearly thought out her disclosure and it seems that she will work with her daughter to process this new information. In the second case, Luz and Marco have definitely not planned the disclosure and the consequences of his being found out seem to be, at this juncture, quite devastating for him and his family. Most families bring themselves out of a crisis without professional help, others will need support or assistance so that the family will remain intact and its members grow through the experience (Fraser, Pecora, and Haapala 1991; Kaplan 1986; Tracy et al. 1991). The benefits of a family support and family preservation strategy have particular relevance in each of these four cases.

THE ROLE AND RESPONSIBILITIES OF THE FAMILY PRESERVATION PROFESSIONAL

Family-centered services, particularly family preservation services are often called "crisis intervention services" (Kinney, Booth, and Haapala 1991; Kinney et al. 1991). Families experiencing high stress, such as the disclosure of a gay or lesbian sexual orientation, may find that their regular coping mechanisms have broken down, leaving them open to change in either a positive or negative direction. The family member's increased vulnerability under these conditions can serve as a catalyst to seeking help to resolve their immediate issues (Tracy 1991; Weissbourd and Kagan 1989). If professionals trained in family preservation techniques can be available and gently encouraging, the pressure families feel can motivate them to change and to share their concerns. The immediate goal of this intervention is clearly to move the family out of crisis and to restore it to at least the level of functioning that existed before the crisis (Kinney et al. 1991:16). Many family preservation professionals go well beyond that goal, increasing families' skill levels and resources so that they function better after the crisis than they did before. Utilizing a family-centered approach (Brown and Weil 1992; Hartman and Laird 1983) for working with families, the following sections suggests some guidelines for practitioners.

Intervention

Addressing issues of sexual orientation disclosure requires professionals to explore their own personal, cultural, and religious biases about persons who are homosexually oriented. Although many professionals might believe that they are nonbias in their approach to gay/lesbian persons, all professionals must first examine their own biases and be at ease dealing with issues that are seen by most people in Western society as "sensitive." Although most professionals receive little, if any, formal training on dealing with issues of sexual orientation in child welfare, there are several recent books (Appleby and Anastas 1998; Mallon 1998a) that can be helpful for professional development.

Initial Preparations

Keeping people safe is one of the primary goals of this intervention. Workers should be aware that issues of sexual orientation can frequently lead to violence within the family system. Being able to predict the potential for violence is an essential skill for workers.

Preparing for the initial meeting by gathering information, for example by talking to the referring worker (if the case has been referred), or by gathering information directly from the family members by calling them to schedule an interview can help form a positive relationship that might make things easier when the worker arrives at the home. In some situations, as in Marco and Luz's case, it might be a good idea to schedule the initial meeting outside the family's home in a public-structured environment, such as a restaurant or a community center. When situations are potentially volatile, meeting in a public place can make it easier for family members to maintain their self-control.

The Initial Meeting

Usually, whenever possible, the initial meeting should take place in the family's home. In three of the four cases presented above, this would be advisable. Meeting clients on their own turf, in their home, is an integral part of the philosophy of family preservation. Professionals should be conscious of being considerate of and careful with all family members. When a disclosure of sexual orientation is involved, family members might think that the person who has come out or been found out is the only person who needs help.

In some cases family members should be met with one at a time. This is particularly true for the family members who are most upset, pessimistic, or uncooperative. They should also be the ones who are talked with first. Such individuals need to feel important and understood. De-escalating such family members and gaining their confidence will help in supporting the process and encouraging other family members to participate. Engaging in active listening techniques—using "I" statements (Kinney et al. 1991:ch. 4); permitting the professional to share their own feelings about the situation; notifying family members of the consequences of their actions; calling for a time-out; seeking the assistance of a supervisor, if necessary; perhaps reconvening at a neutral location or even actually leaving the home if the situation escalates to a point where police intervention is necessary are all options that professionals may need to consider and act upon during the initial visit.

The first session is usually the most fragile one. The family who has had a member disclose an unexpected sexual orientation is, as noted, in a crisis mode. Family members in crisis feel vulnerable and anxious. Some may be angry, others mistrustful. Many families feel secretive about disclosing family business to a stranger, especially when it pertains to a sensitive issue like one's sexual orientation. The goal in the first session is usually to calm everyone down. Establishing trust and forming a partnership between family members and the professional are next.

Subsequent Contacts—Helping Families Learn

In subsequent sessions, the worker will need to assist the family in organizing information about its crisis. Professionals should work with family members to minimize blame and labeling and instead focus on generating options for change. This may be facilitated by helping the family reach consensus about the fact that a family member is, in one way, not as the family thought he or she was, but at the same time, is still the same person that he or she has always been. Guiding family members in shaping less negative stereotypes about a gay or lesbian identity is an important place to begin. Helping families to define problems in terms of their own skill deficits by setting goals, taking small steps, prioritizing issues of concern for the family, and being realistic with family members can lead families back toward homeostasis. In the context of an emerging managed care environment, and as a means toward addressing issues of accountability, utilizing standardized outcome measures to test the veracity of clinical interventions with clients has increasingly become a significant aspect of practice (Bloom, Fischer, and Orme 1995; Blythe, Tripodi, and Briar 1994; Fischer and Corcoran 1994).

One of the most salient elements apparent in each of the case vignettes above is the lack of accurate and relevant information about gays and lesbians. The standard myths and misconceptions influencing families are graphically present in their initial concerns about molestation, about the need for therapy, and about the possibility of reversing one's sexual orientation. Changing a family's notions about a gay or lesbian family member is not always a smooth or easy process. A great deal of the worry that families have about gay and lesbian persons is based on irrational fear and shame. The disclosure of a gay or lesbian sexual orientation within a family context spreads the societal stigmatization of homosexuality to all family members. Goffman called this phenomenon "courtesy stigma" (Goffman 1963).

Although Kinney et al. (1991:95) caution about developing realistic expectations for all families, they posit that there are several ways to facilitate learning with clients: 1) direct instruction; 2) modeling; and 3) learning from one another. These strategies can be useful in helping families affected by issues of sexual orientation as highlighted below.

DIRECT INSTRUCTION   The family preservation professional who is working with a family troubled by issues of sexual orientation should be prepared to offer a great deal of direct instruction with family members. Providing a family with accurate and relevant information about the child or family members' orientation is an essential part of thee process. Bibliotherapy, offering families reading material, is an integral component. of this strategy. Although finding such information is not the problem that it once was (now a plethora of information is available), workers may have to access this information by visiting a local gay/lesbian bookstore or via the Internet as they are frequently not carried in mainstream bookstores.

Increasing the family's knowledge about homosexual orientation (Baker 1998; Borhek 1983, 1988; Dew 1994; Fairchild and Haywood 1989; Griffin, Wirth, and Wirth 1986; Strommen 1989; Switzer 1996; Tuerk 1995) and knowing about resources that support families, like Parents and Friends of Lesbians and Gays (PFLAG 1990; www.pflag.org; www.glpci.org) are important ways to strengthen and support the families of gay and lesbian persons.

Furnishing young people with literature, especially work written by gay and lesbian young people for gay and lesbian young people, is one of the most beneficial techniques that can be employed (see Alyson 1991; Due 1995; Heron 1994; Kay, Estepa, and Desetta 1996; Miranda 1996; Monette 1992; Reid 1973; Savin-Williams 1998; Valenzuela 1996; Wadley 1996a, 1996b). Videos and guest speakers also can and should be a part of this process. Such information is assists gay/lesbian-oriented youngsters in abolishing myths and stereotypes and correcting misconceptions about their identity. Moreover, such information can also help educate nongay teens about their gay and lesbian cohorts (Berkley 1996; Greene 1996).

Although the Internet and World Wide Web have liberated gay and lesbian young people from their extreme isolation, supplying them limitless opportunities to communicate with other young gays and lesbians in chatrooms and bulletin boards, most of these adolescents have little access to information about their emerging identity and few adult role models from whom to learn. In recent years the Internet has grown exponentially. Its growth has liberated thousands of gay/lesbian persons who may not be able to get to libraries or bookstores, or who may live in geographically isolated areas. There are several important web sites for youth: see www.youth.org; www.qrd.org/qrd/youth/; www.vector.net/cariboo/youth), and many others that can be identified by using a search engine (i.e., Yahoo, Webcrawler, Metacrawler, Lycos, or Infoseek) to locate addresses.*

Unfortunately there is a very limited body of literature focusing on the impact of disclosure on the nongay spouses of gay and lesbian persons (Gochros 1989, 1992), but there is an excellent website known as the Straight Spouses Network located at www. glpci.org/~ssn, that offers valuable support to the partners of gay or lesbian spouses. Ali 1996; MacPike 1989; Saffron 1996 have all addressed issues of parental disclosure to their children. An excellent web site that addresses the concerns of the children of gay and lesbian parents (Children of Lesbian and Gay Parents Everywhere— COLAGE) is located at www. colage.org/

Although published sources can be purchased at gay and lesbian bookstores in metropolitan areas (i.e., A Different Light, New York, San Francisco, Los Angeles; Crossroads Market, Dallas, Houston; Giovanni's Room, Philadelphia; Glad Day Bookshop, Boston; Lambda Rising, in Washington, D.C., Baltimore, Rehoboth Beach, Del., Norfolk, Va.; Our World Too, St. Louis, Mo.; The Faubourg Marigny Book Store, in New Orleans), these sources and many others not mentioned here can also be ordered via the Internet at the following address: www. Amazon.com or www. Barnesand-Noble.com.

MODELING   If we ourselves act as models for behaviors that are accepting and understanding in order to show clients how to do so, we follow a very useful strategy for working with families dealing with issues of sexual orientation. The gay/lesbian who comes out, or the family members affected by such a disclosure might benefit from attending a support group with other individuals or other family members who share the same experience. Individuals and family members, anxious about attending a support group for the first time, might very much benefit from a professional who agrees to accompany them to the session. Accompanying the client to the

---

*As internet addresses sometimes change, it is advisable to first check the site before providing an internet address to a client. Search engines can also be useful in locating current addresses.

bookstore to purchase books about gay and lesbian topics or attending a gay/lesbian-run function with clients can be other ways for workers to model acceptance for the client. Linking clients to religious leaders in their communities and of their faith, who have an affirming stance about gays/lesbians, can also be a useful modeling experience for family members.

LEARNING FROM ONE ANOTHER   Families can also learn from one another by connecting with other families where sexual orientation is an issue. If connections with other families cannot be made in person because of geographic distance, the Internet can be a useful substitute. There are many sites that include opportunities for gay and lesbian individuals and families affected by issues of sexual orientation to communicate with one another. It is the responsibility of the professional working with the family to identify and access resources for support within the community where families live. Workers need to be aware of these resources and visit them prior to making such referrals to clients.

Workers must also be prepared to assist families in overcoming barriers that will inevitably appear while they are in the learning process. Acknowledging, validating, and rewarding small signs that family members are considering new options and beginning to try them is also an important task for workers.

SOLVING PROBLEMS   Family preservation workers trained in problem resolution strategies must incorporate issues of sexual orientation into such designs. Family reservation workers focus on listening to and helping families to clarify what is causing them the most discomfort. Intervening with clients to assist them in intrapersonal problems can occur via direct interventions, cognitive strategies, values clarifications, and behavioral strategies—all methods suggested by Kinney, Haapala, and Booth (1991:121–124).

Most families dealing with issues of sexual orientation need help controlling and clarifying their own emotions. Assisting families to develop effective communication skills and problem-solving strategies is a major focus of the family preservation model, which can be effective with gay and lesbian children, youth, and families.

All family-centered services, notwithstanding issues of sexual orientation, from family support to family preservation, maintain the position that children and adolescents are best reared by their own families. Viewed ecologically, both assessment and intervention with families must focus primarily on the goodness of fit (Germain and Gitterman 1996) between the gay or lesbian individual and those other systems with which he or she is in transaction, the most central of which, in this case, is the family. Many of the issues that surface when a family member discloses or is dealing with aspects of sexual orientation can be best dealt with by a competent social worker trained in family systems. Such issues must be viewed as deficits within the environment, dysfunctional transactions among environmental systems, or as a lack of individual or family coping skills or strategies (Loppnow 1985). Providing education and intensive training effort for family-centered practitioners (Faria 1994; Laird 1996) that would help them feel competent about broadly addressing issues of sexual orientation could provide support for families in crisis and prevent unnecessary family disruption. Family-centered practitioners must also be prepared to serve as advocates for their clients, including a gay/lesbian child or adolescent, a parent who identifies as gay or lesbian, or a couple where one of the partners identifies as other than heterosexually oriented.

Family preservation and family support programs with their primary goal of keeping families together can deliver these services within the context of the client's natural environment—their community. Programs like the Homebuilders model (Kinney et al. 1991) have opportunities to help families grappling with issues of sexual orientation. Community-based family and children's services centers also provide many opportunities for addressing issues of sexual orientation within the family system. These approaches also have relevance for other situations where spouses or parents come out as gay or lesbian. Working with family systems in their communities makes social workers in family-centered programs ideally situated to see what is really going on in a family's natural environment. By being located in the home or in the community, the worker is able to make an accurate assessment and design an intervention that would support and preserve the family system. With a greater awareness of issues of sexual orientation, family-centered practitioners could educate parents, ease the distress experienced by couples where one partner is gay or lesbian and the other is heterosexual, as well as model and shape new behaviors that can transform lives for young gay and lesbian persons.

CHAPTER 3

Protecting Gay/Lesbian Children and Youth: Issues of Abuse, Neglect, and Familial Violence

Over the years child protection has been the focus of much controversy (A glimpse into hell, 1997; Herbert 1998) and the subject of extensive research (Ahn 1994; Daro 1988; Garbarino 1980, 1992; Hutchison 1994; Melton and Barry 1994; Pelton 1994; Rose and Meezan 1996; Thompson 1995; Wolfe 1994). Although the upsurge of familial violence and heightened incidence of substance abuse has caused figures to grow exponentially, these events have also caused heightened awareness on the part of individuals and as such there is a higher percentage of recognition and reporting (Crosson-Tower 1998: ch. 9). Child welfare services have long intended to support children's safety and well-being in their families. The Adoption Assistance and Child Welfare Act (AACWA) of 1980 (P.L. 96–272) embodied those intentions and focused services on safely main taining abused and neglected children in their biological families whenever possible in preference to out-of-home placement. The very foundation of child welfare services rests on the value of family-centered child protective services that posits that practitioners should always act "in the best interest of the child."

By virtue of the fact that they are an often invisible population or in some cases because they are perceived as being "different" by their families (Mallon under review), gay and lesbian children and adolescents are at high risk for neglect, abuse, and violence within their own family systems. In case after case, self-identified gay and lesbian children and adolescents, and those perceived to be so because of gender-nonconforming behaviors or mannerisms, reported that they were the victims of abuse, neglect, and violence at the hands of their own families (Mallon 1998a).

In this chapter, drawing on insights gained from actual interviews and based on clinical practice experiences with gay and lesbian children, youth, and their families, I present a conceptual framework for examining, understanding, and intervening with these people who are at risk for abuse or neglect. In presenting such a framework, I again will utilize case examples to address the issue of child protection within the family system—first, by exploring the phenomenon of parental neglect based a parent's lack of knowledge or recognition of the child's gay or lesbian identity; and second, by examining the experience of various forms of abuse perpetrated on gay/lesbian children and adolescents within their family systems based on their perceived or actual sexual orientation. Guidelines for child welfare practitioners concerned about how and in what ways they can work to protect gay/lesbian children and youth from abuse and neglect are presented within a risk assessment framework of family-centered child protective services at the end.

A REVIEW OF THE LITERATURE

Despite the manifest risk factors that gay and lesbian children and youth appear to exhibit for possible maltreatment by their families, child welfare advocates, and especially those in child protection, have not heretofore written about, investigated, or explored the incidence of abuse and neglect in this population. A careful content analysis of contemporary generic child welfare literature (Cohen 1997; Golden 1997; Goldstein et al. 1996; Gustavsson and Segal 1994; Rycus and Hughes 1998) and more specifically the child protection literature (Costin, Karger, and Stoesz 1996; Daro 1988; Garbarino 1977, 1980, 1989; Melton and Barry 1994; McCurdy and Daro 1994; Straus, Gelles, and Steinmertz 1980; Olds and Henderson 1989; Videka-Sherman 1991) does not yield a single citation or make one reference to the level or existence of abuse or neglect that this population of children has endured. Yet countless case anecdotes and carefully collected and analyzed qualitative interviews with self-identified gay and lesbian youths refer to the experience of perceived family abuse. Lack of professional attention to this "closeted" issue is no surprise, but the fact that the leading child protection experts in the United States and Canada have never discussed or even mentioned this abuse and neglect suffered by these young people at the hands of their own families should concern both scholars and practitioners.

An Overview of the Issue

Serving children, youth, and families who are lesbian or gay requires that organizations and practitioners identify and address social problems—in this case child abuse and neglect—that affect them individually and collectively. These include the discrimination practiced in children and family services organizations, in health care systems, in educational settings, and in family courts, as well as the violence perpetrated against gays and lesbians.

Addressing such problems requires child welfare professionals to advocate with and on behalf of lesbian and gay clients, to be vigilant against institutional discrimination against gay and lesbian clients, and to be visible in joining with the lesbian and gay communities to address community and social problems. The following vignette illustrates the relevance of these dimensions.

José

José, a 12-year-old Spanish-speaking youth, was sent from Puerto Rico where he had resided with his 49-year-old maternal grandmother since he was three months old to live in Manhattan with his biological mother. This move was precipitated when his grandmother alleged that he was engaging in same-gender prostitution activities. When he arrived in New York his mother, who he had not seen since he was three months old, had remarried and started a life apart from him.

José was at his mother's home for five days when his stepfather, who he did not know and who did not speak Spanish, immediately became concerned about his perceived feminine mannerisms and his late hours. When José arrived home late one night, his stepfather became physically abusive toward him—punching him in the face and verbally abusing him, screaming: "I will not have a faggot in my house." As a response to insuring his own safety, José left the house and wandered around Manhattan. Unfamiliar with the New York City area since he had arrived from Puerto Rico only days before, José, lost and confused, asked a stranger for assistance. The woman took José into her home and permitted him to remain there until she could contact the police.

The police returned José to his parents' home. His mother refused to keep him in her home, saying that she could not deal with him if he was "like that." At this juncture, his mother brought him to Family Court where she filed a PINS (Person In Need of Supervision) petition against him, citing his late hours and incorrigible behavior as reasons for the court's intervention. Although bruises were apparent on his arms and neck, no one made note of the abuse that this child had endured. Since the judge, the child's social worker, and his attorney were uncomfortable with the issue of José's sexual orientation, no one addressed the abuse issue in the courtroom. In fact, when the social worker was told by a Spanish-speaking colleague what, in fact, had happened to José, her response was: "What do you want the parents to do? No parent wants their child to be 'like that.' Sometimes families try to beat it out of them."

José was separated from his family, and placed by the City in a group home where no one spoke Spanish and where no one was trained to deal with the unique issues that his sexual orientation presented. The issues pertaining to his abuse and neglect were never addressed.

Jose's case is not an isolated incident.

PROTECTING THE CHILD WHILE PRESERVING THE FAMILY

Although the Child Abuse and Neglect Act of 1974 provided funds to create demonstration projects in states, child services have been the responsibility of child welfare workers in the United States and Canada for over a century (Stein 1984; Watson 1990). By the philosophical principle of acting in the best interest the child, the field of children and family services has had responsibility for protecting children from abuse and neglect. In the past social workers have been characterized as quick to separate a child from his or her family if they believed that risk was involved. What was not known at the time was that the effects of separating children from their families and placing them in out-of-home care were also significant. Efforts to preserve and strengthen the family have caused professionals in the field to move toward more comprehensive services to protect children (Hartman and Laird 1983, 1985). This reframing of the focus of child welfare practice has changed the ways that the field, in recent years, has responded to children, youth, and families. Indeed, the issue of preserving the family and protecting the child are age-old tensions in children and family services.

DEFINING CHILD MALTREATMENT

Child abuse and neglect falls into specific categories with different symptoms and often different etiologies. The four categories most often used are physical abuse, physical neglect, sexual abuse, and emotional or psychological maltreatment (Crosson-Tower 1998:229). The term "child maltreatment" encompasses a wide range of parental acts or behaviors that place a child at risk of serious physical or emotional harm (Hutchison 1994). Abuse can be emotional, physical, or sexual and all three were observed in the cases evaluated for this study.

Child neglect places a child at risk of serious harm through acts of omission by the parent or caregiver (Rose and Meezan 1991). In most cases a neglectful parent fails to provide minimal levels of care and supervision to a child, even though the parent has the means and ability to do so. According to Thompson (1995:16) the largest proportion of maltreating parents are identified as neglectful, not physically abusive. The association between child neglect and poverty are strongly correlated (Pelton 1994). These conditions were also reflected in the gay and lesbian youths who experienced familial neglect in these case examples. Neglected children and adolescents encompass those who are abandoned by their parents, malnourished, ill, and who do not receive necessary medical care, as well as children and youths who live in a dangerous physical environment, who lack basic physical care and hygiene, who are inadequately clothed, and who are not old enough to care for themselves but who are left unattended and unsupervised. Emotional neglect, a slightly different phenomenon, includes chronic emotional deprivation, where the child or adolescent is denied attention and affection, is ignored, made to feel unwanted and unloved, is isolated and denied interactions with other people, or is exposed to the conflict, discord, and often erratic behaviors of an unstable parent.

According to Steele (1987) there are four dynamics that are almost always present in families in which child abuse occurs and might also contribute to child neglect:

1. Parents must have the psychological predisposition to abuse or neglect their children.
2. Abused children are often perceived by abusive parents as different, or in some way unsatisfactory.
3. High stress and crisis in the family usually contribute to maltreatment. Abuse is usually precipitated by some external stress on an already vulnerable family.
4. Maltreating parents often lack interpersonal or environmental supports.

Steele suggests that when all four of these dynamics are present, the likelihood of child abuse is extremely high. All of these conditions are reflected back in the clinical case examples of abused and/or neglected gay/lesbian children and youth reviewed for this chapter.

NEGLECT BY FAMILIES

In clinical work with families affected by issues of sexual orientation, many parents reported that they frequently were caught off guard when their gay/lesbian son or daughter disclosed their gay/lesbian identity. In fact, many parents were so staggered by that disclosure that their response could be characterized as psychologically neglectful.

PETER

Peter came into the kitchen while his father and I were having a snack. He looked so serious that we asked him if something was wrong. At first he didn't answer and he fixed himself a snack, then he sat down at the table with us. It took him a while before he looked at us. After what seemed like an eternity, he said, "I have something to tell you and it's not an easy thing to say." I felt myself steel against whatever it might be, a plethora of things ran through my mind: was he doing drugs? did he get someone pregnant? was he dropping out of school? did he have an accident with the car? We all seemed frozen in place waiting to hear what it was. Then he said, "I'm gay!" I couldn't believe it. I felt as though this child whom I had raised was an absolute stranger. I thought, "Oh, no, not my son. I would have known this, why didn't I ever see this coming?" It was like being told that he was dead. Suddenly the person sitting across from me wasn't my son anymore. I felt as if we were talking with a stranger. I've lost my child.

Are some of the parents of gay and lesbian children neglectful by child welfare standards? It is an important question for child welfare practitioners to consider. The feelings of most parents of gay and lesbian children, so well illustrated in the excerpt from the case above, found parents who were shocked and completely dumbfounded by their child's disclosure of a gay or lesbian identity. These thoughts represented an internal response that they, at least initially, could not bear.

Why don't the parents of gay and lesbian children notice that their child is different? If they did, would it make a difference in how they were treated? Perceived "difference," which was also identified as a contributing factor for child maltreatment (Steele 1987), is an important factor to consider. The case below provides an example of a situation where a child was perceived as different by his family at a young age.

CARL

Carl, a 7-year-old Caucasian boy, lives with his mother, father, and two siblings, a 9-year-old sister, and a 3-year-old brother in a small single-family home in a rural suburb of Chicago. Carl is soft-spoken, bright, and described as "a sensitive boy" by his parents. Last Christmas, when his sister received a doll, Carl spoke up and said that he would like one too. Carl's parents immediately insisted that boys do not play with female dolls. They offered him a G.I. Joe doll as an alternative, Carl insisted that he wanted a doll like his sister's. His parents are concerned and feel that maybe he needs to be less sensitive and more involved in traditional "boy" activities. They wonder if they should involve Carl in more sports activities.

If Carl is in fact gay and not just sensitive as his parents describe him, is their way of dealing with him, which suggests a reparative theme, psychologically neglectful? There are several questions that should be explored. Are parents who attempt to change their child's sexual orientation neglectful? Because of their own fear that he might be gay and their own lack of knowledge about a gay or lesbian orientation, will his parents be able to fully parent him and meet his emotional needs? Will they be able to support his emerging identity as he grows into adolescence or will they persuade him to suppress his identity? Will the family be able to endure the stigma that comes with having a gay or lesbian family member?

In the cases where I have conducted clinical work with the parents of gay/lesbian children and youth, the response from many parents can best be described as a "corrective" to an emerging gay identity, which is viewed as shameful and stigmatizing. Although the thought of parenting a gay or lesbian child is enough to send some families into a complete crisis, not all families respond negatively. Ryan and Futterman (1998:69) suggest that there are actually three adaptations—rejection, ambivalence, and acceptance—the last of which involves a reframing process for the family. The following vignette illustrates an affirming approach held by one parent:

PAUL

Ten-year-old Paul, an African-American child, lives with his mother, Barbara, in a quiet neighborhood in Los Angeles. Paul is a calm, sweet child, and not at all interested in the usual rough-and-tumble activities of other boys his age. He prefers reading, drawing, and playing on his computer at home.

One day the counselor in his after-school program approached Paul's mother to tell her that some of the other parents were concerned that her son was very effeminate. The counselor, who was inexperienced and not professionally trained, suggested that she should consider involving her son in more masculine sports activities. Barbara laughed and asked if the counselor and the other parents were afraid that her son might be gay? The counselor uncomfortably acknowledged that this was indeed their fear.

Barbara's reply was, "My child will be who he is. If he is gay, fine. If he is not gay, fine. All the so-called masculine activities in the world are not going to make him straight if he's gay. And it doesn't matter to me what sexual orientation he is as long as he is a good person."

Barbara withdrew Paul from the after-school program and sought a different one with a more enlightened staff and perhaps less judgmental parents.

Limited research with the parents of gay and lesbian children (Cantwell 1996; Mallon under review) suggest that there could be a gap of eleven years between the time that, for example, a gay child was aware of his gay identity and the point at which he disclosed his identity to his parents. One mother interviewed in my study recalled:

> I always knew someplace deep inside that my son was different, but I guess I just repressed that observation. When he did come out to his father and me when he was 26, I asked, after getting over the initial shock of the disclosure, how long he had known and when he responded since he was 15, I felt so bad. How could my child have suffered in silence for so long. I felt guilty too, how could I have been so blind to him?

Empirical evidence (D'Augelli and Hershberger 1993:433) suggests that most young people when coming out do not first come out to their families. These researchers note that the majority of gay/lesbian youth (73%) disclosed first to a friend. Mothers were told first only 7 percent of the time; fathers, or both parents, were told first 1 percent of the time. The fact remains, however, that parents are not privy to integral information about their child's sexual identity should cause concern on the part of professionals and parents. Such an unawareness of an integral part of a child's identity could be characterized, I believe, as psychological neglect.

While I posit that from a clinical perspective it would be more helpful for parents to know of their child's being "different" at an earlier age, Baker (1998:19), a mother of two gay sons, expands further:

> I cannot help but wonder if we had known that our children might grow up to be gay, what would have been different in the way we treated them? Would we have loved them as unconditionally as we did or would we have been anxiously trying to shape their sexual orientation? Would we have looked upon some of their characteristics as less endearing? Would we have tried to force them to play football and basketball rather than spend their time reading and studying nature? What damage might we have done to their personalities, their emotional development, if we had known? These are all questions that cannot be answered but that call attention to the particular problems in child rearing that arise from anti-gay prejudice and parental ignorance about sexual orientation.

Baker's (1998:29) feelings of guilt and helplessness are further explicated in this recollection:

> We, as parents, had been of absolutely no help to our children with their growing up gay. It would have been so simple if, at times during their childhood and adolescence, we had only known enough just to have explained homosexuality to our children, to have told then that some people fall in love with people of the same sex, and that it isn't a sickness or deviance, it is just the way some people are. We could have told them that if they should grow up to be gay, it wouldn't mean they couldn't have a normal life. But, sadly, my husband and I never told them any of those things . . .
>
> As parents, we weren't informed enough and we weren't understanding enough. We had been mainly silent about the topic.

Parental attitudes toward a child's disclosure are mediated by stereotypical perceptions of what it means to be gay or lesbian. In fact, one study (Robinson, Walters, and Skeen 1989) suggested that many parents view their child's gay/lesbian sexual identity disclosure as an occasion akin to mourning a death. Clearly, accurate information about sexual orientation, including open discussions that address gay and lesbian orientation, could assist parents in dispelling myths that are parent-blaming and erroneously link a gay or lesbian identity to an unhappy childhood and a disturbed relationship with parents. Although changing cultural values and beliefs about homosexuality, oftentimes reinforced through personal or religious bias, will take many years, in the case of young gays and lesbians who find themselves the victims of parental or familial violence, there is a great deal that child welfare practitioners can do immediately.

PHYSICAL ABUSE

The literature clearly suggests that lesbian and gay children and youth are at risk for abuse within their homes and in their communities (Hunter 1990; Mallon 1998a; Rivers 1997; Savin-Williams 1994, 1998). Runaway and homeless youth (see chapter 7) may experience familial abuse at higher levels (Bucy and Able-Peterson 1993; Janus, Archambault, and Brown 1995; Kruks 1991; Kurtz et al. 1996; Luna 1995; Zide and Cherry 1992). Abuse of gay/lesbian children and youth, like the abuse of their heterosexual coun-terparts, takes the form of physical abuse, emotional abuse, and sexual abuse, as illustrated by the following cases.

ROBERT

Robert is a 17-year-old Jamaican-born adolescent who lives with his mother, Rosa, who is a homemaker, his stepfather, James, who is a carpenter's assistant, and three younger brothers. Robert is an effem-inate youth who has been teased by peers and his family about being a "fag" ever since he can remember. Robert and his stepfather have always had a acrimonious relationship; he and his mother have gen-erally been close, but his mother's religious beliefs frequently come into conflict with his sexuality.

One evening when Robert came home from being out with his friends he returned to find his mother crying in the kitchen, reading letters that his boyfriend had written to him, letters that he had kept in his "secret box." He immediately knew that there would be trouble when he realized what his mother was reading. As Robert entered the kitchen Rosa began screaming at him that he was a "faggot," that she always knew it, and now she had proof. She jumped up from the kitchen table and began punching him on the back and slapping him across the face. He tried to protect himself, but Rosa did not stop.

When Robert's stepfather, James, heard the commotion he came running into the kitchen. Rosa was screaming that Robert was a fag-got and rather than attempting to stop the violence, James joined in, taking off his belt and beating Robert with his belt. Robert finally escaped from the beating by pushing his mother down and running out of the apartment. He had no where to go, but decided to go to the police. When he arrived at the station and explained what hap-pened he was told, "if you're going to live that kind of lifestyle, that's what you'll have to expect." He had no where to go, but knew that he couldn't go home. It was not a safe place for him to be.

Many gay and lesbian youths report physical abuse by their parents directly linked to their sexual orientation. According to the youths and families interviewed, fathers had a more difficult time accepting homosex-uality than did mothers, which may account for issues having to do with gender biases toward a gay or lesbian identity (Reiter 1991). Overwhelmingly, the comments of most young people who had endured abuse concurred with Reiter's findings and suggested that female care providers were better suited to working with gay and lesbian young people than were male care providers. Control issues and macho attitudes were identified by young people as impairing most males' ability to care for gay and lesbian young people.

The siblings of a gay/lesbian child or adolescent may also respond in an ambivalent manner to a family member's disclosure. While some siblings may be supportive, others could join in the familial abuse of a gay/lesbian brother or sister. Sibling reaction to a the disclosure of a family member is evidenced in this occurrence recalled by a sixteen-year-old gay man in Los Angeles:

> It wasn't bad enough that my Mom was freaking out and beating on me, but my older brother was also really upset when I came out. He was so mad. I remember him saying, as he was punching me in the face, "if you think I am gonna defend you in school, you're crazy—you stupid faggot. Why did you have to go and tell everybody you're gay?—why couldn't you just keep it to yourself." I guess he was worried that people might think that if he had a brother who was gay, then maybe he might be gay too. I didn't count on him joining in with the bashing.

EMOTIONAL ABUSE

Emotional abuse, which most self-identified gay/lesbian youths claimed to endure as an almost daily occurrence, can be associated with physical abuse or neglect, or can be a separate psychological phenomenon. The emotional harm that occurs without physical abuse or neglect often falls beyond the legal and practice scope of child welfare intervention. Nonetheless, except for physical scars, emotional abuse has pervasive emotional consequences. Unpredictable emotional trauma from a parent can cause extreme anxiety and feelings of worthlessness for a gay or lesbian young person. Darrel, a fifteen-year-old from New York experienced emotional abuse firsthand by his family.

Darrel

"Hey sissy boy!"

"You fucking homo, faggot, sissy, queer"—these were words that Darrel had hurled at him ever since he could remember. It was bad enough that kids in school harassed him, but when his own family joined in, it really hurt. It seemed that whenever anything went wrong at home these were the words that his brothers, his sister, and even his mother and father used to deride him. It wore him down, it made him feel terrible.

One night Darrel had had enough and tried to end his life. He took a mixture of prescription drugs that his mother kept in her medicine chest. They found him in his room, rushed him to the emergency room, and couldn't figure out why he was so upset that he would try to end his life. He told his social worker that it was the words . . . they were hurtful, they made him feel inferior, when your own family hurts you like that, what can you expect from the rest of the world?

But it was more than just the words, it was the emotional battering that he had endured which caused him to try to end it all.

Parents are a child's most important source of praise and support needed to develop confidence, self-worth, self-esteem, and a sense of accomplishment. Parental approval and support are a vital prerequisite to healthy emotional development and the most powerful predictor of mental health for young gays, bisexuals, and lesbians interviewed in one study (Hershberger and D'Augelli 1995). Gay and lesbian children who are emotionally belittled and verbally assaulted can suffer serious emotional consequences and are at high risk of emotional harm. Feeling of self-worth comes about for some abused youth only after they leave an abusive environment and find a positive view of their sexual orientation and acceptance from a peer group.

A study by Pilkington and D'Augelli (1995) found that 36 percent of the young gays and lesbians surveyed had been insulted or verbally abused by at least one member of their immediate families. Although parental reactions to a child's disclosure of homosexuality are varied, in addition to verbal taunts and physical violence, gay/lesbian children and youth are confronted with more surreptitious and insidious forms of rejection, including withdrawal of affection or exclusion from family activities (Rivers 1997).

Parental indifference, which is at times a consequence of a child's disclosure, may have even more potential for emotional damage. The message of parental indifference is that nobody cares; that the child is not even worth a negative thought or interaction; and that the child is not worth anything. Parental indifference further robs children of a chance to earn parental approval, rewards, and reciprocal caring relationships, as evidenced by Rose's narrative:

> Once my parents found out that I was lesbian, my home became like a tomb for me. No one talked, no one asked me how my day went, our relationship went from pretty good to terrible in such a short period of time. It was horrible and it made me feel so bad. I wound up spending more and more time away from my home, not because I wanted to, but because I just couldn't stand the silence anymore.

Because it can also be difficult to identify risk assessment criteria with respect to emotional abuse that warrant agency intervention and family disruption, physical abuse and neglect have been child welfare's priorities for intervention. Although it is often difficult to assess the extent of emotional abuse, or to predict future pathology which can result, emotional abuse has devastating effects which, left untreated, often prevent gay and lesbian children from developing into emotionally healthy adults.

SEXUAL ABUSE

Sexual abuse refers to "contact with a child where the child is being used for sexual stimulation by another person"—it is assumed that the abuser is older than the child (Crosson-Tower 1998:240). Although child sexual abuse is a more complicated phenomenon than I am able to discuss here, sexual abuse perpetrated by adults against gays and lesbians is not uncommon. The basic cause of child sexual abuse is the pathology of the perpetrator, exacerbated in some cases by the preposterous notion that the perpetrator can change the gay or lesbian child through sexual abuse, as in Leah's case:

LEAH

"Oh, you're a lesbian? All you need is a good man to show you what it's like and then you'll never want another woman again." That night my stepfather came into my room, locked the door behind him, pushed his body on top of mine, and raped me. I never expected that my stepfather would do this to me. I was so ashamed, I was so embarrassed, I was so hurt. I left home the next day and went to live with friends. I never told anyone, until now, about that night. All I was being was myself, I wasn't hurting anyone, I was just trying to be myself. I didn't deserve what happened to me—no one does.

Because of the complexity of child sexual abuse cases, it is not possible for those in the child welfare field to respond effectively without the assistance of law enforcement, prosecutors, mental health professionals, and the courts. An effective response also requires that child welfare professionals master a variety of new, complex, and specialized skills. Those professionals whose positions require intervention in child sexual abuse cases are urged to read related material (Finkelhor 1984; Gomes-Schwartz, Horowitz, and Cardarelli 1990; Gilgun 1990; Haugaard and Reppuci 1988; Kolko 1987; Sgroi 1982), attend specialized classes, and train with skilled experts before working within this area of child maltreatment.

It should be abundantly clear from these case illustrations that all forms of abuse—physical, emotional, and sexual—against gay and lesbian youths are perpetrated by some caretakers and family members. In some cases, the incidence of child maltreatment is discounted for what it truly is because protecting a child from the stigmatizing nature of a gay or lesbian identity is seen by some parents as the "divine right of a parent" and preferable to having a child who is gay or lesbian (Mallon under review).

TREATMENT OF CHILD ABUSE AND NEGLECT

The risk-assessment process, which is the primary strategy utilized by child welfare practitioners to begin the process of treating child maltreatment, is (according to Rycus and Hughes 1998) akin to a fact-finding mission, which gathers pertinent information to make the following determinations:

1. Has the child been physically, emotionally, or sexually abused or neglected?
2. Is the child at risk of further harm or maltreatment?
3. Is the child in need of immediate protection?
4. If the child is at imminent risk, what must be done immediately to protect the child?

The following illustration of child maltreatment, which will also be used to illustrate a risk-assessment process, is derived from an actual case in New York City:

JORGE

Hector Allesandro is a 41-year-old divorced father who lives with his son, Jorge, age 14, and his daughter, Beatrice, age 17. Hector is employed full time in construction work, which necessitates his leaving home at an early hour and returning feeling spent from the physical aspects of his work. Beatrice cooks for the family, is responsible for keeping the apartment clean, and watches out for her younger brother.

Jorge is a soft-spoken teenager who does well in school, and is not involved in negative social activities. His father always teases him that he needs to "toughen up," to be more macho, because he feels that Jorge is "too soft." Jorge usually laughs off these comments, but sometimes, he admits, it hurts his feelings that his father does not approve of the way he acts.

One day, Jorge, who had been given money by his grandparents for his birthday, went out to the store to buy shampoo and other hair-grooming products. Amongst his purchases was a can of hair spray. When he returned home, as he unpacked his purchases his father, seeing the can of hair spray, flew into a rage. He began screaming at Jorge, "What is this shit? What are you, a woman? Men don't buy this shit! I'm not going to have any son of mine being a faggot. If I have to, I'll beat that faggot shit out of you." He began to punch Jorge who fell on the floor crying, "It's just hair spray, what's the big deal? So what if I'm gay. Is that what you're so afraid of?" Beatrice tried to stop her father from hitting Jorge, but he just pushed her away. Jorge ran out of the house when he could get away, and called the police. The police arrived and arrested Mr. Allesandro. Jorge sustained several injuries, including bruised ribs, a cut requiring several stitches over his left eye, and a sore scalp.

Fearing for his safety, Jorge asked if he could go someplace else. The police brought him first to the local hospital Emergency Room for treatment and then to the New York City's Administration for Children's Services, where he was placed in a diagnostic center for evaluation. He was scared, away from his family, and felt that he was being punished for just being himself.

The caseworker assigned to the case from the local social service district went to the Allesandro home to conduct an assessment to determine whether Jorge had been abused and to calculate the risk of returning him home. The caseworker talked to Mr. Allesandro, who had been released from detention after one night, about the alleged physical abuse and inquired about why it had occurred. Mr. Allesandro did not deny the physical abuse. He said further that he was glad that Jorge was "put away." If his son was homosexual, said Mr. Allesandro, he did not want him in his home. As a good Latino father, he asserted, it was his "right" to beat Jorge to try to change him.

Beatrice was very upset that her brother was away from home and upset by the behavior of her father, who said that he would refuse to allow Jorge to have home visits. Beatrice expressed concern about her brother and confided to the worker that her father was a "hothead" but usually came around after he had time to cool off. Mr. Allesandro, who prided himself on caring for his family, had never been arrested and was furious that his son had called the police. He maintained that as a father he had a right to beat his son, especially if he was trying to correct what he perceived to be his son's homosexual behavior.

The caseworker explored Mr. Allesandro's previous relationship with Jorge. Mr. Allesandro said Jorge was always "soft," even as a young child. He believed that Jorge was soft because he was "not around him [Mr. Allesandro] enough to show him how to act like a man." He said he tried hard to be a good father and to support his family, but "I just cannot have a son who is a faggot. It's not right, what would everybody think of me as a father?"

The caseworker tried to explain that sometimes parents do hurt their children when they are angry, or when they feel stress, or when they per-

ceive their child to be "different," as in the case of a child who is gay-identified. She explained that it was her job to help him learn more about his
son's gay identity, so that physical abuse wouldn't happen again. Mr. Allesandro responded, "Well if you can't change my son so that he is not a faggot, you can forget it! It will happen again, because if I need to beat him
again to change him, I will." Mr. Allesandro made it clear that he was not
open, at this point in the case, to learning about or to discuss his son's gay
identity. Beatrice, however expressed the wish to visit her brother and to
maintain close contact with him.

A Risk-Assessment Process with a Gay Youth and His Father

Utilizing a scheme devised by Rycus and Hughes (1998) the following risk-
assessment rating represents an examination of the risk variables and the
formulation of a risk rating for this case. Assisting child protection workers
to quantify risk objectively, rather than permitting their own subjective
bias to cloud the issue, is a strategy of risk-assessment process that could
prove useful in evaluating risk for a gay or lesbian youth. The degree of risk
to a child or adolescent as risk for abuse ranges on a continuum from no
risk to high risk. The following is a example of a risk-assessment scheme
for Jorge and his family.

Risk Assessment

Age of the child:
At age 14, Jorge is at low risk. LOW

Child's temperament, conditions, and behaviors:
Although homosexuality is societally stigmatized, Jorge is well mannered and appears to
have no unusual conditions or behaviors. LOW
Mr. Allesandro perceives Jorge's gay identity to be deviant. HIGH

Type of injury or harm:
Stitches, bruises from attack. HIGH
Injuries appear to be situational, none prior. LOW

Parental context:
Abuse occurred in a rage, the punishment was unreasonable. HIGH

Role of emotional harm:

Abuse was situational, but involved police and the emergency placement of Jorge. HIGH

Parent's willingness to acknowledge maltreatment:

Mr. Allesandro readily admits his responsibility for the injuries, but demonstrates no guilt, shame, or remorse, stating that it was "right" as a parent to correct his son, even if it is was through physical abuse. HIGH

Parent has condition/mental illness that affects parental ability:

Mr. Allesandro is not a substance abuser, has no known physical or mental health conditions that would affect his ability to parent. LOW
Mr. Allesandro has work-related stress. MODERATE
Mr. Allesandro believes his harsh treatment to be corrective and warranted. HIGH

Parenting skills and abilities—age appropriate:

Mr. Allesandro has culturally defined rigid views of masculinity and femininity and very limited understanding of a gay identity. Parenting in other areas has been adequate. MODERATE

Access to child:

Jorge lives full time in the care of his father. There are no other adults in the home. Mr. Allesandro's access to Jorge is unlimited. HIGH

Condition of the home:

Physical home environment is good. LOW

Previous reports:

There are no previous reports of maltreatment. LOW

Susceptibility to crisis:

Mr. Allesandro has high stress at work, as a single father, and in being new to the idea of parenting a child who he has suspected, and now knows is gay. He is angry that his son is what he most feared he was, he is angry about being sent to jail for one night, and he is angry that his family is now known to the ACS system. HIGH

Strengths and safety factors:

Beatrice loves her brother and is a resource for him.
Mr. Allesandro has been known to cool off after a period of time.
Mr. Allesandro has been a successful parent in other parenting areas.
Coming out can be a situational stress and crisis for the family. Interventions to stabilize the family and to educate Mr. Allesandro in the future about gay adolescent development could minimize risk. MODERATE

Overall level of risk:

Without intervention, there is a strong likelihood that Jorge could be harmed again by his father. The fact that the abuse was situational would usually warrant a low or moderate risk rating, however Mr. Allesandro's insistence that it was his "right" to beat his son is an important factor to consider. Additionally, Mr. Allesandro's threat to "beat him again" and his unwillingness to allow Jorge to have home visits suggests that he is not willing to accept immediate services. HIGH

Safety plan:

1. The caseworker should explore the possibility of placing Jorge with relatives. If this is not possible, caseworker should explore the possibility of placing Jorge in a gay-affirming family foster home.
2. The Family Court should order Mr. Allesandro to receive supportive counseling with a therapist who has gay-affirming training.
3. Beatrice should maintain frequent contact with Jorge and visit him where he resides.
4. Mr. Allesandro should receive parent training in gay adolescent development.
5. Jorge should receive counseling to help him to adjust to living apart from his family and should be connected to age-appropriate services for gay adolescents in his community.
6. The caseworker should work with the entire family unit within a cultural context toward rebuilding relationships now that everyone is aware that Jorge is gay. The worker should involve everyone in problem solving to work toward reunification when and if it is deemed that Mr. Allesandro is no longer a risk to maltreating Jorge.

The risk assessment outlined above is obviously an idealistic scenario, but not one that is unobtainable. Placing greater emphasis in professional training on the dynamics of culture with a particular emphasis on issues of sexual orientation could assist child protection practitioners in this neglected area.

Scraping below the already unpleasant veneer of child neglect and maltreatment one can sometimes find an additional concealed layer, one that when revealed is clearly linked to issues of sexual orientation. Competent definitions of child maltreatment must avoid extreme heterocentrism. Just as a general lack of training and knowledge about cultural diversity has hampered child protection efforts (Ahn 1994; Hong and Hong 1991; Korbin 1994), so has heterocentrism in child welfare hampered professionals in the system from responding effectively to a growing number of gay and lesbian children who come to the attention of child protection services.

Heterocentrism disregards sexual orientation differences and imposes a single standard for all child care practices. This is potentially harmful to children and adolescents who identify as gay or lesbian as it downgrades their sexual orientation. It is also potentially harmful to child protection efforts in that one strategy (that of heterosexual assumption) will be implemented for all young people regardless of their individual sexual orientation. Furthermore, Western society's tacit acceptance of some parents' attempts to "correct" their child's real or perceived gay or lesbian identity, viewed as shameful and stigmatizing, through physically, sexually, or emotionally abusive means should cause consternation for child welfare advocates or anyone who claims to be concerned about the protection of all children.

IMPLICATIONS FOR PRACTICE

Protective services for gay/lesbian children, youth, and families can be improved in three areas: improvement of staff training, prevention, and advocacy.

Training in competent practice with these persons, not just one-shot deals, but training that is consistently integrated into the core protection curriculum is essential. In addition to agency-based training, colleges and universities must become more active in providing skills-based training in child protective services that incorporates issues of sexual orientation (Brown and Weil 1992; Mallon 1998b). It is quite likely that child protection workers will find issues of sexual orientation at the root of a variety of child maltreatment situations.

One cannot discuss the need to improve child protection services for gay/lesbian children and youth without stressing the importance of prevention. Prevention should not simply be seen as consciousness-raising through awareness programs, but also as primary prevention, including integrating content of issues of sexual orientation in parenting programs and mediation programs in educational sites.

Finally, those child welfare advocates who claim to be concerned about the welfare of all children must also include protection issues as they pertain to gay/lesbian children and youth. To do otherwise is an abhorrent and unethical violation of our values as a profession.

In this chapter I wanted to drive home the urgency of developing comprehensive, informed approaches to evaluating potential and realized risks for these human beings. It is my hope that the cases presented provide a beginning context to understand the potential for such conditions.

CHAPTER 4

Sexual Orientation and the Law: Legal Issues in Child Welfare

Acutely conflicting attitudes toward a lesbian or gay sexual orientation share an uneasy existence in Western society. This variety of perspectives is reflected in legislation, legal decision making, social policy design, and academic scholarship. Attitudes ranging from disapproval to pity to insouciance to respect appear in both the legal and social welfare communities and are firmly rooted in heterocentrism.

Although some courts and social welfare analysts are supportive to claims for equal treatment by lesbians and gays, many professionals within these communities retain negative views of anyone with a minority sexual orientation. Skepticism about the very existence of gays or lesbians, which further marginalizes that population, is an additional strategy of nonaction deployed by families, social institutions, and the law.

The legal system has increasingly played an important role in either insuring or denying the rights of those whose lives are affected by their sexual orientation (Flaks 1994; Guggenheim, Lowe Dylan, and Curtis 1996; Rivera 1987; Stein 1996). Parents seeking child custody or visitation rights, gays and lesbians seeking the right to be recognized as legal parents through adoption, states that ban gays and lesbians from being foster or adoptive parents, and child welfare agencies' policies based on recognition of same-gendered couple benefits, a child's right to protection from harm while in state custody, and a minor's consent to treatment procedures are all issues affected by the legal system and the laws imposed by individual states. This chapter reviews the issues, utilizing individual and organizational case data to analyze the role that the law plays in the lives of children and families affected by issues of sexual orientation.

Issues in Family Law That Involve Children

In the United States, gay/lesbian children, youth, and families are denied most of the rights afforded to nongay/lesbian children, youth, and families. Fewer than one-fifth of the states offer full civil rights legal protection to gay/lesbian persons. Courts routinely refuse to provide gay/lesbian relationships the legal recognition they need and deserve, and often go so far as to treat lesbian/ gay families with contempt. All family law issues are governed by state law. As such, most court cases are argued on a state-by-state basis, sometimes even on a court-by-court one. This requires that litigation on these issues must occur again and again in state after state—each victory has particular importance in the larger struggle to gain full legal recognition for lesbian/gay children, youth, and families in every state.

Because gay and lesbian children and youth are socialized to hide their orientation, and because of the systemic bias that makes it necessary for many of them to hide for their own safety, there are no figures to document how many children and youths in child welfare systems are affected. In the United States there are only two agencies, the Gay and Lesbian Adolescent Social Services (G.L.A.S.S.) Agency in Los Angeles and Green Chimneys Children's Services in New York City, that provide services specifically for gay/lesbian children, youth, and families. The Children's Aid Society in Toronto provides similar services in Canada (see Mallon 1998; O'Brien, Travers, and Bell 1993).

This out-group faces many social and legal obstacles in the areas of child protection, family support, out-of-home placement, and most clearly with respect to gay and lesbian parenting (Sullivan 1994). The following examination evaluates the impact of the law concerning parenting by gays and lesbians in several areas: custody and visitation, adoption and foster parenting, second-parent adoption, issues related to procreation and parenting, a child's right to protection from harm while in state foster care custody, and minors' participation in treatment programs.

Custody and Visitation Rights

Custody cases often arise involving lesbian/gay parents and their children. It is useful to distinguish between three types of custody and visitation disputes: those between a child's biological parents; those between a legal parent and a nonparent; and those that result in termination of parental rights with respect to the child. Courts employ different standards in each of these settings. In disputes between biological parents the courts are required to determine custody and visitation on the basis of the "best interest of the child" (Goldstein et al. 1996; Hunter and Polikoff 1976; Kleber, Howell, and Tibbits-Kleber 1986). Laws governing disputes between legal parents and nonparents vary from state to state, but generally there is a presumption that exists in favor of granting custody to the child's legal parent (Clark 1988; Polikoff 1986). In cases that lead to termination of parental rights with respect to the child, regardless of the parties involved, all states preserve the parent's rights unless the parent is found unfit or that continuation of the relationship would be harmful to the child (Clark 1988).

Regarding disputes between biological parents, many lesbians and gays are the parents of children born to them from heterosexual unions. In some cases, when a child's nongay parent discovers that the vis-à-vis parent is gay or lesbian, he or she may attempt to limit the parenting role of the gay/lesbian parent. Challenges have also been brought by other relatives or government agencies. In these cases,[*] the sexual orientation of the lesbian or gay parent is often used to foment prejudice—to insinuate the myths and stereotypes about gay or lesbian parents in order to achieve a denial of visitation or custody.

In general, the legal standards applied to child custody and visitation cases are vague. Since courts award custody based on the standard of the "best interest of the child," courts frequently consider the parent's sexual orientation to be relevant to the child's best interest and several courts have used the "best interest" standard to deny custody to gay and lesbian parents (Raymond 1992). These laws vary from state to state, depending on existing laws and statutes, and usually vest a great deal of discretion on the judge. Some states have created irrebuttable presumptions against granting custody to a gay or lesbian parent. Other states have rebuttable presumptions that require a gay or lesbian parent to prove that his or her sexual orientation will not harm the child. Courts in at least ten states have held that they will not deny custody to a parent on the grounds of sexual orientation without proof that the parent's sexual orientation would adversely affect the child.

---

[*] The highly publicized Sharon Bottoms story, in which a lesbian mother lost custody of her daughter to a grandparent, epitomizes the double standards and outright heterocentrism facing gay and lesbian parents in many state courts. The antigay standards used to judge this Virginia mother's fitness as a parent represents a minority view among state courts.

Most courts have adopted an approach known as "the nexus approach," which requires a clear demonstration that a parent's sexual orientation actually causes harm to a child before it is deemed relevant. Under this approach legal experts claim, the child's best interest becomes and remains the proper focus of the case (ACLU 1997; Lambda 1996, 1997). As of May 1995, twenty-nine states have adopted some variant of a nexus test. As of this writing, several localities have explicit laws guaranteeing that sexual orientation by itself cannot be used as a factor in determining custody or visitation (Lambda 1997:2–3; M. Peguese, Lambda Legal Defense and Education Fund, February 4, 1999).

Moral issues frequently come into play. Some courts treat a parent's sexual orientation as determinative despite the statutory requirement that custody decisions be based on the child's overall best interest. Courts that deny custody or restrict visitation by a gay or lesbian parent typically use one or more of five rationales to conclude that granting custody or unrestricted visitation to such a parent is not in the child's best interest. The first rational is that the child will be harassed or ostracized by heterosexuals (*Jacobson v. Jacobson*, 1981). Second is the fear that the child might become gay or lesbian (*J.L.P.[H.] v. D.J.P.*, 1982). Third, courts believe that living with or being visited by a gay or lesbian parent may harm the child's moral well being (*Roe v. Roe*, 1985). Fourth, courts worry about child molestation (*J.L.P.[H.] v. D.J.P.*, 1982). Finally, courts point to state sodomy statutes that they claim embody a state interest against homosexuality (*Constant A. v. Paul C.A.*, 1985; Verhovek 1997; Williams 1997).

In truth, none of these rationales are sufficiently related to the child's best interest to justify denying custody or restricting visitation by a gay or lesbian parent. Furthermore, none of these fears are borne out or supported by evidence (Dunlap 1996; Patterson 1994, 1995, 1996). All research to date has reached the same unequivocal conclusion about gay and lesbian parenting: the children of lesbian/gay parents grow up as successfully as the children of heterosexual parents (Elovitz 1995). Not one study has found otherwise. Likewise, not one study has found that the children of lesbian/gay parents face greater social stigma. Additionally, there is absolutely no evidence to support the belief that the children of lesbian/gay parents are more likely to be abused, nor is there evidence to suggest that the children of gay/lesbian parents are more likely to be gay or lesbian themselves.

A judge's view of a child's moral well-being may not be the same as the child's "best interest." Although it is difficult to state definitively what beliefs regarding sexual orientation are best for a child, judges should avoid legislating their own sense of morality through custody decisions.

The court's fear that gays and lesbians will molest their children is also not borne out in the research (Groth and Birnbaum 1978; Herek 1991; Jenny, Roesler, and Poyer 1994; Newton 1978). The majority of child molesters are heterosexually oriented men. Women, regardless of sexual orientation, rarely molest children. If courts were to make custody decisions based solely on the risk of molestation, they would probably award custody to the mother whether or not she was a lesbian (*Harvard Law Review* 1989:130).

Finally, the state's desire to promote policies underlying its sodomy statue is not a statutorily permissible predicate for a custody denial or visitation restriction because it is irrelevant to the child's best interest. Moreover, because most state sodomy statutes prohibit opposite-gender as well as same-gender sodomy, these statutes cannot justify custody denials only to gays and lesbians. Most courts who have denied child custody to gays and lesbians have not heard evidence proving that the gay/lesbian parent has violated the sodomy statutes, or that the nongay/nonlesbian parent has not.

Adoption and Foster Care

Every state has an obligation to protect the health and welfare of its children. Adoption and foster care provides homes for children who cannot or should not live in their own homes with their own biological families. Although the psychosocial issues associated with gays and lesbians creating their own families will be more fully covered in chapter 5, this section focuses on the legal consequences of adoption and foster care.

Adoption terminates the rights and responsibilities of biological parents and vests them with an adoptive parent or parents. Adoptions are officially sanctioned through public or state-licensed private agencies or via private placement arrangements. Courts, guided by the child's best interest, must review all adoption petitions; in addition, the consent of the agency is required for agency adoptions and, in most states, judges hearing private adoption petitions must consider agency or social worker recommendations.

In contrast, foster care is intended to provide a temporary home for a child. Permanency planning mandates and the intent of the Adoption and Safe Families Act of 1997 stipulates that after a period of no more than eighteen months in foster care, a child should either be reunited with his or her biological family or freed for adoption. In some cities—New York, Philadelphia, Los Angeles, Denver, and San Francisco—although no statistical information is available, foster home placements have been made for gay and lesbian adolescents with gay or lesbian foster parents. Many states, however, make it difficult for lesbians or gays to be foster parents (Groninger 1996). In North Dakota, for example, only married couples are allowed to be licensed as foster parents. In other states, although many child welfare agencies and social workers may be opposed to placement in gay or lesbian homes, such placements occur either because the social workers are unaware of an applicant's sexual orientation or because they unofficially recognize that the gay or lesbian applicant will provide a good home for the young person (Achtenberg 1990; Kessler 1997; Ricketts 1991; Ricketts and Achtenberg 1987, 1990; Sullivan 1995).

The recent repeal of the New Hampshire ban leaves Florida as the only state in the country with a law on the books prohibiting gays and lesbians from adopting children (Frieberg 1999:11). Florida's law is also to be challenged in court later this year (Epperly 1999). Although the majority of states no longer officially deem lesbians and gays as "unfit" to rear a child, each state decides independently who can adopt, and bills barring adoptions by gays/lesbians continue to be introduced into state legislatures every year. During the past two years, several bills have been introduced to ban gays and lesbians from adoption and foster parenting. In Arkansas, a regulation that would prohibit anyone from being a foster or adoptive parent if any adult member of the household is homosexual received approval from the governor-appointed Child Welfare Review Board (Green 1999). Two bills have been proposed in Texas—one barring the state from placement of children in adoptive or foster homes where "homosexual conduct is occurring or is likely to occur," and the other, which would mandate the removal of a child already placed with gay or lesbian foster parents. Texas Governor George W. Bush has gone on record (Hennie 1999:1) as saying that he would sign the first bill if it should come to his desk. The head of Utah's Child and Family Services Board has proposed a regulation to prohibit gay and unmarried couples from adopting; and in Indiana, an elected statewide official has introduced a bill to prevent gay people from adopting or becoming foster parents (Freiberg 1999).

While there have been openly gay and lesbian adoptions in a number of jurisdictions, including the District of Columbia, Ohio, New Mexico, and California, the most common practice is for a single individual to apply for adoption as the "legal" adopter of the child. Couples who desire joint custody then apply for a "second-parent adoption," which will be explored in the following section.

Restrictions on whether gays and lesbians can be allowed to provide foster or adoptive homes for needy children run counter to the welfare of children needing such homes. States' and agencies' refusals to place children with gays and lesbians are also sometimes based on the perceived potential harm to children, as discussed earlier. Refusals to permit lesbians and gays to adopt or become foster parents stem in part from a fear of appearing to accept same-gendered relationships to any degree that would resonate with the experience of heterocentrism.

Deciding whether a particular placement is in the child's best interest should always involve balancing that specific placement against other available alternatives (Goldstein et al. 1996). The benefits of placing a child in a gay or lesbian home are especially clear for "hard-to-place" children, and most self-identified gay and lesbian adolescents are, by virtue of their orientation, "hard-to-place." Many states have a shortage of foster or adoptive parents, many children end up in inappropriate settings such as diagnostic centers, psychiatric hospitals, or congregate care institutions (Mallon 1992) if they cannot find a home with the right "fit." Since a permanent home is a requirement for all children and is critical to their development, gay/lesbian individuals and couples can provide a much-needed source of potential foster and adoptive parents for such young persons.

Since refusals to permit gays or lesbians to become foster parents do not serve the affected children's best interest (Raymond 1992), they can in some cases be challenged in court. In all states except Florida, a would-be foster or adoptive parent challenging a judge's refusal to grant a private placement adoption petition can argue that the denial does not serve the child's best interest. In other situations, however, such a denial of a foster care license, or when an agency refuses to place a gay/lesbian individual or couple on its wait list, the would-be parent has no state law cause of action with which to challenge the denial. Class action law suits (Bernstein 1999; Boerner 1999; Price 1999; Stein 1991, 1998:202), focusing on best-available placements for children in foster care (i.e., *Joel A. v Guiliani*, 1999; *Joseph, A. v. New Mexico Department of Social Services*, 1983; *Marisol v. Guiliani*, 1996; *Wilder v. Sugarman*, 1974) can also be used as grounds for legal action to guarantee appropriate placements for gay and lesbian young persons.

Second-Parent Adoption

Until recently, in most lesbian- and gay-headed families, only one parent was recognized as the legal parent. Dissimilar from the traditional form of adoption, which recognizes only the parental right of the biological parent as the current legal parent(s), second-parent adoption leaves the parental rights of one legally recognized parent intact and creates a second legally recognized parent for the child. While second-parent adoption is currently the only way for both partners of a gay or lesbian couple to become the legal parents of a child, it has also become fairly routine for nongay adoptive parents.

One of the first cases tested occurred in New York, the 1992 *Matter of Adoption of Evan*. Two women living together in a committed long-term relationship, which they perceived as permanent for fourteen years, decided to have a child together. Pursuant to their joint plan, the women were alternatively inseminated with sperm obtained from a male friend, who formally relinquished any parental rights to the child. When Evan was born, he lived with both women. They both participated in raising him over the following six years. Evan viewed both women as parents.

In considering the best interest of Evan, the court evaluated home study reports, which described the nonbiological parent as loving, warm, and nurturing who was committed to Evan and was an effective parent to him. Having concluded on the facts presented that the adoption was in Evan's best interest, the New York County Surrogates Court ultimately also granted adoption to the nonbiological mother.

A similar case, which was one of the most highly publicized changes in the area of child adoption laws for lesbian and gay couples, can be seen in the "Massachusetts Adoption of Tammy" case. By a 5 to 4 decision, after months of testimony attesting to the best interest of the child, the Supreme Judicial Court of Massachusetts upheld the adoption of the child by a lesbian couple who had raised her since birth.

In the *Matter of Jacob* (NY Nov 2, 1995), the New York Court of Appeals ruled in a 4 to 3 decision that "the unmarried partner of a child's biological mother, whether heterosexual or homosexual, who is raising the child together with the biological parent, can become the child's second parent by means of adoption." The ruling established for all New York State that the adoption code does permit "second-parent adoption."

Similar groundbreaking decisions have been made in New Jersey (Smothers 1997; Szymanski 1997). In October 1997, Jon Holden-Galluccio and his partner, Michael Galluccio, challenged the New Jersey law that prevented same-gender couples and unmarried heterosexual couples from jointly adopting a child, in this case, Adam (at the time of writing, four years old), who had lived in their home as a foster child since age three months. Judge Sybil R. Moses of Superior Court in Bergen County granted the joint adoption, saying that it was in the best interest of the child. Two months later, all legal barriers to joint adoption by unmarried same-gender and heterosexual unmarried couples were removed in a broader consent decree negotiated by the judge, state welfare officials, and attorneys with the Lesbian and Gay Rights Project of the Civil Liberties Union, who represented the men and several other gay couples. New Jersey became the first state to establish a policy treating gay and unmarried couples the same way it treats married couples regarding adoptions (Smothers 1998:B5).

As of April 1997, second-parent adoptions by lesbian and gay couples had been approved by courts in the District of Columbia and twenty-one states. In most cases the approvals were from the lower courts (Lambda 1997:6).

Issues Related to Procreation and Parenting

Gays and lesbians are as capable of procreation as bisexuals or heterosexuals (Money 1988). Many are choosing to have children via alternative insemination, surrogacy, or through sexual intercourse. Legally defining rights and responsibilities of the other biological parent and consideration of the rights of the co-parent are factors today confronting legal experts and child welfare professionals. Clearly, unless a child is adopted, his or her natural mother is the legal parent. Whether the father is the legal parent is more complicated and depends on the mother's marital status, the reproductive technique utilized, and applicable state statutes. If the child is conceived through sexual intercourse and paternity is established, the father generally has equal rights and responsibilities. If the child is conceived through alternative insemination, the donor's status depends on whether the state regulates alternative insemination of unmarried women.

As with many family laws issues, laws governing donor insemination vary from state to state. Most states' laws apply only to married heterosexual women, which excludes lesbians. Some states do not have any laws governing insemination. In a majority of states there is some form of legal protection to the lesbian mother, provided that the insemination was performed in a doctor's office (Bernfeld 1995; Lambda et al. 1997). Although donor insemination requires virtually no medical expense and can be performed at home without any involvement by state officials or medical professionals, it is not without legal risks.

When a lesbian or gay couple chooses to have a child, only the biological parent is automatically the child's legal parent. If the legal parent dies, the surviving partner, or co-parent, could lose custody to the child's other biological parent or to other relatives of the child, especially grandparents. In addition, if the couple separates, the legal parent may be able to prohibit contact between the co-parent and the child.

Same-gendered couples can attempt to avoid these difficulties in several ways. They could file for second-parent adoption, insuring that both partners have equal rights and responsibilities with respect to the child. The biological parent could appoint the co-parent as testamentary guardian in the case of the biological parent's death. Finally, if the couple separates or the biological parent dies without specifically implying guardianship, the co-parent could claim custody or visitation rights under the "psychological parent" theory[*] (Goldstein, Freud, Solnit 1996:90); Goldstein et al. 1996:90.

The infamous "Baby M" case in New Jersey brought the legal and ethical complexity of surrogacy to light. This particular case, wherein Mary Beth Whitehead contracted with William Stern and his wife to bear a child, was a media event and a lightning rod for both sides of the surrogacy issue. Surrogacy agreements are one means by which gay men are opting to create a family. Surrogacy arrangements, as Martin (1993:166) notes, "contracts for the sale of reproductive services." Surrogacy as a means of parenting is so new that the legal issues are still confusing and at times conflicting. In Arizona, surrogacy is illegal; in Kentucky, Michigan, and Utah it is illegal only if a woman is paid to bear a child. Regardless, there is an important distinction between statutes that criminalize surrogacy and those that do not automati-

---

[*] A psychological parent is an adult who, regardless of biological relationship to the child, on a continuing day-to-day basis fulfills the child's psychological need for a parent, as well as the child's physical needs.

cally uphold surrogacy contracts. If all parties involved in a surrogacy arrangement are satisfied, there is usually nothing to worry about; legal problems arise only when the surrogate mother either changes her mind and keeps the child, or when the biological father is unwilling to accept the child once it is born. The major legal hurdle for a gay father with respect to surrogacy is to establish that he is the legal father of the child, and to enforce the mother's contractually stated intention to surrender her parental rights.

A Child's Right to Protection from Harm

Children and adolescents in state custody, which includes gay and lesbian youths, may live in family foster homes, institutional settings, residential treatment centers, group homes, or family foster homes. When the state separates a child from his or her caregiver and places the young person in foster care, a special custodial relationship is created. At this juncture, the state assumes the duty, rooted in the Due Process clause of the Fourteenth Amendment, to protect the child from harm (Stein 1998:186). This duty imposes on key players in the state an obligation to protect those in their custody. This duty may be violated when the state shows "deliberate indifference" by failing to take action when the state believes that a child has been abused in foster care, thus placing the child at a known risk for injury. States have an obligation to take steps to protect the safety and well-being of children in foster care.

The state's duty to protect young people in foster care has particular implication for gay/lesbian children and youth in foster care as they have been said to be "victimized twice," first by their families and then by the Child Welfare system (Mallon 1998:152). When gay/lesbian children and youth, many of whom are invisible to a system which is unskilled at identifying them or meeting their needs, are in state custody, the state is obliged to treat them in a humane manner and to protect them from harm. In this case, gay/lesbian youths in foster care have a clear advantage over their at-home counterparts, as the U.S. Supreme Court has refused to extend protective obligation for children and adolescents not in state custody, even though the state knows that they are being abused (Stein 1998:189).

Litigation on behalf of gay/lesbian children and adolescents in New York's foster care system (Bernstein 1999; Boerner 1999; Joel A. v Guiliani) has sought to bring some of these issues to light to protect their Fourteenth

Amendment rights and insure that gay and lesbian youths in state custody are protected from harm. Other states have been exploring similar legal action and may soon follow suit on behalf of these particular individuals in their custody.

MINORS' RIGHT TO PARTICIPATE IN SERVICES

Ryan and Futterman (1998:33–35) provide an excellent discussion of the issues pertaining to confidentiality and legal issues for gay and lesbian youth. Adolescents aged 18 and older are legally considered adults in almost all states and therefore can consent to availing themselves of social services, including participation, without parental permission, in a community-based gay and lesbian youth group. Those under 18 are considered to be minors, and although parental consent is generally required for participation in most social services, all states have laws that allow minors to consent to certain community-based services. Several studies (Gittler, Quigley-Rick, and Saks 1990; Kaser-Boyd, Adelman, and Taylor 1986; Weithorn and Campbell 1982) all corroborate the notion that adolescents over the age of 14 are competent as adults to make their own health care decisions, including the ability to understand the risks and benefits of treatment and to give informed consent. Consent issues for gay and lesbian minors should also be considered by child welfare practitioners.

This chapter has introduced the reader to the role that the law plays in child welfare services for persons affected by issues of sexual orientation. Court decisions, legal actions, and legislation frame the discussion concerning the rights of gay and lesbian children and adolescents, adoptive parents, and biological parents. Child welfare practitioners and policy makers must work in collaboration with attorneys and other in the legal professions to insure that persons affected by issues of sexual orientation are treated justly and equitably.

For many years it was almost impossible for a person to be gay or lesbian and rear a child, but in today's Western society gay men and lesbians are raising children and are involved in the lives of children in many ways. Some children are from heterosexual marriages, others are adopted or foster children; an increasing number of gays and lesbians are choosing to birth children by alternative insemination, surrogacy, and via natural means.

Regardless of the circumstances of the child's birth, the legal treatment of the parent/child relationship should not rest solely on the parent's sexual orientation. Rather than promoting prejudicial attitudes based solely on decisions made on false stereotypes or perceived environmental intolerance, courts, legal experts, legislatures, and social workers should instead focus on their need for a stable home and a supportive environment.

In the United States, lesbian and gay persons are denied most of the rights afforded to nongay persons because of dominant heterocentric societal attitudes. Courts routinely refuse to provide gay and lesbian relationships with the legal recognition they need and deserve, many often go so far as to treat lesbian- and gay-headed families with contempt. As this chapter has argued, because sexual orientation alone is irrelevant to parenting ability, gays and lesbians should not be denied custody/visitation rights, or the possibility of becoming adoptive or foster parents. Second-parent adoptions and other parenting issues related to alternative procreation techniques are also important areas for social workers to develop their knowledge base to effectively work with gay and lesbian children, youth, and families affected by issues of sexual orientation.

Recent litigation on behalf of these individuals (*Joel A. v. Guiliani*) has sought to bring some of the salient legally based issues to light in an effort to protect their Fourteenth Amendment right and insure that gay and lesbian youths in state custody are protected from harm. Other states, interested in exploring similar legal action, are also exploring the possibility of similar actions.

Gays and lesbians have increasingly gained in visibility and public acceptance during the latter part of the twentieth century, but for the most part, the lesbian and gay community has existed in a parallel world—separate and apart from mainstream culture, not by their own choosing, but because they have been debarred from full protection because of intolerant societal attitudes. The next frontier requires that gays and lesbians continue to lead the way out of the closet, becoming skilled at using legal means to achieve not special rights, but full and equal rights as protected by the law and the Constitution in the same areas where heterosexual persons and families are guaranteed corresponding protection.

CHAPTER 5

Gays and Lesbians as Adoptive and Foster Parents

A family is a family when two or more persons decide they are a family.
—Hartman and Laird (1983)

Initiating a dialogue about gays and lesbians adopting or foster parenting children makes many people, including some child welfare professionals, uncomfortable. The last decade has seen a sharp rise in the number of gays and lesbians forming their own families through adoption and foster care. Indeed, today, despite best estimates that suggest that there are between 6 and 14 million children being raised by gay and lesbian parents (Patterson 1992), and although not all of these children are adopted, the issue still evokes controversy and strong, emotionally charged negative feelings for some.

In response, many states have moved toward safeguarding the interests of children in the care of gays and lesbians by strengthening their legal relationships with their families (Smothers 1997a, 1997b; Szymanski 1997). According to the Legal and Gay Rights Project of the ACLU (www.aclu.org), at least 21 states have granted second-parent adoptions to lesbian and gay parents, ensuring that their children can enjoy the benefits of having two legal parents. Recognizing that lesbians and gays can be good parents, state agencies and courts now apply a "best interest of the child" standard to decide cases where child custody or visitation is in question.

Nonetheless, some states led by "family values" ideologues who play on people's misinformation, fears, ignorance, and uncertainty about lesbian and gay persons have relied instead on myths and stereotypes and have attempted to use a person's gay or lesbian sexual orientation to deny him or her the privilege of adoption or foster parenting care (see Arizona law 1997; Arnold 1997; Baldauf 1997; Court refuses 1997; Florida judge 1997;

Freiberg 1999; Georgia ban 1998; Green 1999; Johnsrude 1997; Kessler 1997; McFarland 1998; Tanner 1996). Currently, Florida is are the only state that statutorily explicitly prohibit adoption by lesbian and gay persons. Legislation introduced in the New Hampshire legislature to repeal the ban there was successful (St. Pierre 1999). Gay and lesbian parenting is, at the time of this writing, under attack in four states: Arkansas, Texas, Utah, and Indiana.

It appears that as a more general acceptance of lesbians and gays in North American culture has increased, attacks from the radical right have become more vociferous (Hartman and Laird 1998:265). As debates continue across the country over whether gay and lesbian individuals should be allowed to raise children at all, three factors deserve attention: first, that the desire to be a parent recognizes no distinctions based on sexual orientation; second, in many cases children who were considered to be unadoptable have found a welcome, loving home with gay or lesbian parents; and third, as lesbian and gay adoptive parents become more visible, word is getting around that they make good parents.

Recognizing that gay/lesbian persons who wish to be adoptive parents are an untapped resource for many child welfare providers interested in securing permanent homes for children, I base this chapter on the relevant research literature on gays/lesbians as parents and on actual case examples drawn from qualitative data culled from in-depth interviews with gay/lesbian adoptive parents in four states. In line with the recent Adoption and Safe Families Act of 1997 (P.L. 105–89), which recognizes the need to move children from foster care and into permanent and loving homes more expeditiously, I call for the child welfare community to become more inclusive of gays/lesbians as adoptive parents. Specific policy recommendations and a discussion about the consequences of inaction are also provided.

DEBUNKING THE MYTHS

Although there has recently been a flood of literature about gay and lesbian parenting (Benkov 1994; Bigner 1996; Bozett 1987; Martin 1993; Muzio 1993, 1996; Pies 1985; Pollack 1995; Rothman 1996), the reality of gays or lesbians as heads of a family rearing children is still an idea that is novel to many (Roberston 1996; Vaughan 1996). The myth of gays and lesbians as child molesters (Groth 1978; Newton 1978) is so powerfully ingrained in the psyche of most people in Western society that the idea that they would be allowed to parent seems, to some, to be almost unbelievable. The fact is, however, that "The qualities that make good parents or good adoptive parents are universal. The ability to love and care for a child is not going to be determined by one's sexual orientation" (Board proposes 1998:6). The desire to parent is not exclusively the domain of those individuals who are heterosexually oriented, but is a powerful desire of many men and women who are gay and lesbian (Iasenza 1996; Shernoff 1996).

Self-awareness, a key to all competent social work practice, has particular relevance to the field of children and family services (Mallon 1998c). All social workers have personal beliefs that have an impact on their professional work. In the specific area of adoption and foster parenting by gay/lesbian persons, some professionals may hold prejudices or make prejudgments regarding the suitability of them to be adoptive parents. Such biases emanate from several sources—family influence, cultural affiliation, and religious connections. Many child welfare professionals, ill-trained by schools of social work or agency-based in-service training programs, also hold firm to a belief system that is grounded in the numerous negative myths and stereotypes about gays and lesbians (Mallon 1999). Professionals worry that gay men might molest a child in their home, or that children placed in their home might be encouraged to be gay or lesbian, or that two men raising a child or two women raising a child might not really be suitable as parental role models for a child. Negative media images of gays/lesbians have also been internalized by many professionals. Such attitudes, whether verbalized, visualized, or contemplated, have a major effect on the child welfare professional's work, including his or her assessment of gays/lesbians as potential adoptive parents.

Programmed by the multifarious images of gays and lesbians portrayed by the media and through societally sanctioned myths and stereotypes, the public's view of gays and lesbians as parents is frequently clouded by many misperceptions. Those who oppose the idea of gays/lesbians as adoptive parents use one or more of five rationales to conclude that licensing a home to such a parent is not in the child's best interest: 1) some believe that the child will be harassed or ostracized by heterosexuals; 2) some fear that the child might become gay or lesbian; 3) courts believe that living with or visiting with a gay or lesbian parent may harm the child's moral well-being; 4) some worry about child molestation; 5) finally some, as in the recent Bledsoe case in Texas, point to state sodomy statutes that they claim embody a state interest against homosexuality (Verhovek 1997; Williams 1997).

In fact, none of these reasons are sufficiently related to the child's best interest to justify denying a gay or lesbian individual from parenting. Furthermore, none of these fears are borne out or supported by evidence (Dunlap 1996; Patterson 1996). All research to date has reached the same unequivocal conclusions about gay and lesbian parenting: the children of lesbian and gay parents grow up as successfully as the children of heterosexual parents (Elovitz 1995; Patterson 1994, 1995, 1996; Tasker and Golombok 1997). Not one study has found otherwise. Likewise, not one study has found that the children of lesbian and gay parents face greater social stigma. Additionally, there is absolutely no evidence to support the belief that the children raised by lesbian and gay parents are more likely to be abused, nor is there evidence to suggest that they are more likely to become gay or lesbian themselves. The published social science literature (Cramer 1986; Groth 1978; Groth and Birnbaum 1978; Herek 1991; Newton 1979) also corroborates that the myth of molestation of children by gay men is a toxic fallacy. Molesting children, which has to do with pedophilia, is the attraction of an adult to children for sexual gratification and has nothing to do with whether or not a person is heterosexual or homosexual. The most recent study (Jenny, Roesler, and Poyer 1994) that looked at hospital records, 269 cases of sexually abused children, found that they were unlikely to have been molested by identifiably gay persons. Of the total number of cases studied, only two offenders were identified as gay. These findings suggest that a child's risk of being sexual molested by the heterosexual partner of a relative is more than 100 times greater than by somebody who might be identifiable as being gay, bisexual, or lesbian.

Adoption and foster parenting by gays and lesbians is not a new phenomenon. Children have always been placed by public agencies in gay- and lesbian-headed homes. In many cases these placements were made openly, other times they were finalized, without asking about the adoptive parent's sexual orientation. Other gays and lesbians have adopted children independently from private agencies or have made private adoption arrangements with individual birth mothers.

CRITERIA FOR ADOPTION AND
FOSTER PARENTING

The placement of children for adoption and family foster care has as its main objective the best interest of the child. Thus, the needs of each child should be the primary determinant used in placing a child in a family's home. Issues of the adoptive parents' sexual orientation may be important to consider in this decision-making process, but sexual orientation itself is not listed as an exclusionary criterion in the CWLA Adoption Standards (1988:50) or in the CWLA Standards of Excellence for Family Foster Care Services (1995:5–8). In fact, section 5.8 of the Adoption Standard states "sexual preferences should not be the sole criterion on which the suitability of adoptive parents is based. Consideration should be given to other personality and maturity factors and the ability of the applicant to meet the specific needs of the individual child."

In March 1998, the North American Council on Adoptable Children (NACAC) adopted a policy statement on gay and lesbian foster and adoptive parenting that reaffirmed the statement made by the Child Welfare League of America, saying: "Everyone with the potential to successfully parent a child in foster care or adoption is entitled to fair and equal consideration regardless of sexual orientation."

The truth is that gays and lesbians become adoptive parents for some of the same reasons that nongay persons adopt children (Mallon 1998b; Pies 1990). Some pursue adoption as a single person, some seek to adopt as a same-gender couple. The following vignette illuminates some of the features of this process for a lesbian couple:

CYNTHIA AND DONNA

Cynthia, a 42-year-old Latina lesbian, who along with her partner Donna, Caucasian and aged 38, adopted two children from a private agency in Oklahoma. Donna and Cynthia have been in a committed relationship for 25 years. They own a private home in a suburb of New York City, have solid, financially secure careers. Both women are in good health and are open about their sexual orientation to their families and to most of their coworkers. Cynthia and Donna began to explore the idea of adopting a child six years ago after a great deal of thought and discussion with one another and with their friends.

Their decision to adopt was primarily motivated by their desire to create a family. Like most gay or lesbian persons they never thought that they could have children, but they always felt that "something was missing"in their lives. Once they made the decision to pursue adoption, they couldn't wait to have a child placed in their home. Cynthia and Donna decided to present themselves as an openly gay couple rather than trying to hide the fact that they were gay and try to adopt as a single person. Because gay and lesbian persons cannot, except in New Jersey, adopt together legally as a same-gendered couple, the couple decided that Cynthia would be the legal parent. Because Cynthia is Latina and Spanish-speaking, the couple surmised that this might increase their chances of adopting a Latino child.

After they had completed the adoption paperwork, had physical exams, obtained references, and passed a home study, a two-week-old Mexican-American baby boy was identified for the couple. Donna and Cynthia named him Joseph. When Joseph was 2 years old, after they had made the initial adjustment to parenthood and adapting to the demands of changing family dynamics, they explored the possibility of adopting another child. In addition to enjoying the experience of parenting, the couple did not want Joseph to grow up being an only child. Shortly after having their home study updated, their family grew as baby Peter was placed in their home.

Two years after their second child was placed in their home, both women successfully petitioned the court to award them second-parent adoption.

Although the literature on lesbians choosing to parent is plentiful (Mitchell 1996; Pies 1985; Patterson 1996; Riley 1988), lesbians who choose to parent may confront challenges that may have less to do with societal expectations of women who parent and more to do with perceptions that heterosexual culture is generally not accepting of lesbian lives (Albro and Tully 1979; Chafetz, Sampson, Beck, West, and Jones 1976; Hall 1978; Laird 1999; Levy 1992; Lewis 1980; Lewis 1984; Loewenstein 1980; Muzio 1996).

The literature focusing on gay men choosing to adopt is uneven (Frommer 1996; McPherson 1993; Sbordone 1993; Shernoff 1996) as fewer gays have pursued adoption as a means toward creating families. The following vignette provides an illustration of the process that one gay couple went through in making the decision to become adoptive parents.

Paul and Jason

Paul, age 34 and African-American, and Jason, age 40 and Caucasian, have lived together as a couple in a committed relationship for five years. They own a condominium in an urban area in the western part of the United States. Paul is a banker; Jason owns his own business. Over the years, both men have discussed the possibility of parenting, Jason is more enthusiastic about the idea than Paul, but both have always wanted to have their own family. Like many gay people, they thought that being gay excluded them from being parents. After reading April Martin's (1993) book *The Lesbian and Gay Parenting Handbook* and meeting another couple who had adopted, the two decided to explore the possibility of adoption. After a great deal of discussion, Jason and Paul decided to present themselves as an openly gay couple rather than trying to hide the fact that they were gay or to try to adopt as single persons. Because their city has a nondiscrimination clause based on sexual orientation, they believed that they would be given a fair chance at adopting a child.

As part of the process they were told that they would have to attend several Model Approaches to Partnership in Parenting (MAPP) training classes at the agency, complete a lengthy application form, obtain three references from people who could vouch for their reputations and attest to their ability to parent, complete financial disclosure statements, submit to a physical exam, and participate in a series of visits to their home and interviews with them called a home study process. Paul and Jason agreed to all of the conditions and completed all of the interviews and necessary paperwork in a timely fashion.

During the course of this process, Jason and Paul were challenged by the social worker (who seems to have been fairly well versed on how to work with gay people) to look at their reasons for wanting to parent and to look at how parenting would change their lives. The social worker asked each of the men to explore with her the roles that men play in parenting a child. She asked that they discuss how they think they might deal with parenting roles as two males rather than as a male and a female. The social worker also informed them that even though they were open about their relationship, that only one of the men could be the legal parent and therefore be the legal parent listed on the adoption papers. The men decided that since Jason was the one who was most enthusiastic that he should be the legal parent. They agreed that Paul would be the legal guardian and work with their attorney to make these arrangements.

Three months after the home study was completed, the agency identified two African-American brothers. One child was a year old and the other was six years old. The younger child was HIV positive.

Clearly, even for these men who were highly prepared to adopt, there are several issues that are common for gay men choosing to be parents. Although many of the perceived stresses illustrated above have more to do with first-time parenting issues than with issues of sexual orientation, there are some unique features to this case example. Unlike their heterosexual counterparts who couple, get pregnant, and give birth, gay and lesbian individuals and couples who wish to parent must consider many other variables in deciding on whether or not to become parents. First the couple must decide how they should go about creating a family—adoption (Colberg 1996), foster parenting (Ricketts 1991; Ricketts and Achtenberg 1990), surrogacy (Bernfeld 1995), or alternative insemination. Second, the couple must decide whether or not to be open about their sexual orientation. Although it is legal for gay men and lesbians to adopt, some couples, fearing that they would not be able to adopt if they disclosed their orientation, opt for silence. Many gays and lesbians do choose to be open about their sexual orientation, others identify as "friends" who will raise the child together. Since only one parent can be recognized as the legal parent, this establishes, as Hartman (1996:81) points out, "an asymmetrical relationship between the two parents and the child." This asymmetry occurs on multiple levels: from school visits, to medical permission forms, to eligibility for Social Security survivors' benefits in the case of the death of a co-parent, to lack of support from family-of-origin members that would most likely have been present for most heterosexual couples who chose to parent, and to requirements for support and visiting arrangements in the case of a separation.

Many families created by gays and lesbians have been greatly assisted by participating in a group for gays and lesbians who are considering parenting. The presence of a supportive network of other gay/lesbian parents can be found in many local communities, or a virtual community via the Internet (see www. glpci.org; www. adopting.org/gaystate).

Gay and lesbian individuals who choose to adopt as a single parent also face stresses that probably are more due to single parenting than to their gay or lesbian identification. Those who choose to create families have the advantage of redefining and reinventing their own meaning for family and parenting precisely because they exist outside of the traditionally defined family and parenting roles based on gender (Benkov 1994). In creating their own families, gays and lesbians offer their own uniqueness and gifts to the children they rear and to the larger society's concept of the family and parenting experience.

Trends in Adoption: The Adoption and Safe Families Act

In most North American cities, the need for adoptive and foster parents far exceeds what is available for the number of children and youth needing adoption or family foster care. Throughout contemporary history gays and lesbians have always been adoptive parents. Some of these individuals have been open about their sexual orientation, others have hidden their gay or lesbian identity from child welfare professionals out of fear that their application to be an adoptive parent would be denied. The policy of "don't ask, don't tell" has a firm hold not only in the U.S. military, but also in the U.S. child welfare system (Groninger 1996), as this excerpt from an interview with a child welfare worker in Connecticut suggests:

> We have a number of women who applied as single women to become foster or adoptive parents whom we assumed to be lesbian, but no one ever came right out and asked them, and they did not volunteer that information either. Some of the staff made some comments about their suspected lesbianism in the office, but no one could dispute that they were excellent foster parents. Their sexual orientation was never an issue because we never discussed it with them. I would assume that we have others, but no one ever comes right out and asks and we don't have any policy that I am aware of.

Numerous child welfare agencies across the country have broken through their own organizational bias against gay men and lesbians and are already placing children with gay and lesbian parents. But by and large, there are few child welfare agencies that seem to be openly discussing this process out of concern about attracting undue attention to their agency or to the issue. There is a large adoption and foster parenting network within gay and lesbian communities across the country as well as a virtual community found on many Internet web sites, all of which assist gays and lesbians interested in adoption or foster parenting in identifying the names and addresses of "safe" child welfare agencies where they can be certified (see www.aclu.org/issues/gay/parent; www. Aclu.org/issues/gay/child www.lambdalegal.org).

A gay male couple in Orange County, California, recalled their journey toward foster care and adoption in this quote:

> We always wanted to be parents, but we just assumed that because we were gay that we would be discriminated against and not permitted to be parents. At a Gay Pride event about two years ago we saw a table with information from G.L.A.S.S. (Gay and Lesbian Adolescent Social Services in Los Angeles). The social worker at the table told us about the foster parenting process and we couldn't believe this might be possible for us. We went home and talked about the idea about becoming foster parents and almost immediately signed up for the MAPP training courses for foster parents. Then we did all of our paperwork, had our home study completed (we were so nervous about that one, we cleaned for days to prepare for it) and waited for a child to be placed with us. We said that we could take siblings, so in three weeks we got a call to say that they had two brothers for us, a 2-year-old and a one-and-half-week-old. We were scared, but excited. It was tough in the beginning, our lives really changed when we became parents, but it was the greatest thing that we have ever done. The boys were freed for adoption last year and we adopted them. It was such a relief to know that the boys were ours permanently. The day the adoption was finalized was the greatest day of our lives. If it weren't for G.L.A.S.S., we never would have been able to have our family.

Moving Toward a Policy of Inclusiveness

President Clinton's signing of the historic Adoption and Safe Families Act (ASFA) of 1997 (P.L. 105–89; Baker 1997) signaled the culmination of over two decades of work toward making it easier to move tens of thousands more children out of foster homes into permanent families. This includes, although not specified in the legislation, families headed by gays and lesbians. The new law provides unprecedented financial incentives to states to increase adoption and helps child welfare providers to speed children out of foster care and into permanent families by setting meaningful time limits for child welfare decisions, by clarifying which family situations call for reasonable reunification efforts and which do not, and places the safety of children as the paramount concern in placement decisions (CWLA 1998). The evidence documenting the damage to children caused by long-term foster care placement is unambiguous (Maas and Engler 1959; Fanshel 1982; Fanshel and Shinn 1978; Festinger 1983). Minimizing foster care drift and emphasizing permanency planning for children (Maluccio, Fein, Olmstead 1986; Pierce 1992; Pelton 1991) has been a primary focus of children and families services for close to two decades and was reaffirmed in Clinton's signing of AFSA.

Historically, perceived as a preferential service granted only to those couples who were usually Caucasian and infertile, who could afford to take a healthy same-race infant into their home, adoption is now viewed in a much broader context. Contemporary adoption has made it possible for a broader range of children to be adopted—children of color, children with a range of disabilities, as well as those with medical and developmental issues, preschoolers, and adolescents.

Similarly, policies have made it possible for a broader range of adults to adopt, including foster parents, families of color, single individuals (both male and female), older individuals, individuals with disabilities, and families across a broad economic range. At one time or another many of these groups were excluded from the adoption process. In fact, the inclusion of some of these groups caused great controversy when initiated. In the process of moving toward inclusiveness, many professionals voiced concern about lowering the standard of adoption and damaging the field.

These trends toward inclusiveness over the past score of years has had a major impact on the over 500,000 children in out-of-home care, some of whom have waited two or three years for permanent homes. Such changes have signaled that thousands of children previously considered unadoptable, or not suitable for family foster care can be provided with loving homes with caring adults. Although accurate statistics on the number of gay and lesbian persons do not exist, it has been estimated that up to 10 percent of the population (25 million individuals) identifies as having a sexual orientation other than heterosexual. Excluding 25 million individuals from becoming adoptive parents, solely on the basis on sexual orientation, seems preposterous considering how many children are in need of loving families to care for them.

Although some child welfare agencies are struggling to develop policies, many agencies appear to believe "the less said the better" (Sullivan 1995:3). Some of this diffidence undoubtedly stems from the fear of being stigmatized as "the gay adoption agency" if they are widely identified as an agency that will not discriminate against gays or lesbians seeking to be adoptive parents. Organizational structures, which operate in the absence of written policies, frequently impel staff members to develop their own policies. The lack of written policies, I believe, in and of itself is a strategy that many child welfare agency executives and boards have permitted to exist with respect to the issue of gay and lesbian adoption and foster parenting. When individuals design their own policies to guide agency practice, then, agencies run the risk of personal, cultural, and religious bias to guide practice. Child welfare agencies that continue to avoid written policies do not provide the opportunity for the community to resolve the issue. Policies that speak to the needs of children and families need to be written and clearly communicated to all interested groups.

POLICY DEVELOPMENT VERSUS PREJUDICE

The creation of adoptive homes by gay/lesbian persons is an intensely emotional topic that divides people into groups on the basis of conflicting personal values and beliefs. Settlements to emotionally charged topics are seldom satisfactory to all involved. The child welfare field's challenge, however, is not to please everyone, but to develop a rational position that is based on professional values and experiences, and one that can be defended when challenged.

Child welfare agencies that wish to develop policies regarding adoption and foster parenting by gays and lesbians need to reflect on a number of questions. How should a child welfare organization respond to gay/lesbian persons who want to adopt or foster children? If a child welfare agency accepts such an applicant, what will be the response of its board, its community constituents, and its funding sources? How should a child welfare organization respond to media attention or attacks from the radical right? Do gays and lesbians automatically have the "right" to adopt? Is it fair for a child to be placed in a gay or lesbian adoptive or foster home? If a child welfare agency does not accept a gay or lesbian applicant, is there potential for legal liability? Can an agency be sued for failing to accept or for accepting a lesbian or gay applicant? How much do professionals in a particular child welfare organization know about gays and lesbians as potential adoptive or foster parents?

Developing a Sound Policy

A sound policy is developed when it is based on information available from external sources and from child welfare practice wisdom. Unfortunately most policy is developed with less than complete information and sometimes without a thoughtful process of discernment. All policies have political consequences (DiNitto 1995; Taylor 1994). Policies, however, are not carved in stone. Flexibility is required to accommodate changing environmental conditions and situations that require policy modification or change. During the past two decades, the child welfare community has responded in an adaptable way in several key areas: to cultural diverse communities, to substance abusing populations, and to those affected by HIV/AIDS. All are good examples of the need for flexibility in policy development.

Utilizing the rich array of resources from the gay and lesbian parenting community (Kids' Talk 1998; www. gaycenter.org/kidstalk; Family Tree 1998) and those resources that are available through the practice wisdom of professionals who have worked with gays and lesbians is also critical. Additionally, the National Adoption Information Clearinghouse (NAIC, n.n.; www.calib.com), the Northwest Adoption Exchange (Nelson 1997); and the Adoption Resource Exchange for Single Parents (Beers 1977; Solot 1998; www.adopting.org/aresp/) have also been essential organizations that have developed and disseminated valuable resources for gay and lesbian adoptive parents. Such information can provide an accurate impression of the range of family options that exist in the gay and lesbian community and can highlight their potential as adoptive resources for children in care awaiting foster or adoptive homes.

The following considerations for professionals developing policy are adapted from Sullivan (1995:5–8):

1. The primary client is the child in need of an adoptive family. All families are potential resources for the child. The issue is not "Do gay men and lesbians have the right to adopt?" No family *ipso facto* has the right to adopt or to be a foster parent—these are privileges afforded to those families who meet a standard, not a right. All individuals should be given equal consideration as adoptive parents.

2. All placement considerations should focus on the best interest of the child. Child welfare professionals should ask, "What is the best family resource for this child at this time?"

3. No single factor, including sexual orientation, should be the determining factor in assessing suitability for adoption or foster parenting.

4. The capacity to nurture a child and a parent's sexual orientation are separate issues. These must not be confused in decision making.

5. Gay and lesbian applicants should be assessed using the same criteria as all other adoptive parents. Although gay and lesbian adoptive parents may present unique situations, they should not have to pass extraordinary means tests to prove their worthiness as parents. Child welfare professionals should make use of an excellent publication made available by Adoption Resource Exchange for Single Parents—*Guidelines for Adoption Workers: Writing Lesbian, Gay, Bisexual, and Transgender Homestudies* (Solot 1998). Those working to certify gay and lesbian parents should ask themselves in making such an assessment: "What are their individual strengths or weaknesses and what is their capacity to nurture a child or children who were not born to them?"

6. Each placement decision should be based on the strengths and needs of the child and the perceived ability of the prospective adoptive family to meet those needs and develop those strengths.

Given the responsibilities of child welfare agencies to the children whom they place in adoptive homes, child welfare professionals should thoughtfully identify the array of issues involved in a family where a gay or lesbian parent or parents raise a child. Child welfare agencies should examine all families for emotional maturity, flexibility, and openness. If there are two partners who are applying to be adoptive parents, professionals should be able to evaluate the commitment they have toward one another and the stability of the relationship; if the potential adoptive parent is single, professionals will need to carefully examine the individual's existing support networks. Furthermore, professionals will also be called upon to evaluate the parent's experience with children and the ability to distinguish a child's needs from one's own.

There are differences with respect to some aspects of foster parenting or adoption by gay or lesbian persons. Child welfare organizations should evaluate the following issues:

1. In most states, only one same-gender partner can be legally recognized as a parent. Although this is changing in some states (e.g., New Jersey), child welfare professionals should be aware of the consequences of having a legal and nonlegal parent and must also assist potential adoptive parents in negotiating a careful discussion about this issue.

2. How willing are the parents to be open about their sexual orientation within their community? Having a child who attends school, makes use of health care services, and attends other child-oriented recreational events causes parents to make decisions about their own comfort level with being out in the community.

3. How willing are the parents to deal with and openly address the multiple levels of "differentness" that they and their adoptive child will experience? All adopted children face issues related to their sense of differentness about being adopted—some differentness is easier to deal with than others.

4. As in all placements children should be involved in the decision-making process whenever possible. For example in placing a 12-year-old with a gay or lesbian couple, it would be important to determine what the child knows about gay and lesbian persons and gauge his or her understanding of the benefits and challenges evident in placement with a specific family.

5. Although the deficits of gays and lesbians are frequently pointed out, they are resilient individuals and as such bring many strengths to a family. Gays and lesbians know firsthand how important it is to allow children to develop naturally without having preconceived notions about what a child should be. Child welfare professionals should be aware of the multiple strengths of a gay or lesbian headed family.

Consequences of Inaction

Agencies that seek to avoid the issue of adoptive parenting by gay- and lesbian-headed families by not acting or maintaining status quo are likely to find themselves confronting the following consequences:

1. A continuation in the trend toward private independent adoptions rather than agency adoptions as prospective parents who are gay or lesbian will find other means to fulfill their desires to parent.

2. An increased likelihood of legal actions against agencies. Many states constitutionally or statutorily prohibit discrimination on the basis of sexual orientation. Increasingly, gay and lesbian individuals are turning to litigation in response to discrimination.

3. An increased likelihood of class action suits and/or consent decrees. All too often, such actions result in a court making the decisions that the professionals should—but were unable to—make themselves.

4. The continued expenditure of public funds to maintain children in out-of-home care for longer periods than would be necessary if all families were explored as resources.

5. The likelihood that a number of children (and children born HIV positive were an example of this population) who would not be placed in a family at all, when they could have been adopted by a gay- or lesbian-headed family.

Not all gay or lesbian persons should be adoptive parents, but the same could be said of nongay persons. Many gays and lesbians, as evidenced by the case examples discussed here and the thousands of untold narratives of others, make wonderful, caring, and loving parents for children who need a permanent home and a family. The question is not whether gays or lesbians will be approved as adoptive parents, but how publicly it will be done and whether these families will be offered the same opportunities as others to adopt. Sidestepping the issue of adoption and foster parenting by gays and lesbians does not protect children. It runs counter to the new Adoption and Safe Families Act legislation and prevents some children from being part of a loving family, which all children deserve. Child welfare agencies are responsible for ensuring a timely and appropriate adoptive family for every child who needs one. In meeting this responsibility child welfare agencies must explore all potential resources for all children awaiting placement in a family, including gays and lesbians who have a desire to parent and long to share their lives with children who need a family to love and nurture them.

CHAPTER 6

Meeting the Needs of Gay/Lesbian Children and Youth in Out-of-Home-Care Placements

Most gay and lesbian young people are not placed in out-of-home-care child welfare settings (i.e., group homes, foster homes, or independent living programs). In fact, the majority live with their families and never interface with the child welfare system at all. Those children and adolescents who come to the attention of the child welfare system are young people who have experienced significant difficulties with their family system to such a degree that they cannot or should not continue to live at home.

Although some gay and lesbian children and youth are thrown out of their homes when they disclose their sexual identity or when they are "found out" by their families, not all of them enter care because of issues directly related to their sexual orientation. Like their heterosexual counterparts, the majority of gay/lesbian young people in out-of-home care were placed there before or during the onset of adolescence (Mallon 1998a), and were placed for many of the same reasons that other young persons are: family disintegration, divorce, death or illness of a parent, parental substance abuse or alcoholism, physical abuse and neglect.

This chapter focuses on the unique situation for gay and lesbian children and young people who are involved with the out-of-home-care child welfare system. This includes both those who clearly identify themselves as gay or lesbian and those who continue to struggle with their emerging sexual orientation. It is based on data obtained from previous work (Mallon 1994, 1998a; O'Brien, Travers, and Bell 1994), and from practice experiences in the child welfare field working with children, adolescents, and their families whose lives are affected by out-of-home services, primarily group homes and foster boarding homes.

Group Homes

Living apart from one's family is seldom easy. Out-of-home child welfare systems have long been and continue to be an integral part of the child welfare continuum of services. The structure of the different types of residential programs varies widely and can take many forms. They range from small community-based group homes and short-term respite care or shelter facilities to large group-care facilities that provide long-term or custodial care. All of these different types of services share one common feature, however: they provide care for children and young people on a 24-hour-day basis.

Group home programs, which is where the majority of adolescents in care live, are not one entity but a diverse group of programs. They provide a less restrictive level of care than do large institutional congregate care settings, but offer more structure than family-based foster homes. Generally, most group homes are staffed by individual child care workers or counselors who are employed by an agency to work in shifts to cover the 24 hours in a day.

The child care workers who work in group home settings play a very important role in the lives of the young people in their care but are, nevertheless, the lowest paid and generally the least educated and trained practitioners in the child welfare system. The daily stress of working with adolescents in this setting, combined with the poor pay, make it especially difficult for staff to be empathetic and compassionate in their dealings with the young people, and it also accounts for a high staff turnover. Social workers, whose offices are not usually in the group home itself, generally do not have as intimate a relationship with a young person in comparison to the child care workers. This is because they are not there as much but visit the house on a regular basis to provide counseling and to work with families.

Administration

Group home programs are supervised by agency administrators who are charged with insuring that agency guidelines are maintained and legal requirements satisfied. In most group home programs, however, it is the program director who decides who will be allowed in, who will be discharged, who will stay, and under what conditions. Most directors are also quick to point out that they have the sole and final say about what is, and is not, acceptable behavior in the group home.

Group Home Living

Young people are generally clustered in group homes according to their sex and age. They are expected to attend school in the community, participate in household chores to maintain the environment of the facility and to adhere to a series of formal and informal rules. In addition to observing the usual injunctions against alcohol and drug use, carrying weapons, fighting, and using abusive language, the residents of group homes are often required to sign contracts whereby they promise to modify their behavior by getting up promptly in the morning, keeping their rooms clean, attending counseling and independent living skills classes, and simply put, working on your "issues."

Most group homes for adolescents focus on preparing these young people for independent living—on or before their twenty-first birthday in some locations, such as New York, and by age eighteen in other places, such as California. Although most group homes are guided by rules and regulations established by the state or province, each group home program has its own norms and unique culture. Some group homes are warm, loving and accepting of diversity and some are unnurturing, cold, and rigid. Gay and lesbian young people live in and speak about both. Since most young gays and lesbians in out-of-home care live in group homes, this chapter will focus on those experiences occurring in that context.

FAMILY FOSTER HOMES

Family foster homes are individual homes, licensed by individual state departments of social services, to provide care for children who cannot or should not live at home with their biological families and for whom this level of care is appropriate. Foster parents can be single persons or couples. In many cases, foster parents have biological children of their own living in their homes. In most states, foster parents can be licensed to have up to four foster children in their home. Foster families are paid a room-and-board rate for each child living in their home. This rate is determined by the agency with which they are affiliated. Medical expenses are usually covered by state Medicaid programs and semiannual clothing allowances are also provided in addition to the room-and-board rate.

The goals of family foster care are to protect and nurture children who are placed with agency-approved foster families to meet the physical, mental health, developmental, social, and educational needs of children placed with them. Foster families also play an important role in supporting the relationship between the children in their care and the children's biological families in an effort to develop a plan of permanency.

Although foster parents are directly linked to child welfare agencies and have a close relationship with them, these agencies do not own a foster parent's home. As such most foster parents have a large sayso over who is placed in their home, and who they might request to have removed from their home. For this reason, gay/lesbian children and young people are particularly vulnerable in foster boarding home settings.

Most foster parents receive training on a variety of issues that pertain to their role, however the majority have probably not received adequate training in issues of human sexuality. Undoubtedly most foster parents have not received training in working with a gay or lesbian foster child. Like most biological families, foster families usually accept the myths and stereotypes about gays and lesbians persons as their guide. Most probably they look for gender nonconforming behaviors or mannerisms (which do not necessarily indicate a gay or lesbian sexual orientation) and take the absence of these "traits" as confirmation that they do not have a gay or lesbian youth in their home. Although there are undoubtedly many gay and lesbian children and youths living in family foster care, it would be safe to say, given that most hide their orientation, that most foster families probably are unaware of their presence.

GAY AND LESBIAN ADOLESCENTS IN OUT-OF-HOME CARE

There have always been gay and lesbian young people in out-of-home-care settings (foster homes, group homes, and group-care type placements) but it has often been difficult for professionals to recognize their existence for three reasons: 1) many of these youths do not fit the nonconforming gender stereotypes that most practitioners associate with a gay or lesbian orientation; 2) many gay and lesbian young people are socialized to hide their orientation (Martin 1982); and 3) many child welfare professionals hold moralistic attitudes and are contemptuous of a homosexual orientation. In addition, most professionals are completely lacking in knowledge about normal gay and lesbian adolescent development (Mallon 1997). Many administrators of child welfare agencies are fearful that acknowledging a self-identified gay or lesbian young person in their program might be seen as "encouraging" or "promoting" homosexuality. The end result is that gay and lesbian youth often remain hidden and invisible in the child welfare system, and if they do come out, they are not provided with the same quality of care that is extended to their heterosexual counterparts.

The reflections of one gay young man about his placement experience in Toronto are representative of the views of many and provide a framework for examining the salient features of this issue. John is a 17-year-old Jamaican-American who currently resides in a group home in New York.

JOHN

I wasn't even sure that I was gay, but I knew that I liked guys. One day when I was talking on the phone to this guy that I liked, my mother overheard our conversation and figured out what was going on. She started screaming at me, telling me I was sick, that I was crazy, and saying that I needed some kind of help.

I was so upset, because she really caught me off guard. I wasn't ready to tell her anything about myself—she just found me out. After an hour of screaming she kind of calmed down and told me it was just a phase that I was going through. Things were tense during that week—she didn't tell my father, she was afraid of what might happen if she told him. He often lost his temper and sometimes when he was angry he would hit me. Toward the end of the week my mother told me that she was going to send me to Jamaica for the summer—"there" she said, "they will cure you." I had no choice, I had to go.

In September, I returned, obviously I hadn't changed, but I lied and told her that I did. She realized after two weeks that I had not changed and things just deteriorated from that point.

Finally, the silent treatment really got to me and I asked my mother to place me. I had some friends in group home and I thought maybe I'd be better there. Most kids don't ask their families to place them, but I did, I just couldn't take living at home anymore.

Once I was in placement, I thought it would be better, but it just got worse. I was scared to tell anyone that I was gay because I saw how the gay kids got treated—even if they thought you were gay you were treated badly. Gay kids were not treated equally, they were treated like they were not normal, like they were not human. It was hell to live there —I felt like I was trapped in some fucking cage, I had no one to talk to, I wasn't happy.

It was like I was abnormal—like I didn't fit in the crowd. Most of the kids were pretty cruel to gay kids, but the staff . . . they were worse. One night this group of kids approached me about having sex with them, but I told them "No." They were really aggressive and told me that if I didn't give it up, they'd tell the staff that I approached them. Well . . . I didn't give it up and they did just what they said they'd do—they told staff that I had made sexual advances toward them. The staff met with me, I told them what really happened, but they didn't believe me. They said, "All you fags are just into the same thing—we've seen this before."

The next day the people from the City came and placed me in another group home. That one was worse. I got jumped by a couple of kids on the first night and the staff there wouldn't even talk to me. It was terrible there. I was treated so badly, I would just go in my room and cry. One day, after all the teasing and harassment, I just couldn't take it anymore and I complained to the social worker who was kinda new herself. She said she understood and then helped get me placed in another group home, one that she said was gay friendly. This worker ended up being the only person who was cool with me. Months later I figured out that she was gay too.

This social worker always said she knew I was gay and that I should come out, but I denied that I was. She tried to reassure me that she could work with me—but I knew better. I saw how they treated the kids who were openly gay and I saw how they treated me because they thought I was gay, so there was no way that I was going to confirm it for them. I didn't want to reveal it to them because I was afraid of how they would treat me if they knew for sure. She kept pressuring me, but I refused to tell her anything. I always tried to act so straight to fit into their crowd—to fit into what they did—but I couldn't.

One day, the day when I told her I couldn't take it anymore my social worker told me that there was this place where I would feel comfortable—she said it was a place for "people like me," a place where I would fit in. But even then, I kept denying that I was gay. They scheduled a visit for me anyway. Even though they made it seem like I had a choice about whether to go there or not, I guess that they didn't really want me, I guess they wanted me out—so I was transferred to Green Chimneys [a gay affirming agency in New York] and there I felt comfortable right away.

Finally I had people that I could relate to, people who I could talk to. When I first got here, I was so happy—they had this sign that said "Here, we respect everyone! Regardless of race, religion, sexual orientation, culture, class, gender, and ability." I was so relived, I didn't have to hide nothing from nobody. I could dress the way I wanted to, I could walk the way I wanted to, I could be free, I didn't have to hide—I could be myself. It was the first time I ever felt that way.

Stories like John's are not uncommon. Gay and lesbian young people in out-of-home care report both positive and negative responses to their sexual orientation. However, the negative stories outweigh the positive. Several themes emerge from the above vignette. These themes, discussed below, are useful in understanding the experiences of gay and lesbian youths in out-of-home-care settings.

INVISIBILITY AND HIDING Because of their survival instinct to conceal their sexual identification, gays and lesbians in out-of-home care are frequently an invisible population. This allows administrators and staff to convince themselves that there are no gay or lesbian young people in their care. Professional staff and administrators often associate homosexuality with gender nonconformity. They believe that they would be able, without hesitation, to identify gay and lesbian clients—if there were any. Only those individuals who do not conform to traditional gender stereotypes (i.e., the butch girl or the effeminate boy) are identified as gay or lesbian, and are subsequently treated with disdain. The majority of young gays or lesbians are silent and hidden witnesses to the negative attitudes of staff, administrators, and peers toward those who staff are believed to be gay or lesbian. Most gays/lesbians in out-of-home care get the message—from multiple sources: "Stay in the closet! We don't want to deal with this!"

STRESS AND ISOLATION   Living in the closet, as so many gays/lesbians in foster care are forced to do, is the source of a high level of stress and isolation in their lives (Hunter and Schaecter 1987). The comments of Brenda, a 20-year-old lesbian from a Los Angeles foster home, exemplifies these issues:

> I tried to hide it 'cause I saw how they treated those kids who they thought were gay or lesbian. I mean, they were treated terribly—just because the others thought they were gay. I knew that I was gay, so imagine how they would treat me if they ever found out. I felt so alone, so isolated, like no one ever knew the real me. I couldn't talk to anybody about who I was. It was a horrible experience—trying to hide who you really are is very difficult and exhausting. Sometimes I felt so bad I just wanted to kill myself.

MULTIPLE PLACEMENTS   Moving from one's family to an out-of-home-care setting is, in and of itself, stressful, but subsequently being moved from one placement to another has been pinpointed as a major difficulty in out-of-home care (Fanshel 1982; Fanshel and Shinn 1978; Maas and Engler 1959). The constant challenge of adapting to a new environment is unsettling, provokes anxiety, and undermines one's sense of permanence. Unlike other adolescents in out-of-home care who move from setting to setting because of individual behavioral problems, gay and lesbian youths report that their sexual orientation itself led to multiple and unstable placements.

Young people report experiencing unstable placements for four reasons: 1) they are not accepted because staff has difficulties dealing with their sexual orientation; 2) they feel unsafe because of their sexual orientation and either "awol" (as the young people say) from the placement for their own safety or request re-placement; 3) they are perceived as a management problem by staff because they are open about their sexual orientation; and 4) they are not accepted by peers because of their sexual orientation.

Maura, an 18-year-old white lesbian from New York, provides a narrative that illustrates many of these points:

MAURA

I couldn't live at home with my mother, because she couldn't deal with the fact that I was a dyke. So, let me give you the sequence, I currently live at the Jane Residence, which is a part of St. Peter's. But I was first placed in a diagnostic center, the Children's Center. But I left there after about ten minutes when I could tell that they couldn't deal with my orientation. I awoled from there and stayed at my grandmother's house. They didn't say anything about me being a lesbian but it was damn obvious that they had a problem with me. If I felt that they couldn't deal with me, I just awoled, I mean my feeling was, I couldn't live at home because my mother couldn't deal with it, and if the staff in the group home can't deal with it either, then why bother sticking around? After that I went back to my mother, then to Grand Street Group Home, and then to John Street Group home, which is another of St. Peter's group homes, then to where I am now, Community House.

Viewing them as a major problem, many agencies simply get rid of gay and lesbian youngsters because staff cannot deal with their sexual orientation. Many of them have been in multiple placements by agencies at all levels of care. Wilem, a 19-year-old Latino from New York, provides this account, which is representative of many young people's stories:

WILEM

I have had so many, I can't even remember. Too many to remember, all of those overnights . . . a lot of places. I was 14 when I went to my first one, I've been to lots of them, but I kept running away because I just couldn't live there. I even was running away from home because I didn't want anyone to know that I was gay. The best was The Meadows and the worst was Mount Laurel. It wasn't horrible but it still wasn't the best place to be. I stood at The Partnership for awhile because I met some gays there that I knew from outside, so we hung out together and they showed me the ropes and we hung out together.

These cases exemplify the ways in which gay and lesbian young people are continuously faced with having to negotiate new environments, many of which are inhospitable and lacking in the conditions necessary for healthy psychological development.

RE-PLACEMENT AND FEELINGS OF REJECTION: The majority of gay and lesbian young people sense that they are not welcome in most child welfare settings. They perceive that they are reluctantly accepted into some placements and consequently feel isolated and have negative reactions to their out-of-home-care placement. Many are impassioned about their maltreatment in these settings, as this comment from Wilem illustrates:

WILEM

How was I treated? You mean the way we were treated? It sucks, it sucks. I mean I wouldn't want to go back to one. It's hard enough being in a situation when you are away from your family and then having somebody else put you down . . . I mean, it's just not fair.

Some young people report that they left their placement once they realized that they were not welcomed. Maura recalls this experience vividly:

MAURA

As soon as I get discriminated against, I leave. I mean when I was on a psychiatric ward they were trying to give me aversion therapy and I mean they were supposed to help me with my depression, not by telling me that I'm wrong. Where I am now, they are fine, but in other places definitely there were problems. I mean when I was in St. Clare's, they were giving me my own room because I was gay and to keep the other kids away from me. It's the kids and the staff that treat you differently.

Frequently, young people who leave placements become lost in the system as their multiple placements creates a sense of impermanence and drift (Maas and Engler 1959). This may account for the high percentages of youth on the street who identify as gay or lesbian (Mallon 1994, 1998a; Seattle Commission 1988; Victims Services 1991).

VERBAL HARASSMENT AND PHYSICAL VIOLENCE Many young people enter foster care because it offers sanctuary from abusive family relationships and violence in their homes. However, with the constant threat of harassment and violence within the system, gay and lesbian youth report being unable to feel completely secure or confident. Although violence and harassment may be an unfortunate component of foster care from time to time for all young people, lesbians and gays, unlike their heterosexual counterparts, are targeted for attack specifically because of their sexual orientation (Comstock 1991; Garnets et al. 1992; Herek and Berrill 1992). In addition, the stigma attached to being gay or lesbian often prevents them from reporting this victimization, and even when they do report it, and their allegations of abuse are believed, the victims themselves are blamed.

Tirades and taunts from family members, peers, and in some cases staff members that begin with the epithets—"you fucking faggot," "bulldyke," "homo," and "queer" sometimes escalate into punches, burnings, and rape. One young person summed it up concisely when he said: "The kids are bad, but the staff are worse. If the staff are cool with you then so are the kids, but if the staff are all hung up about someone being gay or lesbian, then the kids just take that as a signal to go to town on that person."

Gay and lesbian young people are considered to be disposable individuals, deserving of being pushed into line or told to stay in the closet. Frequently they find themselves in environments that are so void of nurturance, where the fit between their needs and the situation at the placement is so bad, that many feel as though they literally have to flee for their lives. Some manage to find a safer environment. Others find even less favorable circumstances when they end up on the streets.

CREATING SAFE ENVIRONMENTS: INDIVIDUAL RESPONSES

Professionals faced with such harsh realities might ask: What can be done? The most important response to such an inquiry is the reminder that all child welfare professionals have the ethical and moral responsibility to create and maintain safe environments for *every* young person in their care. The foundation of this safety is at the very core of all child welfare practice.

Solutions cannot be found simply by trying to identify gays and lesbians. Safe environments are essential for young people who are gay or lesbian to come out, if they choose to come out. How are such environments created? On the basis of my own experiences in the field, I have developed ten recommendations for developing a safe agency environment that affirms the identity of every young person:

1. Acknowledge that there are gay and lesbian young people are among your clients. Do not assume that all your clients are heterosexual. The only way that you can ever know someone else's sexual orientation is if that individual tells you. Many times staff make assumptions based on inaccurate information or misperceptions. Just as clients will tell you who they are when, and if, they feel ready, lesbian and gay clients will come out if and when they feel that there is a safe environment in which they can disclose this information.

2. Educate yourself and your coworkers about gays and lesbians. Familiarize yourself with the literature, bring in speakers, or ask an openly gay or lesbian professional to act as your "cultural guide" to teach you and others in your agency about gay and lesbian issues.

3. Use gender neutral language. If a practitioner uses language that assumes a person is heterosexual (i.e., inquiring about a woman's boyfriend or husband), a gay/lesbian client may not feel that the professional is knowledgeable about his/her orientation and may not share valuable information. The use of words and terms such as "partner," "significant other," or "someone special in your life" are appropriate—and it is important to use them.

4. Use the words "gay" or "lesbian" in an appropriate context when talking with clients about diversity. As mental health practitioners we try to be inclusive by specifically referring to the diverse groups of people that we encounter—Latino, African American, Asian American, developmentally challenged—being inclusive means also mentioning gay and lesbian people.

5. Have visible signs in the waiting room or in your office that speak to the fact that it is a gay and lesbian affirmative environment. Magazines, pamphlets, posters that have the words "gay" or "lesbian" printed on them let clients know that you are sensitized and that your office or your agency is a safe place for them.

6. Be prepared to change the culture of your organization. Condemn all slurs about all persons, let colleagues know that you do not think a joke is funny if it is at the expense of any group. This sends an unambiguous message that oppression hurts everyone.

7. If a client discloses to you that he or she is gay or lesbian, acknowledge it and talk about it. Don't just move on to other subjects; talk

about what it means to this client to be gay or lesbian. Process the feelings with the client.

8. Do not confuse transsexuality, transvestism, and homosexuality. Be aware that clients who are transsexual or transvestite are also members of sexual minority communities, although they may not be gay or lesbian. They may require services that are unique to meet their needs.

9. Research resources in the gay and lesbian community. Identify and become familiar with the resources that exist for gay and lesbian people in your geographic area. If there are services in your area, visit them. Be prepared to escort clients who might be scared to go to a gay agency for the first time.

10. If you are gay or lesbian yourself consider coming out! Visibility is powerful.

Systemic Responses: The Need for Alternatives and Strategies

In order to create consistently safe environments, there must be system-wide policies and practices in place to support the individual responses described above.

First, providing information alone is not sufficient. There must be a system-wide recognition of the extent to which negative attitudes toward homosexuality and discrimination against lesbian and gay youth contribute to the difficulties that these people encounter. Child welfare professionals need to acknowledge that young gays and lesbians do exist and then they need to develop ways to educate themselves as well as the families of children in care in order to understand the significance of sexual orientation in young people's lives and to help overcome the discrimination and oppression contributing to the difficulties these young people encounter.

The mandate of child welfare is to protect the child while supporting the family. Instances in which a child is gay or lesbian are no exception even though the apparent difficulties encountered in interactions between most gay and lesbian adolescents and their families have discouraged many child welfare professionals from attempting to reunite these children with their families. Although family reunification is generally not the typical outcome once a gay or lesbian adolescent enters into an out-of-home child welfare placement, reunification must not be completely rejected as a possible goal. In some cases, after a period of cooling down following the initial shock of disclosure, families are ready to work toward reunification with their children.

Supporting children and their families requires a service provider trained in family systems who is also competent to address sexual orientation issues in a sensitive way with children and families. Part of the service provider's role is to work toward increasing the parents' knowledge about gay and lesbian adolescents, and to model and encourage nonjudgmental and accepting attitudes and behavior toward the child. However, if reunification is not possible, gay and lesbian adolescents should be prepared for independent living and alternatives for those who require out-of-home care should be explored.

There are three alternatives which would provide a safe environment for gay and lesbian youth. The first is family foster care with gay or lesbian adults as foster parents (Ricketts 1991; Ricketts and Achtenberg 1987, 1990). The second is to provide specifically designed group home programs for gay and lesbian youth (Mallon 1994).

These alternatives are controversial. Conservative factions of the public frequently voice the opinion that gay/lesbian adults are not "fit" parents. This is, however, an opinion grounded in myths and stereotypes, not in fact. But it is a problematic public relations issue particularly if the system does not have a clearly defined policy that includes proactively providing appropriate services for lesbian and gay youth.

There is sometimes concern that providing separate services for lesbian and gay youth serves to further stigmatize them, and allows mainstream services to avoid their responsibility to provide safe and appropriate placements for them. Although this concern must be addressed, in the meantime, separate services do provide the environment and the care that lesbian and gay youth need right now. Both of these options for care have been implemented successfully in cities such as Los Angeles, New York, Toronto, Washington D.C., and Philadelphia. These programs offer safe, nurturing environments for young people who have had difficulty finding a good fit with their own families or within existing child welfare systems.

The third alternative is to transform the system into one that is responsive to the needs of lesbian and gay youth. Hiring openly gay and lesbian staff in group homes is one step in this process. Systematic and ongoing staff training and professional development for all levels of child welfare personnel, including foster parents, are also necessary.

GENERIC SERVICES VERSUS SPECIAL SERVICES

There has been some debate about the need to mainstream gay and lesbian young people into already existing child welfare programs as opposed to developing an array of specialized child welfare services for them, including group homes and foster homes. Opponents of special services note that young gays and lesbians need to interact within the larger heterosexual context of society and allege that such programming promotes segregation rather than integration. This assumption is self-contradictory because the child welfare system has historically grouped children according to special service needs. One respondent, interviewed for Mallon's 1994 study, put it best when he made this statement:

> I believe that if possible all children should be mainstreamed, if possible, that's the ideal, and we don't live in an ideal situation, but if you speak of the foster care system, the foster care system segregates children from the get go. We have specialized programs, because we feel that we should offer specialized programs to serve the children better. We have put specialized programs together for all types of children and we segregate them if we know initially that they have a particular issue, we segregate them. If we know that a child is HIV positive, then we place him or her in a special program for HIV positive children, right away that is a segregation, that child is not being mainstreamed into a regular foster home, he's being put into a specialized foster home. Or if we are unable to locate a specialized foster home he goes to a congregate care facility which is specialized, right there is an example of not mainstreaming and why? Because we feel that that child can be served better by not being mainstreamed; it's not that we want to segregate them for the virtue of segregating, it's that we think he can be served better. We do it for children who we call "hard-to-place," we segregate them into our specialized programs, not because we want to segregate again, but because we feel that that child will be better served; it's sort of a triage

that occurs. We do it for children who are physically handicapped, we send them to specialized programs, we do it for children who are emotionally disturbed, you know we do an initial triage and we send them to specialized residential facilities, if children are court adjudicated, we do a triage and send them to special facilities, we try to mainstream the bulk of the population but we do realized that there are certain services that do require a specialty.

I see the gay and lesbian group home as a specialized need for children that we think require enhanced services and can't be served elsewhere, it's just part of a spectrum of specialized programs that we have developed. I mean we do it! And to say that we don't do it, that is an argument that I had with _____ they said we don't segregate, I said, that's not true! We segregate all the time, but we don't call it segregation, we call it a service need, we do it on the basis of services because we think the kids will receive better services and I said that is the same thing with a gay and lesbian group home, for certain children, they will receive better service, because they need that better service, that's all. They need a place to feel safe and comfortable. It's based on service needs. But to say that we mainstream every child in care is just denying what we do.

Proponents of specialized services note that child welfare practitioners are uncomfortable, unskilled, and untrained in working with gay and lesbian youth and moreover that out-of-home-care settings are generally unsafe places for a self-identified or even perceived gay or lesbian young person to live. Moreover, they point out that these specialized services would not be necessary if mainstream child welfare agencies were held accountable for providing quality care to all children, including gays and lesbians. They therefore advocate that an array of specialized child welfare services, including agency-operated boarding homes, therapeutic foster boarding homes, group homes, and foster boarding homes, be offered as an option for self-identified gays and lesbians.

While recognizing that it is preferable for all young people to remain at home with their own families of origin, most professionals recognize that if children need to be placed, they should be placed in the least restrictive, mainstreamed, existing child welfare out-of-home-care settings. But the reality is, as Mallon's (1994) findings make clear, that staff are untrained and unskilled in working with homosexually oriented adolescents and that, in general, it is unsafe for these adolescents to be cared for in the majority of existing group and foster homes. As such, an array of specialized child welfare services needs to be developed by agencies (and supported by the appropriate city and state officials) that have a history of effectively working with self-identified gay and lesbian young people. Until child welfare practitioners and their agencies become more knowledgeable and skilled in working with homosexually oriented adolescents, until out-of-home-care settings can be made safer for these young people, it is strongly recommended that specialized child welfare programs, including agency-operated boarding homes, therapeutic foster boarding homes, group homes, and foster boarding homes, be developed and funded to provide an array of child welfare service options and safe places in which this underserved population can live and thrive. These services need to be particularly targeted to the following groups as there are currently no programs to meet their needs: adolescent lesbians, transgendered youths, gay and lesbian youths between the ages of 12 and 15, and seriously emotionally impaired gay and lesbian youths between the ages of 12 and 20.

If child welfare administrators are truly committed to diversity, they must be willing to include sexual diversity as a part of that commitment. This means that consideration must be given to these matters at the policymaking level (Children's Aid Society of Metropolitan Toronto 1995; Child Welfare League of America 1991; Child Welfare Administration of New York City/Council of Family and Child Caring Agencies 1994). When professionals operate in the absence of clearly stated polices as guides, out of necessity they utilize their own personal experiences based on their own cultural, religious, and societal biases (Forrester and Huggins 1981). Written, formal policies help prevent discrimination, harassment, and verbal abuse of gay and lesbian young people, and of those perceived to be gay or lesbian.

The problems encountered by gay and lesbian adolescents and their families are frequently ignored and largely unrecognized by the majority of child welfare professionals—analogous to the ways in which the child welfare system has been deficient in addressing the specific needs of diverse ethnic and racial minorities. An understanding of the impact of societal stigmatization of gay/lesbian individuals and their families is crucial to the recognition of and response to the needs of this population.

Effecting changes in attitudes and beliefs in pursuit of competent practice with these individuals requires education, training (Mallon 1998b, 1998c, 1998d), and self-exploration on both the individual and institutional level. The development of competence in this area holds promise for preserving and supporting families and for the establishment of appropriate gay-/lesbian-affirmative child welfare services for young people and their families.

CHAPTER 7

Runaways and Homeless Gay and Lesbian Youth

Inasmuch as services for runaway and homeless youth fall outside the domain of traditionally defined child welfare services (Fitzgerald 1996), lesbian and gay youth are present in a variety of youth-serving systems and are disproportionately overrepresented in the young runaway and homeless population because a substantial proportion of these youths have fled the child welfare system when they determined that it was a hostile environment that constituted a poor fit (Holloway 1998; Rosenberg 1998; Seattle Commission 1988; Webber 1991). The National Network for Youth suggests that approximately 1.3 million young people run away from home each year. One in seven will run away from home sometime between the ages of 10 and 17. On an average day in the United States, 3,228 youth leave home (National statistics 1998; Runaway and homeless, n.d.).

The following vignette illustrates the relevance of the issues faced by gay/lesbian runaway and homeless youth. Frank is an 18-year-old gay Latino "system kid" who has lived on the streets of New York City for the past four years:

FRANK

When I was about 7 or 8 I went into foster care placement. My mother was like majorly into drugs, she was like burnt out and she neglected us a lot and a lot of the neighbors saw that and there was a lot of complaints made and so BCW [New York City's Bureau of Child Welfare, now Administration for Children's Services] ended up coming to the house and finding my mother not there, or going there and finding my mother there but finding no food in the house, or finding the house a mess, you know, or finding drug paraphernalia, or finding drug behavior of some type, you know, so we were placed in foster care. We were taken in and out of foster homes a lot, taken away, then given back to my mother, four months in, then given back, three months in and then given back, a week in and then given back, you know, and then as we got older it progressed, it got worse. I mean we went from going to foster homes to going to group homes, to going to boarding schools, to going to Division for Youth facilities, to going to lock up, to going to Rikker's Island [a detention center in New York City], and then to going to jail upstate.

I was about 16 when I was released from jail and that's when I hit the streets. I couldn't go home—didn't have a home, and I wasn't going to go back to a group home, I just kinda started to hang out, you know, staying at friends' houses. Finally I started to just spend more and more time on the streets. I spent a few nights in shelters, but then I'd either get fed up with the rules or kicked out for getting into conflicts with other residents—to be honest it didn't always have to do with my sexuality.

I started to like a lot of the things I found out on the street, I mean I started hustling at that point, you know, prostitution and in the beginning I thought that I wasn't going to be able to get into this, then I ended up liking it, you know, and getting into it. I made a lot of money. But I also got into drugs big time—coke, heroin, hard stuff—I guess it's hereditary. I did it all out there. About two months ago I took the HIV test and found out that I'm HIV positive. Sometimes folks in the drop-in center try to help me get it together and there's times when I'd like to get it together, you know, to have a home, but then I think—maybe it's too late for me.

Like Frank, many runaway and homeless youths do not seek out social services for help. Many have been in the child welfare system or are still in the official custody of the state, and their experience has been that the system gives them nothing of value. Some choose the streets over the child welfare system because they have determined that traditional child welfare settings are unsafe and unwelcoming (Mallon 1998). Still others have run away from homes where emotional, physical, or sexual abuse were commonplace (Janus, Archambault, and Brown 1995; www. acf.dhhs.gov/programs/fybs/faq). Although shelter is a primary need (O'Brien, Travers, and Bell 1993), lesbian/gay runaway and homeless youth have distinctive health and mental health care needs that are the result of societal stressors and may engage in high risk behaviors.

The reality of these runway and homeless youths is a complex phenomenon. Calling on actual case examples from youths interviewed in Toronto, Los Angeles, and New York, this chapter examines the factors associated with lesbian and gay youths and offers recommendations to policy makers and practitioners responsible for their care.

TYPOLOGY OF RUNAWAY AND HOMELESS YOUTH

One of the foremost difficulties in addressing the needs of runaway and homeless young people is to attempt to quantify the population (Caton 1990; Zide and Cherry 1992) who, for a myriad of reasons, are difficult to identify. Quantifying lesbian and gay youths is additionally burdensome because they are socialized to hide, which makes service provision indisputably more complex. Although data on street youth remain scant (*The Blade* 1999), the studies that exist provide some direction for program and policy makers. In three separate studies conducted over a three-year period (1987–1990), involving a total of 235 youths, The Streetwork Project in New York City's Time Square area, a project of Victim Services, found that 42 percent of the youths surveyed reported that they were lesbian, gay, or bisexual; 57 percent reported that they had been in a foster home or group home; 73 percent reported that they were engaged in prostitution; and 87 percent reported an involvement with drugs (Victim Services/Travelers Aid 1991). Of those interviewed by Remafedi (1985), 26 percent said that they were forced to leave home after they disclosed their sexual orientation.

From a legislative perspective, the Stewart B. McKinney Act was passed in 1987 to meet the emergency of homelessness as such, responding to the issue of temporary relief. The definition of a person who is homeless and thereby eligible for assistance under the McKinney Act includes a person who 1) lacks a fixed, regular, and adequate nighttime residence, or 2) lives in a shelter or institution other than a prison, or in a place not designated for or ordinarily used as a sleeping accommodation for human beings (Able-Peterson and Bucy 1993). Although this legislation provided a clear definition for program and policy makers, some have criticized it as reducing youth homelessness to a definition that focuses only on lacking a fixed address. Although there are several terms (e.g., runaways, street youth, system kids, throwaways) used interchangeably to define homeless and street youths, these categories are distinct and different from one another. The National Network for Youth has suggested some fully rounded definitions for the broad population:

- *Runaways* are those youths who have left home at least overnight without parental permission. Most of these youths probably return home without seeking services, others are reunited with their families with the assistance of runaway shelter staff. Repeat runaways may eventually lose contact with their families and become homeless.
- *Homeless* youths are those without parental, foster, or institutional homes to which they can return. They have often left with the full knowledge or approval of their legal guardians even though they may have not a place to live.
- *Street* kids are young people who have run away several times and have lived on the streets long enough to have internalized a view of themselves as street kids. They are adept at fending for themselves.
- *System* kids are youths who have been removed from their homes for their own protection, by means of a voluntary agreement signed by their families and the local social services district, or ordered by the courts, and have been placed in a series of unsuccessful placements. They leave their placements or are allowed to "go awol" and choose to live on the streets.

Homelessness is a gradual process for many youths. Those who flee to the streets or who begin to flirt with life on the streets are those who have decided not to "take it" anymore. Lesbian and gay youths are highly represented in this population. Because a lesbian or gay identity remains highly stigmatized by heterosexual society, these youths are often expelled from or prematurely leave their homes after coming out or being found out by families (Mallon 1998). The narratives of the young people interviewed by me (Mallon 1998) clearly illustrates that lesbian/gay youths are found in all of the typologies identified above.

THE "SAFETY" OF THE STREETS

The debilitating effects of verbal harassment and physical violence, which embraced the poorest elements of fit, caused more than one half of the young people interviewed in a recent study (Mallon 1998) to migrate to the relative safety of the streets. Finding life in their families, group homes, foster homes, or institutional settings to be intolerable, these youths stated that they felt "safer" on the streets than in their family or out-of-home care setting. Young people who fled to the streets, or who began to spend more time outside of their group home or foster home, were those who were no longer willing to tolerate the poor fit that was manifest in such settings (Holdway and Ray 1992). Those who declared that they were no longer willing to "take it" defined "it" as sexual or physical abuse or severe psychological and emotional neglect (Kurtz et al. 1996).

Escape from dangerous and even life-threatening conditions (note Bucy and Able-Peterson 1993) is actually a healthy response to intolerable situations. In some cases the violence and alienation that these young people experienced on the streets may be less than what they endured with their families or in some out-of-home care child welfare setting. The flight of these young people from their families or group homes to the streets does not actually happen in one swift move, but is usually a gradual process that takes place over a period of time. Because young people perceived that most staff members were unable to respond to their needs and because most felt that out-of-home care settings were unnurturing and hostile environments, they felt that they had no option but to live in the streets. Although the streets of any city would hardly seem like a place to find a good fit, of the 54 young people who were interviewed for this study, fully one half of the respondents (n=27) indicated that they had lived on the streets at one time or another as an alternative to living in a hostile child welfare environment. The following narrative provided by a young African American, culled from Mallon's (1998:ch. 4) extensive interviews with lesbian and gay youths in foster care, best speaks to this experience:

> I couldn't live at home with my family once they found out that I was gay so I was sent to live in a group home. That was worse than living at home. I didn't fit in at home and then I didn't fit in at the group home either. I was living in my fourth group home in like six months and it was horrible. The teasing, the tormenting, the harassment really got to me and one day I just decided that I couldn't take it any more and I left. I had no place to stay, but I didn't even care. I knew that I just couldn't stay one more minute in that group home. I lived with friends, I stayed on people's sofas, I became a "couch kid."

I prostituted—I'm not proud of that, but I did what I had to do—to get money to rent a place. I even lived in an abandoned trailer truck with ten other people, slept in railroad tunnels, and anywhere that was warm. As bad as things got on the streets, it was better than the group homes that I had lived in—at least people cared for me on the streets.

Recalling how he fled the system because his needs were not met, and because he perceived it to be unsafe for him, one youth in Mallon's study vividly recounted his frightening journey:

The city don't like runaways, but they [staff] never paid much attention to me and so when I had to, I just left. I was in this one agency, the Children's House, there was a guy there and he was real effeminate and they treated him like junk, he was a closet case, but everyone knew. They treated him like junk and then they started to treat me like junk too, I used to get beat up by the other residents. That's where I had the hardest time and every time I left, the city would send me back. I just kept running away and they kept sending me back and saying, work it out. One day one lady at CWA said, give it 30 days and if it still doesn't work out, I'll replace you. Thirty days later I was back and she did replace me, that worked for a while, I was there for three years and then I had to be replaced again.

At that point I just went to live on the streets. I slept at first on the trains, but then I started to sleep at this spot in Penn Station along the Long Island Railroad track 18 or 19, not on the track, but sometimes under the platform where there was a little space. It was dark, but it was a place to sleep. Then I went to this place called the Underground, there were about 30 or 40 people living there. It was an abandoned trailer at 34th Street and 11th Avenue. In the winter it was cold there, we kept warm by making a fire in a large can inside the trailer, it was OK, but it got pretty smoky there. We found food to eat outside of the fancy restaurants. . . It wasn't the greatest at the trailer, but it was safe there and no one really bothered you.

I hate to admit it, but I also prostituted myself. It wasn't really one of the greatest things, it really wasn't but it was like a lot of us young people did it and I had never tried it but it's, it's money! You see some people used this money to smoke their lives away but whenever I got this money it was to eat. I did it about three times and after the third time, the girl I was telling you about, she was telling me stories about how certain hookers or male prostitutes or female prostitutes were found hung, heads decapitated, these were not just fake stories, these were true stories in the paper—it made me think.

No one ever went to Mount Laurel. I had been there before and they were not so nice to gay and lesbian people because it's predominantly straight people in there and people always jump you there. All those people do is either call the cops or throw both of you out which really doesn't help because then you're out on the street again.

Adaptations to Life on the Streets

Youths who made their homes in the streets have also had to make many adaptations to their perceived safety in the street subculture. Some of the most resilient young people band together with other young gays and lesbians to find homes and employment, as well as to provide emotional support for one another. Forming alliances with others on the street is an important part of living on the streets. Many of these very resourceful young people re-created new family systems, families of choice that sometimes include older lesbians or gays fulfilling the parental roles in an effort to nourish one another with the familial nutriments that they lacked in their biological family systems. The narrative of one youth spoke about the need for family:

> I met other people who were like me. Some of us lived together for a while. We'd work, share the rent and be, you know, be like a little family. It was really nice. We supported one another, we had fights and all, but we resolved them amongst ourselves. We had people of all ages, some younger, some older. We were tight, we were, like I said, like a little family.

Other youths sought emancipation and moved, often times prematurely, toward independence:

> When I left the group home I tried to make it on my own, but I didn't have a GED, I didn't have any life skills and all I could do was work in

minimum wage jobs. It was all right, but it was hard to budget money and I couldn't really deal with the independence of it all. I mean I loved being on my own, but it's hard out there—it was also lonely and I didn't really have any support from anyone.

Survival Sex

Closely allied to the issue of lesbian and gay homelessness and as a means of earning income, some young gay males have turned to prostitution. Several authors (Boyer 1989; Cates 1989; Coleman 1989) have investigated the issues pertaining to male prostitution and the risk factors involved in this activity.

Many young people who have spent time on the streets have been sexually exploited first in their own homes and then become involved in the sex trade industry as a means to support themselves (Athey 1991; Hunter and Schaecher 1994; Luna 1991). Kruks (1991) reported that gay male youths who have been forced out of their homes because of their sexual orientation are more likely to engage in survival sex than their nongay counterparts. Street youths find that they can earn money dancing in clubs and backrooms, "going on dates," doing pornographic photo shoots or films, and providing "escort" or "massage" services to adult clients. Although not all street youths become involved in the sex trade industry, many lesbian and gay street youths do see it as a means to meet their basic needs—housing, food, clothing, and drugs. Both young lesbians and gays participate in prostitution and sex trade activities. One young person from Los Angeles recalled a history of prostitution:

> Yeah, I was out on Santa Monica and Orange nightly. I made a lot of money having sex with men. I spent it all too! I couldn't make it on minimum wage and trying to apply for a job when you don't have clean clothes, a phone number, and an address is really difficult. I used the one thing that I had—my body. The funny thing is that most times I just used the money to buy drugs to chill myself out from the pain I felt from having to live my life like that. I never planned for this to happen. I was a real mess during that time of my life.

An additional consequence of survival sex is risk for HIV infection. HIV transmission is an ever-present danger in street life. Several factors place lesbian and gay youths at very high risk for HIV transmission including: having to exchange sex for money, unsafe sex, substance abuse, and denial of sexual identity (Cranston 1992; Rotheram-Borus, Rosario, and Koopman 1991). Although virtually all street work programs provide HIV education and prevention, including risk reduction, very few youths feel empowered enough to negotiate safe sex with their clients. Numerous street youths suffer the lifetime traumatizing effects of unwanted pregnancy, sexually transmitted diseases, and sexual assaults.

Substance Abuse

Society provides very few sanctioned outlets for lesbian/gay youth. Many homeless and street youths "self medicate" from their emerging sexual and affectional feelings through the use and abuse of alcohol and other substances. Lacking age-appropriate social, safe spaces, a large number of lesbian and gay adolescents are left with few options besides frequenting bars and clubs that serve the adult lesbian and gay community. These adolescents often find themselves isolated from persons of their own age and absorbed in an abusive pattern of alcohol or substance abuse. Reflecting on his own substance abuse as a contributing factor to his homelessness, Paul, a gay youth from New York made this recollection:

PAUL

I was what you called a "club kid." I was out every night dancing and druggin.' I usually snuck into clubs because I sure as hell didn't have any money. I didn't live at home—my parents couldn't have cared less about me, especially when I came out as gay. I always told people I lived with friends—in reality I lived with a lot of different friends—every night sleeping on someone's sofa. I think I did every drug possible—Ecstasy, Special K, coke, pot, speed, you name it—I did it. I was high all the time. I crashed finally—hit bottom—I was arrested, sentenced to probation, and placed by the court in drug treatment. I wish I could say I have conquered my addictions, but I still struggle with it. It's hard when you don't have family to watch your back.

Health and Mental Health Issues

Living on the streets puts the physical and mental health of youth at constant risk. Lesbian and gay youths typically do not have ready access to health care that recognizes and addresses sexual concerns (Owen 1985; Paroski 1987). In addition to the life-threatening consequences of HIV infection, substance abuse, and street violence, street youths often suffer from upper respiratory infection, body and pubic lice, burns, numerous injuries, sexually transmitted diseases, dermatological problems, and mental health problems. The extremes of temperatures, irregular sleep in exposed places, poor diet, and the lack of hygiene opportunities for regular showers exacerbates the problem. Hunger is also a serious problem for street youths. A study conducted by Robertson (1989) found that 57 percent of those interviewed had experienced at least one day in the past month with no food.

Contrary to the popular myth that young lesbians do not become pregnant, many young lesbians who engage in sexual relationships with men do become pregnant. Pregnant teens who live on the streets find their problems magnified. Prenatal care and living with a child on the streets is a onerous prospect.

Homeless lesbian/gay youths are also at risk for severe mental health problems. They suffer primarily from anxiety and depression. Many have also suffered from childhood sexual abuse or other traumatization related to family violence (Shaffer and Caton 1984) as evidenced in the following account from Sara, a 17-year-old Caucasian lesbian in Los Angeles:

SARA

My family was always a mess. My Mom's boyfriends were always disgusting. Most times they beat on her, sometimes they beat on me and my brothers. One of them molested me for years, starting when I turned 11. I didn't tell my mother, I mean she couldn't even help herself, how was she gonna she help me? My life from the time I was 5 until the time I left home at 15 was a nightmare. Believe it or not, running away from home was one of the best things that ever happened to me. But I still have a lot of bad shit that haunts me about all the stuff that happened to me.

At times, the psychological stress, as evidenced by the above account, is more than many young persons can endure. Some lesbian and gay youths reportedly made suicide attempts (Kournay 1987; Remafedi 1994; Rofes 1983) to escape the isolation and estrangement of their pain as one Toronto youth, named Buzz, recalled:

Buzz

I was high everyday. My life was a mess, I hated myself. I had nothing. I didn't have a family that cared for me, I didn't have a home, I didn't have anyone I thought I could go to. I tried to kill myself three times. They always tried at the shelter to give me a referral for counseling, but I never went. I never trusted them. Finally after a pretty serious suicide attempt (I sliced up my arm with a razor blade), I was hospitalized. When I was released from the hospital they found me a good place to stay and things have been better since then.

Educational and Life Skills

Poor school performance, lack of skills, and poor attitudes about education and employment are fundamental facts of life for young people who are homeless. Assisting street youth in re-entering high school or working to obtain their G.E.D. (General Equivalency Diploma) and working toward the development of life skills for living independently are critical aspects of addressing the needs of street youths. Gays and lesbians may face additional challenges since many have left school because of safety issues.

SERVICES FOR HOMELESS YOUTHS

Although lesbian/gay street youths have some unique service provision needs, most require the same services as their nongay counterparts. Among the services that street youths require are: direct services on the street; drop-in center services; and shelter and transitional living services.

Direct Services on the Street

Life on the streets is a transient and shifting scene. Before programs are initiated, social workers must survey the street scene to determine the "turf"—to determine who hangs out where. Although there is blending, gay/lesbian street kids hang out in different areas in New York, Los Angeles, and Toronto than do heterosexual street kids. In urban areas streetwork begins by visiting youth-oriented gathering areas—parks, street corners, "strolls"(areas where gay and lesbian youths are known to prostitute themselves), specific neighborhoods, restaurants that are tolerant of gay life and where gays and lesbians are known to hang out. They may also hang out around bus or train terminals in the area because these are open late at night. Fast food restaurants in these areas also have late night hours and may attract street youths. Peep shows, bars, and transient hotels in these areas also are places where lesbian/gay street youths may congregate. In rural and suburban areas, they hang out in different ways. For example in rural farming areas, they hang out in cornfields where it is easy to remain unobserved.

Professionals who work with street kids need to assess their own safety levels on the street. Two-person teams are ideal. They create a partnership and workers feel less isolated. Although safety is paramount, hanging out regularly is the first step to becoming part of the street scene.

In some areas lesbian and gay street youths may seem invisible and indistinguishable from heterosexual street youths. However when these groups are observed by workers who are knowledgeable about lesbian/gay persons, they can be differentiated from the others.

Most importantly, street workers must learn to listen to young people. Those who live on the streets have a very low level of trust for adults. Many have been misused by adults and trust will have to be earned. Able-Peterson and Bucy (1993) offer several rules for engaging homeless youths.

Rule 1: First and foremost street workers must learn young people's names. Young people feel important when someone has taken the time to connect and learn their names. Use whatever name they give you—street youths use nicknames regularly. Do not press them to disclose their real names to you in the earliest stages of a developing relationship. It is also important to repeat your name to them every time you see them, so that they will get used to hearing and using yours. A person is not a stranger if first names are used. It is also important to remember that every new face is viewed with suspicion.

Rule 2: It is essential that street workers state very simply who they are, and with whom they are connected. In working with lesbian and gay street youths, workers must be especially attuned to their unique culture and language. Many workers carry cards with their names and their agency's name and services printed

on them. Cards distributed should refer to services that are specific to lesbians and gays. Introductory assessment questions
should be utilized in a conversational manner. Stress food,
clothing, showers, and medical care. Repeat your name and
theirs when you say good-bye.

Rule 3: Street workers need to be patient and consistent. Building a good
relationship with street youths takes time. Young people who
have survived on the streets know that it was their wariness that
has kept them alive. Street workers need to be clear that what
they offer (food, clothing, shelter) comes with no strings
attached. Although trust is developed slowly, there is an easy
comraderie on the streets. After a worker has bumped into a
youth three or four times, they begin to get used to the worker's
presence and may begin to form a relationship with him or her.

Rule 4: Workers need to trust the process. There are no short cuts to
building a relationship.

As the relationship develops between the youth and the street worker, so
usually will the requests for assistance (Bronstein 1996). Case management,
resource identification, and advocacy often begins on the streets, but may
move into the drop-in center as time, need, and the relationship progress-
es (Street outreach n.d.; U.S. Dept. of Health and Human Services 1998a,
1998b).

The Drop-In Center

The drop-in center provides a transition from the work conducted on the
streets and longer-term services. Drop-in centers are places where youths
can take a shower, get clothes, meet with a counselor, attend a life skills
group, participate in a G.E.D. class, take part in a recreational activity,
have a meal, and begin to deepen relationships. Drop-in centers are usually located near areas where youths hang out. Some centers also have
medical vans attached to their programs and provide much needed health
care. Lesbians gays who have spent a great deal of time on the streets
might be initially reluctant to participate in drop-in center activities
because of past negative experiences with insensitive social services
providers. Peer outreach is a key to insuring that the center is a safe place
for all youths.

Shelters and Transitional Living Programs

Since 1974, shelters have been an important part of the array of services available to street youths. Lesbian and gay young people, many of whom have experienced very poor fits in the child welfare system, might avoid shelters or transitional living programs at all costs. Although family reunification was a major impetus for funding shelter programs in the mid seventies, such idealistic goals were evidence of how little policy makers understood the reasons why many young people fled from their homes. Reunification may be possible for many homeless young people, but for others, it is must be acknowledged that it is not a realistic or practical goal. It is important to realize that crisis intervention and residential care for young people whose separation from their family will become permanent is very different from interventions with first-time runners. In most cases, individual host homes, rather than a shelter, may be a preferable alternative for less street-wise youth.

Shelters and host homes that are committed to providing care for lesbian and gay youth must consciously focus on creating an affirming and supportive environment to insure safety for all young people. At the very minimum, shelter staff and host home volunteers, at all levels, should be knowledgeable and trained about lesbian/gay culture and norms; agency literature should include references to welcoming and working with lesbians and gays; health and mental health care providers must be able to "send out the cues," through their language and by their actions, that they are comfortable and confident in working with lesbian/gay youth. Shelters that do not create an affirming environment for them will not be utilized by them.

Transitional living programs (TLPs), funded by the Family and Youth Services Bureau (Transitional living, n.d.), are apartments rented by multiservice youth-serving organizations in the community to house homeless youths. TLPs are excellent program models for adolescents who are moving toward self-sufficiency. In addition to providing safe and stable living accommodations while they are program participants, the programs also provide an array of services necessary to assist them in developing both the skills and personal characteristics needed to enable them to live independently. Among these services are education, life skills development, information and counseling aimed at preventing, treating, and reducing substance abuse, and appropriate referrals and access to medical and mental health treatment. Young people may live in this supervised living arrangement for up to 18 months.

Like adult homelessness, lesbian/gay homelessness is not simply a matter of providing housing for a young person. Nor should youth homelessness be viewed entirely as an indicator of problem youth behavior, but as evidence of society's inability to develop adequate supports for youth and families troubled by economic hardship, substance abuse, sexual orientation issues, incest, and familial violence (Rivers 1998). All runaway and homeless young people face a multitude of problems when on the streets. Lesbian and gay youths are further burdened by lack of family support, unsafe child welfare placements, and societal heterocentrism and homophobia. The dual stigmatization of being lesbian/gay *and* homeless can lead to an overwhelming sense of despair and hopelessness. Making mainstream runaway and homeless youth services accessible to them is an active, ongoing, and evolving process that requires organizational sensitivity and responsiveness. Homeless lesbian and gay youths can be moved from the streets into appropriate homes if they are provided with competent practitioners to work with them and are offered sensitively designed programs to meet their needs.

CHAPTER 8

Locked in the Child Welfare Closet—Who's Got The Key?

Tell them about how you're never really a whole person if you remain silent, because there's always that one little piece inside you that wants to be spoken out, and if you keep ignoring it, it gets madder and madder and hotter and hotter, and if you don't speak it out one day it will just up and punch you in the mouth from the inside. —Audre Lorde (1984:42)

This book emerged from a series of conversations with child welfare colleagues about why the child welfare field has done so little to respond to and address the needs of gay and lesbian children, young people, and families. I wondered why so little concern has been expressed about their needs in national, state, and local policies, in child welfare agency practices, and in professional publications. The lack of attention to this out-group had to be more than flagrant heterocentrism and personal bias, but even after writing the book I am hard pressed to find other compelling reasons for such conspicuous disregard. For the most part, with few exceptions, the situations that gay and lesbian children, young people, and families endure as representative examples of child welfare at its worst. The very existence of this out-group is generally unacknowledged by most child welfare professionals except when a particular case that pertains to sexual orientation is blared across the print news or sensationalized in the mass media. This lack of acknowledgment by child welfare practitioners and policy makers is in stark contrast to the heightened consciousness about this population by practitioners and policy makers evidenced by the runaway and homeless youth programs across the nation.

After almost a decade of traveling in the United States and abroad to challenge and dialogue with child welfare professionals about how they could work effectively with gay and lesbian children, young people, and families, it has become apparent to me that training programs alone will not ameliorate the injury that many of these individuals have experienced under the guise of "services to children and families." Although certain kinds of unfounded beliefs and uncompromising prejudices must give way when tested against the standards of truth and rationality, there will always be a certain number of people who will refuse to give up their convictions that gays and lesbians are "sick, immoral, and perverted"—no matter what counter-information may be given them. Policies and programs that are nonbias in their approach and gay- and lesbian-affirming practices by child welfare professionals are the imperatives necessary to remedy these historic damages.

In this book I have tried to challenge policy makers, practitioners, and those concerned about children, youth, and families to cope with issues of sexual orientation in their deliberations of policy alternatives. I have also provided a clear gay- and lesbian-affirming perspective to assist practitioners, scholars, and policy makers in shaping these deliberations. Clearly, if it is even present at all, sexual orientation has been assigned a low position in public debates about how to improve child welfare practices and programs. The issue is seldom raised as a determining factor in the development of policies for families and children. It is, however, as highlighted in this book, a critical factor in the lives of countless children, young people, and families who are affected on a daily basis by issues of sexual orientation.

Changes in the country's attitudes toward gay and lesbian persons, and civil rights struggles by gay and lesbian persons themselves, demand a conscious effort to include issues of sexual orientation in child welfare practice and policy debates. A deferral will only serve to increase social costs to society and perpetuate harm to the thousands gay and lesbian children, young people, and families in this out-group whose lives are affected by the child welfare system.

One might ask: What could be gained by elevating sexual orientation issues as a factor in the policy-development phase? I would reply by asking: What could be lost by not incorporating the unique needs of gays and lesbians?

WHAT CHILD WELFARE NEEDS TO DO

Resolving the child welfare imbroglio for gay/lesbian children, youth, and families—and all children, youth, and families—requires changes in both the policies and practices of child welfare agencies. These changes must be based on a intentional and deliberate recognition of the uniqueness of anyone's sexual orientation, so that approaches used can enhance family functioning and the well-being of children. Confident but effective initiatives and pilot programs should be launched, particularly those which encourage the development of community-based preventive services, empowerment models, and training for sensitive practice. Openly gay and lesbian child welfare professionals are essential key players in these change efforts, but so are nongay allies. Although the major sources of power and control over the distribution of child welfare services are assumed to be heterosexual, the resources themselves—the nurturance, the sustenance, and the affection—are in gay and lesbian people.

To effectively serve gay and lesbian children, adolescents, and families, professionals in the child welfare system must first accept the fact that they really do have clients who are gay or lesbian. They must also acknowledge that gay and lesbian persons are affected by every level of child welfare services, from adoption to out-of-home care, from child protection to family preservation services. Integration of a gay- and lesbian-affirming perspective into contemporary child welfare policies and practices can promote the well-being of this out-group. Indifference to issues of sexual orientation will result in continued psychological and social assaults. Indefensible policies and practices, as well as personal bias against gay and lesbian persons must be eliminated by child welfare systemic policy reform or by legislation in the form of nondiscriminatory protection by the enforcement of laws. The profession must also ask itself: How has it been possible for our colleagues in runaway and homeless youth programs to acknowledge this population and respond to its needs, and why has child welfare been so reluctant to do so?

The welfare of gay/lesbian children, youth, and families cannot be adequately enhanced as long as the larger society, heterocentrically oriented and heterosexually controlled, ignores their existence. The misguidedness of the political system with respect toward gays and lesbians—their levels of participation, power, and struggle for human rights—is an excellent measure of the bias against them. Many child welfare professionals challenge the notion of creating separate programs for gays/lesbians but then refuse to put funds behind efforts to educate staff on how to respond to their needs. Pharr (1988:21–23) aptly points out that no institutions, other than those created by lesbians and gays, affirm gay/lesbian identity and offer protection. The affirmation and protection usually afforded automatically to most children and families are rights not guaranteed by child welfare agencies to most gay/lesbian children, youth, and families. Of course, there is some variety; some institutions provide more affirming environmental "fits" than do others for gay/lesbian persons. But whether one looks at child welfare, education, health care, religion, culture, law enforcement, the media, or any other dominant system of the larger Western society, we see heterocentrism at work. This force makes gay and lesbian persons and the families of gay and lesbian persons specially vulnerable to life's challenges.

The dominant child welfare institutions in the United States continue to exclude openly gay and lesbian persons even though, despite this exclusion, they exist within all child welfare organizations. This overt heterocentric discrimination has been replaced by a covert but nonetheless effective heterocentrism in the lack of distribution of services to gay/lesbian children, young people, and families. In large urban areas, like New York, Los Angeles, and Philadelphia, where gays and lesbians are protected against discrimination by local legislation, the apparent discrimination has officially decreased, but it exists nonetheless as those services reaching them continue to be administered in a toxic form.

The behavioral heterocentrism reflected in the inequities inflicted on gay/lesbian persons is accompanied by several manifestations of an ideational heterocentrism that in fact serves to perpetuate and protect the behavioral manifestations. As we have seen, efforts for change specifically for gay/lesbian children, young people, and families have almost always been met with a rationale absolving those upholding the discrimination. These rationales all rest on some pervasive negative conceptions of gays and lesbians. Each facet of these rationales reflects the refutation of gay/lesbian people and the gay/lesbian experience. And this same denial of gay/lesbian persons pervades the language of child welfare practice and policy development.

These efforts, which rise and fall in the level of interest allocated by child welfare authorities, according to political pressures or the threat of class action law suits, failed because they have not been sufficiently radical. More specifically, they were not conceived or pursued from a gay-/lesbian-affirming perspective. They did not grow out of a gay/lesbian experience. In addition, they were not based on recognition that some of the dysfunctions were inherent in the existing system of child welfare services.

THE NEED FOR ALTERNATIVES AND STRATEGIES

The lack of accurate and adequate information about children, youth, and families who are gay or lesbian seriously impairs the capacity of both the family system and the child welfare system to provide competent service delivery to this underserved and marginalized population. Information alone is insufficient to achieve competence with respect to issues of sexual orientation in the child welfare system. For proficiency to be achieved, policy and practice considerations must permeate all administrative levels and all types of child welfare programs. Clearly there is (as indicated by Pecora et al. 1992: xvi) "a need to develop alternatives to working with all groups which are hindered by oppression in its various forms . . . but it is also essential that child welfare practitioners be cognizant of these conditions and incorporate strategies for helping clients overcome discrimination if long-term success is to be achieved." Like cultural competence, competent practice with gay and lesbian people at the service delivery level of the child welfare system, can be achieved only with the recognition of the significance of sexual orientation in people's lives.

Administrators of child welfare systems in both the public and private sectors must "make every effort to support the family, to enhance its functioning, and to avoid separation and placement" (Laird 1979: 205). When separation is necessary, the importance of family must continue to be recognized through vigorous efforts to maintain family ties, and to work, whenever possible, toward reuniting the family. These guidelines apply regardless of personal, religious, sexual orientation, or cultural biases to all children and families including children who are gay or lesbian.

As a system that is, by its own definition, designed to provide protective and preventive services for the safety and well-being of a child when the family system fails, child welfare practitioners must ask why this is not being done for gay/lesbian children, young people, and families? The child welfare system already has the structures it needs to encourage competent practice with gay/lesbian persons. What follows are recommendations for practice, policy, and administrative procedures that can enhance competency in responding to this out-group.

- Comprehensive and intensive efforts must be made to keep gay/lesbian children and adolescents in their own homes. Viewed ecologically, both assessment and intervention must focus primarily on the goodness of fit (Germain and Gitterman 1996) between the child or adolescent and those other systems with which he or she is in transaction, the most central of which, in this case, is the family. Many of the issues that surface when a family member discloses or is confronted with aspects of sexual orientation can be best dealt with by a competent social worker trained in family systems. Providing on-going education for protection and prevention workers that would help them feel competent about addressing issues of sexual orientation while gay and lesbian young people are still in their homes, and could support families and prevent the placement of many of these youngsters.

- Family support and preservation programs with their primary goal of keeping families together can deliver these services within the context of clients' natural environments, their homes. Many of the community-based programs, located in every community, and nationally recognized programs, like the Homebuilder model (Kinney et al. 1991), can provide opportunities to help families with a young person who identifies or may later identify as gay or lesbian. Working with families in their natural environments makes social workers in a family support or preservation program ideally situated to see what is really going on in a family's home. By being in the home, the workers could make an accurate assessment and design an intervention that would support (Saperstein 1981) and preserve the family system. With a greater awareness of sexual orientation, family-centered practitioners could educate parents, as well as model and shape new behaviors.
- Increasing the family's knowledge about a family member's gay or lesbian sexual orientation (Borhek 1983, 1988; Dew 1994; Fairchild and Haywood 1989; Griffin, Wirth, and Wirth 1986; Strommen 1989), and identifying resources that support families, like Parents and Friends of Lesbians and Gays (PFLAG 1990), are important ways to strengthen and support the families of gay and lesbian adolescents.
- Family therapy can facilitate reunification, but many child welfare professionals will have to learn how to work sensitively toward openly confronting sexual orientation with children, adolescents, and their families. If reunification is deemed not to be an appropriate goal, gay and lesbian adolescents should be prepared for independent living.
- Gay and lesbian children and youth are frequently the victims of abuse, neglect, and violence at the hands of their own families. In some cases, the violence has gone unchecked by child protection practition-

ers as there has been a tacit acceptance of abuse against gay/lesbian youths as a parental "corrective" to a gay/lesbian sexual orientation. Child protection workers must become keenly aware of the potential for violence in the homes of gay/lesbian children and youths. By responding to the abuse and neglect many gay/lesbian young people experience, protection practitioners will be meeting their ethical obligation to protect all children and youth from abuse or neglect in their homes.

To enhance their competence, protection workers need on-going training and education on competent practice with gay/lesbian children, youth, and families. They also need support—child protection is demanding and emotionally draining work. Advocacy for gay/lesbian children's and adolescents' needs is another critical step in providing better protective services. The child advocate plays an integral role in ensuring that the gay/lesbian child or adolescent and their families are adequately served. Finally, protection workers must be prepared to confront institutional heterocentrism and societal homophobia.

In cases where family preservation or family support programs or child protection efforts have not been able to preserve the family, finding appropriate out-of-home placements becomes a key task. The placement of lesbian/gay children and adolescents in nonsensitive foster and group homes frequently leads to placement failure, a low incidence of family reunification, and, in many cases, homelessness (Mallon 1998a). Making out-of-home child welfare placements safe for all young people, including young gays and lesbians, should be of paramount importance to child welfare professionals. Services to prepare adolescents for independent living (Mallon 1998b) and to develop their potential as youth (Mallon 1997) must also be offered. To do this, child welfare professionals must focus their best energies on creating safe and affirming environments to help all young people grow into healthy, well-adjusted adults—including gay/lesbian young people.

Additional alternatives for meeting the needs of gay/lesbian children and adolescents who require out-of-home placements should also be explored. Two alternatives that I would suggest are family foster care utilizing gay or lesbian adults as foster parents (Ricketts 1991; Ricketts and Achtenberg 1990), and the development of smaller group homes, agency-operated boarding homes (AOBHs), and supervised independent living programs (SILPs) designed specifically for gay and lesbian adolescents who cannot fit into existing out-of-home programs (Mallon 1998a). These alternatives have not been untested, but have most definitely been underutilized by the child welfare community. These programs offer what most mainstream child welfare programs have not been able to provide—nurturing and safe environments for young people who have had difficulty finding a good fit with their own families or within existing child welfare structures.

Thousands of gay/lesbian children and youths flee the foster care system when they determine that their needs are not being met. Many of them become part the nation's runaway and homeless youth population. While historically more responsive than traditional child welfare programs, streetwork outreach programs, drop-in centers, transitional living programs, and youth shelters must continue to be responsive to providing them with safe and competent services.

The untapped resources of gay/lesbian adults as foster parents and adoption resources must be explored. While thousands of children wait for appropriate and permanent homes, thousands of gay/lesbian adults are interested in creating their own families. Innovative, flexible, and gay-/lesbian-affirming approaches to recruitment efforts must be made to involve additional members of the gay/lesbian community. The acknowledgment that sexual orientation has nothing to do with one's ability to be a parent must be recognized.

There are also obvious gaps in our knowledge about what service models exist, which ones work, and how effective they are. Research and policy studies are needed. Legal protections for gay/lesbian children, youth, and families remain nonexistent in most states, as such civil rights issues for gay/lesbian persons will continue to be challenged on a case-by-case basis. It is also clear that many traditional child welfare organizations and funding patterns for research projects have various aspects that are less than supportive of gay/lesbian children, youth, and families and indeed reflect the heterocentrism that is endemic to their basic structure. A primary focus of this book has been to provide information about the effects of child welfare services on this out-group. Further development and application of a gay- and lesbian-affirming perspective will only enhance service delivery to them.

Any serious discussion about issues of sexual orientation in child welfare in the Unites States must begin not with the problems of gay/lesbian persons but with the flaws of the American society—flaws rooted in historic inequalities and long-standing cultural stereotypes. As long as gay and lesbian children, youth, and families are viewed as a "them," the burden falls on gays and lesbians to do all the work necessary for sound sexual orientation relations.

Traditionally, in American society, it is the members of oppressed, marginalized groups who are expected to stretch out and bridge the chasm between the actualities of their lives and the consciousness of those whom oppress them. Lesbians and gays are frequently expected to educate the heterosexual world about their lives. This expectation permits those who subjugate gay/lesbian children, youths, and families to maintain their own positions of power and evade responsibility for their own actions. The implication of this approach is that only a certain kind of American can define what it means to be American—and the rest must simply "fit in." The emergence of a strong and affirming sense of pride among gay/lesbian children, youths, and families is a revolt against having to "fit in." We do not want to be like Procrustes, that villainous son of Poseidon who forced travelers to fit in his guest bed by stretching their bodies on a rack or cutting off their legs.

There are no "quick fixes" to the problems that exist within the child welfare system. No single training program, policy, or practice intervention will eliminate the damage that has already been imposed on gay/lesbian children, young people, and their families. Although we must acknowledge the limits of these strategies, and note the obstacles (Sullivan 1994), the development of practice competence and policy development in this area holds promise for preserving and supporting families and for the establishment of appropriate gay-/lesbian-affirming child welfare services for all of those whose lives are affected by the child welfare system. Effecting systematic change, just like coming through the closet doorway, has never been easy. Addressing the needs of gay and lesbian children, youth, and families requires that child welfare professionals obtain duplicates of the key that will assist them in opening those doors that have ostensibly been hermetically sealed for too long.

References

Able-Peterson, T. and J. Bucy. 1993. *The Street Outreach Training Manual.* Washington, D.C.: U.S. Dept. of Health and Human Services.

Achtenberg, R. 1990. *Preserving and Protecting the Families of Lesbians and Gay Men.* San Francisco: Nation Center for Lesbian Rights.

Administration on Children, Youth, and Families. 1994. *Implementation of New Legislation: Family Preservation and Support Services.* Title IV-B, subpart 2 (Log No. ACYF-P1–94–01). Washington, D.C.: U.S. Dept. of Health and Human Services.

Ahn, H. N. 1994. Cultural diversity and the definition of child abuse. In R. Barth, J. Duerr Berrick, and N. Gilbert, eds., *Child Welfare Research*, vol. 1, pp. 28–55. New York: Columbia University Press.

Albro, J. and C. Tully. 1979. A study of lesbian lifestyles in the homosexual micro-culture and the heterosexual macro-culture. *Journal of Homosexuality* 4(4): 331–344.

Ali, T. 1996. *We Are Family: Testimonies of Lesbian and Gay Parents.* London: Cassell.

Allen, K. R. and D. H. Demo. 1995. The families of lesbians and gay men: A new frontier in family research. *Journal of Marriage and the Family* 57: 111–127.

Allport, G. 1958. *The Nature of Prejudice.* Garden City, N.Y.: Doubleday.

Alyson, S. 1991. *Young, Gay, and Proud.* Boston: Alyson.

ACLU (American Civil Liberties Union). 1997. Lesbian and Gay Rights Project. *ACLU Fact Sheet: Overview on Lesbian and Gay Parenting*, May. New York: ACLU.

American Psychiatric Association, *see* APA.

Anderson, G. 1991. Ethical issues in intensive family preservation services. In E. M. Tracy, D. A. Haapala, J. Kinney, and P. Pecora, eds., *Intensive Family Preservation Services: An Instructional Sourcebook*, pp. 177–184. Cleveland: Mandel School of Applied Social Sciences.

Anderson, S. and D. Henderson. 1985. Working with lesbian alcoholics. *Social Casework* 30(6): 518–526.

APA (American Psychiatric Association). 1974. *Diagnostic and Statistical Manual of Mental Disorders.* 2nd ed. (D.S.M. II). Washington, D.C.: APA.

APA. 1983. *Diagnostic and Statistical Manual of Mental Disorders.* 3rd ed. (D.S.M. III). Washington, D.C.: APA.

Appleby, G. and J. Anastas. 1992. Social work practice with lesbians and gays. In A. Morales and B. Sheafor, eds., *Social Work: A Profession with Many Faces,* pp. 347–381. New York: Allyn and Bacon.

Appleby, G. and J. Anastas. 1998. *Not Just a Passing Phase: Social Work with Gay, Lesbian, and Bisexual People.* New York: Columbia University Press.

Arizona law gives gay foster parents edge. *Phoenix Times,* November 13, 1997, p. A3.

Arnold, T. 1997. Protect foster kids from gay discrimination. *Edmonton Journal,* July 16, p. 31.

Athey, J. L. 1991. HIV infection and homelessness. *Child Welfare* 70(5): 517–528.

Auerback, S. and C. Moser. 1987. Groups for the wives of gay and bisexual men. *Social Work* 32(4): 321–325.

Baez, E. 1996. Spirituality and the gay latino client. In M. Shernoff, ed., *Human Services for Gay People: Clinical and Community Practice,* pp. 69–82. New York: Harrington Park Press.

Baker, J. M. 1998. *Family Secrets, Gay Sons: A Mother's Story.* New York: Haworth Press.

Baker, P. 1997. Clinton signs law to speed adoption process for children in foster care. *Washington Post,* November 20, p. A17.

Baldauf, S. 1997. How Texas wrestles with gay adoptions. *Christian Science Monitor,* December 31, p. 3.

Ball, S. 1996. HIV negative men: Individual and community social service needs. In M. Shernoff, ed., *Human Services for Gay People: Clinical and Community Practice,* pp. 25–40. New York: Harrington Park Press.

Barthel, J. 1992. *For Children's Sake: The Promise of Family Preservation Services.* New York: Edna McConnell Clark Foundation.

Bawer, B. 1998. *Stealing Jesus: How Fundamentalism Betrays Christianity.* New York: Crown.

Beaton, S. and N. Guild. 1976. Treatment for gay problem drinkers. *Social Casework* 57: 302–308.

Beers, A. 1977. *The Tale of Two Families: Gay Men and Lesbians Building Loving Families.* Springfield, Va.: Adoption Resource Exchange for Single Parents.

Benkov, L. 1994. *Reinventing the Family: The Emerging Story of Lesbian and Gay Parents.* New York: Crown.

Berger, R. M. 1977. An advocate model for intervention with homosexuals. *Social Work* 22(4): 280–283.

Berger, R. M. 1982. The unseen minority: Older gays and lesbians. *Social Work* 27(3): 236–242.

Berger, R. M. 1983. What is a homosexual? A definitional model. *Social Work* 28(2): 132–135.

Berger, R. M. 1990. Passing: Impact on the quality of same-sex couple relationships. *Social Work* 35: 328–332.

Berger, R. M. 1996. *Gay and Grey*. 2nd ed. Boston: Alyson.

Berger, R. M. and J. J. Kelly. 1981. Do social work agencies discriminate against homosexual job applicants? *Social Work* 26(3): 193–198.

Berkley, S. 1996. Homophobia in the group home: Overcoming my fears of gays. *Foster Care Youth United.* (January/February): 17–19.

Berkman, C. S. and G. Zinberg. 1997. Homophobia and heterosexism in social workers. *Social Work* 42: 319–333.

Bernfeld, R. 1995. A brief guide regarding donor and co-parenting agreements. In M. E. Elovitz and C. Schneider, eds., *Legal Issues Facing the Nontraditional Family–1995*, pp. 135–169. New York: Practicing Law Institute.

Bernstein, B. E. 1977. Legal and social interface in counseling homosexual clients. *Social Casework* 58(1): 36–40.

Bernstein, N. 1999. Lawsuit says gay youths in foster care are abused: Class action faults child welfare agencies. *New York Times*, January 16, p. A16.

Bigner, J. 1996. Working with gay fathers. In J. Laird and R.-J. Green, eds., *Lesbians and Gays in Couples and Families: A Handbook for Therapists*, pp. 370–403. San Francisco: Jossey-Bass.

Billingsley, A. 1992. *Climbing Jacob's Ladder: The Enduring Legacy of African-American Families*. New York: Simon and Schuster.

Billingsley, A. and J. M. Giovannoni. 1972. *Children of the Storm*. New York: Harcourt Brace Jovanovich.

Bloom, M., J. Fischer, and J. G. Orme. 1995. *Evaluating Practice: Guidelines for the Accountable Professional*. 2nd ed.. Needham Heights, Mass.: Allyn and Bacon.

Blumenfeld W. and D. Raymond, eds. 1993. *Looking at Gay and Lesbian Life*. Boston: Beacon Press.

Blumstein, P. W. and P. Schwartz. 1977. Bisexuality: Some social psychological issues. *Journal of Social Issues* 33(2): 30–45.

Blythe, B., T. Tripodi, and S. Briar. 1994. *Direct Practice Research in Human Service Agencies*. New York: Columbia University Press.

Board proposes banning gays from foster care. *IMPACT*, July 3, 1998, p. 6.

Boerner, H. 1999. City sued over treatment of teens: Foster homes unsafe, agency charges. *New York Blade*, January 22, p. 6.

Borhek, M. V. 1988. Helping gay and lesbian adolescents and their families: A mother's perspective. *Journal of Adolescent Health Care* 9(2): 123–128.

Borhek, M. V. 1983. *Coming Out to Parents*. New York: Pilgrim Press.

Boyer, D. 1989. Male prostitution and homosexual identity. In G. Herdt, ed., *Gay and Lesbian Youth*, pp. 151–184. New York: Harrington Park Press.

Bozet, F. W. 1987. *Gay and Lesbian Parents*. New York: Praeger.

Bronstein, L. R. 1996. Intervening with homeless youths: Direct practice without blaming the victim. *Child and Adolescent Social Work Journal* 13(2): 127–138.

Brown, J. and M. Weil, eds. 1992. *Family Practice*. Washington, D.C.: CWLA Press.

Bucy, J. and T. Able-Peterson. 1993. *The Street Outreach Training Manual*. Washington, D.C.: U.S. Department of Health and Human Services.

Bucy, J. and N. Obolensky. 1990. Runaway and homeless youth. In M. J. Rothman-Borus, J. Bradley, and N. Obolensky, eds., *Planning to Live: Evaluating and Treating Suicidal Teens in Community Settings*, pp. 333–354. Tulsa: National Resource Center for Youth Services.

Cain, R. 1991. Stigma management and gay identity development. *Social Work* 36(1): 67–73.

Cain, R. 1996. Heterosexism and disclosure in the social work classroom. *Journal of Social Work Education* 32(1): 65–76.

CASMT (Children's Aid Society of Metropolitan Toronto). 1995. *We Are Your Children Too: Accessible Child Welfare Services for Lesbian, Gay, and Bisexual youth*. Toronto: CASMT.

Cass, V. C. 1979. Homosexual identity formation: A theoretical model. *Journal of Homosexuality* 4: 219–235.

Cass, V. C. 1983/1984. Homosexual identity: A concept in need of a definition. *Journal of Homosexuality* 9(2/3): 105–126.

Cass, V. C. 1984. Homosexual identity formation: Testing a theoretical model. *Journal of Sex Research* 20: 143–167.

Cates, J. A. 1987. Adolescent sexuality: Gay and lesbian issues. *Child Welfare League of America* 66: 353–363.

Cates, J. A. 1989. Adolescent male prostitution by choice. *Child and Adolescent Social Work* 6(2): 151–156.

Caton, C. 1990. *Homeless in America*. New York: Oxford University Press.

Chafetz, J. S., P. Sampson, P. Beck, and J. West. 1974. A study of homosexual women. *Social Work* 19(6): 714–723.

Chan, C. 1989. Issues of identity development among Asian American lesbians and gay men. *Journal of Counseling and Development* 68(1): 16–20.

Chan, C. 1993. Issues of identity development among Asian-American lesbians and gay men. In L. D. Garnets and D. G. Kimmel, eds., *Psychological Perspectives on Lesbian and Gay Male Experiences*, pp. 376–388. New York: Columbia University Press.

Chestang, L. 1972. Character development in a hostile environment. *Occasional Paper No.3*. Chicago: University of Chicago Press.

Children's Aid Society of Metropolitan Toronto, *see* CASMT.

Child Welfare Administration, *see* CWA.

Child Welfare League of America, *see* CWLA.

Close, M. 1983. Child welfare and people of color: Denial of equal access. *Social Work Research and Abstracts* 13: 20.

Cohen, N. A., ed. 1997. *Child Welfare: A Multicultural Focus*. Needham Heights, Mass.: Allyn and Bacon.

Colberg, M. 1996. With open arms: The emotional journey of lesbian and gay adoption. *In the Family: A Magazine for Lesbians, Gays, Bisexuals, and Their Relations* 2(1): 6–11.

Cole, E. and J. Duva. 1990. *Family Preservation*. Washington, D.C.: CWLA Press.

Coleman, E. 1981. Developmental stages of the coming out process. *Journal of Homosexuality* 7(2/3): 31–43.

Coleman, E. 1987. Assessment of sexual orientation. *Journal of Homosexuality* 13(4): 9–23.

Coleman, E. 1989. The developmental of male prostitution activity among gay and bisexual adolescents. In G. Herdt, ed., *Lesbian, Gay, and Bisexual Youth*, pp. 131–150. New York: Harrington Park Press.

Comstock, G. D. 1991. *Violence Against Lesbians and Gay Men*. New York: Columbia University Press.

Constant A. 1985. 344 Pa. Super. 49, 57, 496 A.2d 1, 5 (1985).

Cooper, D. 1994. *From Darkness Into Light: What the Bible Really Says About Homosexuality*. 3rd ed. Tucson: Cornerstone Fellowship.

Council on Social Work Education, *see* CSWE.

Costin, L. B., H. J. Karger, and D. Stoesz. 1996. *The Politics of Child Abuse in America*. New York: Oxford University Press.

Council of Family and Child Caring Agencies, *see* CFCCA.

Court refuses challenge. 1997. Court refuses challenge to gay foster parents. *Boston Globe*, October 7, p. 43.

Cowger, C. D. 1994. Assessing client strengths: Clinical assessment for client empowerment. *Social Work* 39(3): 262–268.

Cramer, D. 1986. Gay parents and their children: A review of research and practical implications. *Journal of Counseling and Development* 64: 501–507.

Cranston, K. 1992. HIV Education for gay, lesbian, and bisexual youth: Personal risk, personal power, and the community of the conscience. In K. M. Harbeck, ed., *Coming Out of the Classroom Closet*, pp. 247–260. New York: Harrington Park Press.

Cross, T., B. Bazron, K. Dennis, and M. Isaacs. 1989. *Toward a Culturally Competent System of Care*. Washington, D.C.: CASSP Technical Assistance Center.

Crosson-Tower, C. 1998. *Exploring Child Welfare: A Practice Perspective*. Boston: Allyn and Bacon.

CSWE (Council on Social Work Education). 1992. *Curriculum Policy Statement for Master's Degree Programs in Social Work Education*. Alexandria, Va.: CSWE.

CWA/CFCCA (Child Welfare Administration and Council of Family and Child Caring Agencies). 1994. *Improving Services to Gay and Lesbian Youth in New York City's Child Welfare System*. New York: CWA and CFCCA.

CWLA (Child Welfare League of America). 1985. *Standards for Family Foster Care*. Washington, D.C.: CWLA.

CWLA. 1989. *CWLA Initiative to Promote Culturally Responsive Child Welfare Practice: Recommendations of a Colloquium, March 12–13, 1989*. Washington, D.C.: CWLA.

CWLA. 1989. *Standards for Adoption Services*. Washington, D.C.: CWLA.

CWLA. 1989. *Standards for Service to Strengthen and Preserve Families with Children*. Washington, D.C.: CWLA.

CWLA. 1991. *Serving the Needs of Gay and Lesbian Youths: The Role of Child Welfare Agencies, Recommendations of a Colloquium, January 25–26, 1991*. Washington, D.C.: CWLA.

CWLA. 1998. *The Adoption and Safe Families Act of 1997*. Washington, D.C.: CWLA.

Dana, R. H., J. D. Behn, and T. Gonwa. 1992. A checklist for the examination of cultural competence in social service agencies. *Research on Social Work Practice* 2: 220–233.

Daro, D. 1988. *Confronting Child Abuse*. New York: Free Press.

D'Augelli. A. R. and S. L. Hershberger. 1993. Lesbian, gay, and bisexual youth in community settings: Personal challenges and mental health problems. *American Journal of Community Psychology* 21(4): 421–428.

Decker, B. 1984. Counseling gay and lesbian couples. In R. Schoenberg and R. Goldberg, eds., *Homosexuality and Social Work*, pp. 39–52. New York: Harrington Park Press.

De Crescenzo, T. 1985. Homophobia: A study of attitudes of mental health professionals towards homosexuality. In R. Schoenberg, R. Goldberg, and D. Shore, eds.), *With Compassion Towards Some: Homosexuality and Social Work in America*, pp. 115–136. New York: Harrington Park Press.

De Crescenzo, T., ed. 1995. *Helping Gay and Lesbian Youth: New Policies, New Programs, New Practices*. New York: Haworth Press.

De Jong, P. and S. D. Mille. 1995. How to interview for client strength. *Social Work* 40(6): 729–736.

De Monteflores, C. and S. J. Schultz. 1978. Coming out: Similarities and differences for lesbians and gay men. *Journal of Social Issues* 34(3): 59–72.

de Poy, E. and S. Noble. 1992. The structure of lesbian relationships in response to oppression. *Affilia* 7(4): 49–64.

de Vine, J. L. 1983/1984. A systemic inspection of affectional preference orientation and family of origin. *Journal of Social Work and Human Sexuality* 2(2/3): 9–17.

Devore, W. and E. G. Schlesinger. 1996. *Ethnic Sensitive Social Work Practice*. 4th ed. Boston: Allyn and Bacon.

Dew, R. F. 1994. *The Family Heart: A Memoir of When Our Son Came Out*. Reading, Mass.: Addison-Wesley.

Diller, J. V. 1999. *Cultural Diversity: A Primer for the Human Services*. Boston: Brooks/Cole.

Dinitto, D. M. 1995. *Social Welfare Politics and Public Policy*. 4th ed. Englewood Cliffs, N.J.: Prentice Hall.

Dorfman, R., K. Walters, P. Burke, L. Hardin, T. Karanik, J. Raphael, and E. Silverstein. 1995. Old, sad, and alone: The myth of the aging homosexual. *Journal of Gerontological Social Work* 24(1/2): 29–44.

Dorrell, B. 1990. Being there: A support network of lesbian women. *Journal of Homosexuality* 20(2/4): 89–98.

Due, L. 1995. *Joining the Tribe: Growing Up Gay and in the '90s*. New York: Anchor Books.

Dulaney, D. D. and J. J. Kelly. 1982. Improving services to gay and lesbian clients. *Social Work* 27(2): 178–183.

Dunlap, D. W. 1996. Homosexual parent raising children: Support for pro and con. *New York Times*, January 7, p. L15.

Edna McConnell Clark Foundation. 1990. *Keeping Families Together: Facts on Family Preservation Services*. New York: EMC Foundation.

Elovitz, M. E. 1995. Adoption by lesbian and gay people: The use and misuse of social science research. In M. E. Elovitz and C. Schneider, eds., *Legal Issues Facing the Nontraditional Family, 1995*, pp. 171–191. New York: Practicing Law Institute.

English, M. 1996. Transgenerational homophobia in the family: A personal narrative. In J. Laird and R.-J. Green, eds., *Lesbians and Gays in Couples and Families: A Handbook for Therapists*, pp. 15–27. San Francisco: Jossey-Bass.

Epperly, J. 1999. Florida ban on adoptions will be challenged in court. *Bay Windows*, May 27, 1999, p. 14.

Espin, O. 1993. Issues of identity in the psychology of Latina lesbians. In L. D. Garnets and D. G. Kimmel, eds., *Psychological Perspectives on Lesbian and Gay Male Experiences*, pp. 348–363. New York: Columbia University Press.

EVAN. 153 MISC. 2D 844, 583 N.Y.S. 2D 997 (1992).

Everett, J. E., S. S. Chipungu, and B. R. Leashore, eds. 1991. *Child Welfare: An Africentric Perspective*. New Brunswick: Rutgers University Press.

Fairchild, B. and N. Hayward. 1989. *Now That You Know: What Every Parent Should Know About Homosexuality*. New York: Harcourt Brace Jovanovich.

Family Tree. 1998. *The Family Tree*, Autumn. San Diego, Calif.: Family Pride Coalition.

Fanshel, D. 1982. *On the Road to Permanency: An Expanded Data Base for Children in Foster Care*. New York: CWLA.

Fanshel, D. and E. Shinn. 1978. *Children in Foster Care: A Longitudinal Investigation*. New York: Columbia University Press.

Faria, G. 1994. Training for family preservation practice with lesbian families. *Families in Society* 75: 416–422.

Festinger, T. *No One Ever Asked Us: A Postscript to Foster Care*. New York: Columbia University Press.

Finkelhor, D. 1984. *Child Sexual Abuse*. New York: Free Press.

Fischer, J. and K. Corcoron. 1994. *Measures for Clinical Practice: A Sourcebook*, vols. 1 and 2. 2nd ed. New York: Free Press.

Fitzgerald, M. D. 1996. Homeless youths and the child welfare system: Implications for policy and service. *Child Welfare* 75(3): 717–730.

Flaks, D. K. 1994. Gay and lesbian families: Judicial assumptions, scientific realities. *William & Mary Bill of Rights Journal* 3(1): 345–372.

Florida judge. 1997. Florida judge upholds state adoption plan. *Miami Herald*, July 29, p. 33.

Focal Point. 1988. What does it mean to be culturally competent professional? *Focal Point*. Portland, Ore.: Portland State University, Research and Training Center.

Folayan, A. 1992. African-American issues: The soul of it. In B. Berzon, ed., *Positively Gay*, pp. 235–239. Berkeley: Celestial Arts.

Fong, R. 1994. Family preservation: Making It work for Asians. *Child Welfare* 73(4): 331–341.

Forrester, E. G. and J. Huggins. 1981. Homosexuality and homosexual behavior. In D. A. Shore and H. L. Gochros, eds., *Sexual Problems of Adolescents in Institutions*, pp. 154–166. Springfield, Ill.: Charles C. Thomas.

Fraser, M., P. Pecora, and D. Haapala. 1991. *Families in Crisis*. New York: Aldine de Gruyter.

Freiberg, P. 1999. Gay adoption rights under attack. *New York Blade*, January 22, pp. 1, 7.

Freiberg, P. 1999. Gay adoption ban repealed. *New York Blade*, April 23, pp. 1, 11.

Friend, R. 1987. The individual and social psychology of aging: Clinical implications for lesbians and gay men. *Journal of Homosexuality* 14(1/2): 25–44.

Frommer, M. S. 1996. The right fit: A gay man's quest for fatherhood. *In the Family: A Magazine for Lesbians, Gays, Bisexuals, and Their Relations* 2(1): 12–16, 26.

Gambe, R. and G. S. Getzel. 1989. Group work with gay men with AIDS. *Social Casework* 70(3): 172–179.

Gambrill, E. and T. J. Stein, eds. 1994. *Controversial Issues in Child Welfare*. Boston: Allyn and Bacon.

Garbarino, J. 1977. The human ecology of child maltreatment. *Journal of Marriage and the Family* 39(4): 721–735.

Garbarino, J. 1980. What kind of society permits child abuse? *Infant Mental Health Journal* 1: 270–280.

Garbarino, J. 1989. Troubled youth, troubled families: The dynamics of adolescent maltreatment. In D. Cicchetti and V. Carlson, eds., *Child Maltreatment*, pp. 685–706. Cambridge, UK: Cambridge University Press.

Garbarino, J. 1992. Preventing adolescent maltreatment. In D. J. Willis, E. W. Holden, and M. Rosenberg, eds., *Prevention of Child Maltreatment: Developmental and Ecological Perspectives*, pp. 94- 114. New York: Wiley.

Garnets, L., G. M. Herek, and B. Levy. 1992. Violence and victimization of lesbians and gay men: Mental health consequences. In G. M. Herek and K. T. Berrill, eds., *Hate Crimes*, pp. 207–226. Newbury Park, Calif.: Sage.

Gelles, R. J. 1992. Poverty and violence toward children. *American Behavioral Scientist* 35(3): 258–274.

Georgia ban on gay adoption in committee. 1998. *Atlanta Times*, March 10, p. 2.

Germain, C. B. 1991. *Human Behavior and the Social Environment*. New York: Columbia University Press.

Germain, C. B. and A. Gitterman. 1996. 2nd ed. *The Life Model of Social Work Practice*. New York: Columbia University Press

Gil, D. 1970. *Violence Against Children: Physical Child Abuse in the United States*. Cambridge: Harvard University Press.

Gil de Lamadrid, M., ed. 1991. *Lesbians Choosing Motherhood: Legal Implications of Donor Insemination and Co-Parenting*. San Francisco: National Center for Lesbian Rights.

Gilgun, J. F. 1990. Factors mediating the effects of child maltreatment. In M. Hunter, ed., *The Sexually Abused Male*, pp. 177–190. New York: Lexington Books.

Gittler, J., M. Quigley-Rick, and M. J. Saks. 1990. *Adolescent Health Care Decision Making: The Law and Public Policy*. New York: Carnegie Council on Adolescent Development.

Glimpse into hell. 1997. A glimpse into hell for helpless infants, captured on videotape. *New York Times*, November 2, p. A31.

Gochros, H. 1972. The sexually oppressed. *Social Work* 17: 16–23.

Gochros, H. 1975. Teaching more or less straight social work students to be helpful to more or less gay people. *The Homosexual Counseling Journal* 2(2): 24–31.

Gochros, H. L. 1985. Teaching social workers to meet the needs of the homosexually oriented. In R. Schoenberg, R. Goldberg, and D. Shore, eds., *With Compassion Towards Some: Homosexuality and Social Work in America*, pp. 137–156. New York: Harrington Park Press.

Gochros, H. 1992. The sexuality of gay men with HIV infection. *Social Work* 37(2): 105–109.

Gochros, H. 1995. Sex, AIDS, social work, and me. *Reflections* 1(2): 37–43.

Gochros, H. and L. G. Schultz, eds. 1972. *Human Sexuality and Social Work*. New York: Associations Press.

Gochros, J. 1989. *When Husbands Come Out of the Closet*. New York: Haworth Press.

Gochros, J. 1992. Homophobia, homosexuality, and heterosexual marriage. In W. Blumenfeld, ed., *Homophobia: How We All Pay the Price*, pp. 131–153. Boston: Beacon Press.

Gock, T. 1992. Asian-Pacific islander issues: Identity integration and pride. In B. Berzon, ed., *Positively Gay*, pp. 247–252. Berkeley, Calif.: Celestial Arts.

Goffman, E. 1963. *Stigma: Notes of the Management of a Spoiled Identity*. Englewood Cliffs, N.J.: Prentice-Hall.

Golden, R. 1977. *Disposable Children: America's Child Welfare System*. Belmont, Calif.: Wadsworth.

Goldstein, J., A. J. Solnit, S. Goldstein, and A. Freud. 1996. *The Best Interest of the Child*. New York: Free Press.

Goleman, D. 1992. Studies find no disadvantage in growing up in a gay home. *New York Times*, December 2, p. C14.

Gomes-Schartz, B, J. M. Horowitz, and A. P. Cardarelli. 1990. *Child Sexual Abuse: The Initial Effects*. Newbury Park, Calif: Sage.

Gramick, J. 1983. Homophobia: A new challenge. *Social Work* 28(2): 137–141.

Gramick, J. 1984. Developing a lesbian identity. In T. Darty and S. Potter, eds., *Women Identified Women*, pp. 31–44. Palo Alto, Calif.: Mayfield.

Green, A. A. 1999. Board votes to ban gays as providers of foster care. *Arkansas Democratic Gazette*, January 7, pp. 1, 5A.

Green, J. W. 1995. *Cultural Awareness in the Human Services: A Multiethnic Approach*. Boston: Allyn and Bacon.

Greene, B. 1994. Lesbian and gay sexual orientations: Implications for clinical training, practice, and research. In B. Greene and G. M. Herek, eds., *Lesbian and Gay Psychology: Theory, Research, and Clinical Applications*, pp. 1–24. Thousand Oaks, Calif.: Sage.

Greene, Z. 1996. Straight, but not narrow-minded. In P. Kay, A. Estepa, an& A. Desetta, eds., *Out with It: Gay and Straight Teens Write About Homosexuality*, pp. 12–14. New York: Youth Communications.

Griffin, C., M. J. Wirth, and A. G. Wirth. 1986. *Beyond Acceptance*. Englewood Cliffs, N.J.: Prentice-Hall.

Groninger, T. 1996. Foster care recruiting still in the closet. *Youth Today*, March/April, p. 54.

Groth, A. N. 1978. Patterns of sexual assault against children and adolescents. In A. W. Burgess, A. N. Groth, L. L. Holmstrom, and S. M. Sgroi, eds., *Sexual Assault of Children and Adolescents*, pp. 3—24. Lexington, Mass.: Lexington Books.

Groth, A. N. and H. J. Birnbaum. 1978. Adult sexual orientation and attraction to underage persons. *Archives of Sexual Behavior* 7(3): 175–181.

Guggenheim, M., A. Lowe Dylan, and D. Curtis. 1996. Gay and lesbian families. In *The Rights of Families*, pp. 269–294. Carbondale, Ill.: Southern Illinois University Press.

Gustavsson, N. S. and E. A. Segal. 1994. *Critical Issues in Child Welfare*. Thousand Oaks, Calif.: Sage.

Gutierrez, E. 1992. Latino issues: Gay and lesbian latinos claiming La Raza. In B. Berzon, ed., *Positively Gay*, pp. 247–252. Berkeley, Calif.: Celestial Arts.

Gutierrez, L. M. 1990. Working with women of color: An empowerment perspective. *Social Work* 34: 505–509.

Hall, M. 1978. Lesbian families: Cultural and clinical issues. *Social Work* 23(5): 380–385.

Hare, J. 1996. Concerns and issues faced by families headed by a lesbian couple. *Families in Society* 75: 27–35.

Hartman, A. 1993. Out of the closet: Revolution and backlash. *Social Work* 38(3): 245–246, 360.

Hartman, A. 1996. Social policy as a context for lesbian and gay families: The political is personal. In J. Laird and R.-J. Green, eds., *Lesbians and Gays in Couples and Families: A Handbook for Therapists*, pp. 69–85. San Francisco: Jossey-Bass.

Hartman, A. and J. Laird. 1983. *Family-Centered Social Work Practice*. New York: Free Press.

Hartman, A. and J. Laird, eds. 1985. *A Handbook of Child Welfare: Context, Knowledge, and Practice*. New York: Free Press.

Hartman, A. and J. Laird. 1998. Moral and ethical issues in working with lesbians and gay men. *Families in Society: The Journal of Contemporary Human Services*, pp. 263–276.

Harvard Law Review, eds. 1989. *Sexual Orientation and the Law*. Cambridge: Harvard University Press.

Haugaard, J. J. and N. D. Reppuci. 1988. *The Sexual Abuse of Children*. San Francisco: Jossey-Bass.

Helminiak, D. A. 1997. *What the Bible Really Says About Homosexuality*. San Francisco: Alamo Square Press.

Hennie, M. A. 1999. Historic second term may set agenda for presidential bid: Texas Gov. Bush joined the bandwagon opposing gay/lesbian adoption and parenting. *Impact*, January 29, p. 1.

Herbert, B. 1998. How did Jayla die? *New York Times*, November 19, p. A22.

Herek, G. M. 1990. The context of anti-gay violence: Notes on cultural psychological heterosexism. *Journal of Interpersonal Violence* 5(3): 316–333.

Herek, G. M. 1991. Stigma, prejudice, and violence against lesbians and gay men. In J. C. Gonsiorek and J. D. Weinrich, eds., *Homosexuality: Research Implications for Public Policy*, pp. 60–80. Newbury Park: Sage.

Herman, D. 1997. *The Antigay Agenda—Orthodox Vision and the Christian Right*. Chicago: University of Chicago Press.

Heron, A., ed. 1994. *Two Teenagers in Twenty: Writings by Gay and Lesbian Youth*. Boston: Alyson.

Hershberger, S. L. and A. R. D'Augelli. 1995. The impact of victimization on the mental health and suicidality of lesbian, gay, and bisexual youths. *Developmental Psychology* 31(1): 65–74.

Hetrick, E. and A. D. Martin. 1987. Developmental issues and their resolution for gay and lesbian adolescents. *Journal of Homosexuality* 13(4): 25–43.

Hidalgo, H., ed. 1995. Lesbians of color: Social and human services. *Journal of Gay and Lesbian Social Services* [Special Issue] 3(2).

Hidalgo, H., T. L. Peterson, and N. J. Woodman, eds. 1985. *Lesbian and Gay Issues: A Resource Manual for Social Workers*. Silver Springs, Md.: NASW.

Hogan, P. T. and F. S. Siu. 1988. Minority children and the child welfare system: A historical perspective. Social Work 23(6): 493–498.

Holdway, D. M. and J. Ray. 1992. Attitudes of street kids toward foster care. *Child and Adolescent Social Work* 9(4), pp. 307–317.

Holloway, L. 1998. Young, restless, and homeless on the piers: Greenwich Village reaches out to youth with problems. *New York Times*, July 18, p. B3.

Hong, G. K. and L. K. Hong. 1991. Comparative perspectives on child abuse and neglect: Chinese versus Hispanics and Whites. *Child Welfare* 70(4): 463–475.

Hudson, W. and W. A. Ricketts. 1980. A strategy for measurement of homophobia. *Journal of Homosexuality* 5: 357–371.

Huggins, J., N. Elman, C. Baker, R. G. Forrester, and D. Lyter. 1991. Affective and behavioral responses of gay and bisexual men to HIV antibody testing. *Social Work* 36(1): 61–66.

Humphreys, G. E. 1983. Inclusion of content on homosexuality in the social work curriculum. *Journal of Social Work Education* 19(1): 55–60.

Hunter, J. 1990. Violence against lesbian and gay male youths. *Journal of Interpersonal Violence* 5(3): 295–300.

Hunter, J. and R. Schaecher. 1987. Stresses on lesbian and gay adolescents in schools. *Social Work in Education* 9(3): 180–188.

Hunter, J. and R. Schaecher. 1990. Lesbian and gay youth. In M. J. Rotherram-Borus, J. Bradley, and N. Obolensky, eds., *Planning to Live: Evaluating and Treating Suicide Teens in Community Settings*, pp. 297–316. Tulsa: University of Oklahoma Press.

Hunter, J. and R. Schaecher. 1994. AIDS prevention for lesbian, gay, and bisexual adolescents. *Families and Society* 75(6): 93–99.

Hunter, N. D. and N. D. Polikoff. 1976. Custody rights of lesbian mothers: Legal theory and litigation strategy. *Buffalo Law Review* 25: 691–733.

Hutchison, E. 1994. Child maltreatment: Can it be defined? In R. Barth, J. Duerr Berrick, and N. Gilbert, eds., *Child Welfare Research Review*, vol. 1, pp. 5–27. New York: Columbia University Press.

Iasenza, S. 1996. To have not: The lesbian dilemma. *In the Family: A Magazine for Lesbians, Gays, Bisexuals, and Their Relations* 2(1): 21–23.

Icard, L. 1985–86. Black gay men and conflicting social identities: Sexual orientation verses racial identity. *Journal of Social Work and Human Sexuality* 4(1/2): 83–93.

Icard, L. and D. M. Traunstein. 1987. Black, gay, alcoholic men: Their character and treatment. *Social Casework* 68(5): 267–272.

Icard, L. D., R. F. Schilling, N. El-Bassel, and D. Young. 1992. Preventing AIDS among black gay men and black gay and heterosexual male intravenous drug users. *Social Work* 37(5): 440–445.

Jacobsen. E. E. 1988. Lesbian and gay adolescents: A social work approach. *Social Worker/Le Travailler Social* 56(2): 65–67.

Jacobson. 314 N.W. 2d 78 (N.D. 1981).

Janus, M. D., F. X. Archambault, and S. M. Brown. 1995. Physical abuse in Canadian runaway adolescents. *Child Abuse and Neglect* 19: 433–447.

Jenny, C., T. A. Roesler, and K. L. Poyer. 1994. Are children at risk for sexual abuse by homosexuals? *Pediatrics* 94(1): 41–44.

J.L.P.(H.). 643 S.W. 2d 865, 872 (Mo. Ct. App. 1982).

Joel A. v. Rudolph W. Guiliani et al., No 95 Civ. 10533 (RJW)(N.Y. 1999).

Johnsrude, L. 1997. Gay mom loses battle for more foster children. *Edmonton Journal*, November 19, p. 3.

Joseph, A v. New Mexico Department of Social Services, 575, F. Supp. 346 (1983).

Kaplan, L. 1986. *Working with Multiproblem Families*. Lexington, Mass.: Lexington Books.

Kaplan, L. and J. L. Girard. 1994. *Strengthening High-Risk Families: A Handbook for Practitioners*. New York: Lexington Books.

Kaser-Boyd, N., H. S. Adelman, L. Taylor et al. 1986. Children's understanding of risk and benefits of psychotherapy. *Journal of Clinical Child Psyhcology* 15: 151–166.

Kavanagh, K. H. and P. H. Kennedy. 1992. *Promoting Cultural Diversity: Strategies for Health Care Professionals.* Newbury Park, Calif.: Sage.

Kay, P., A. Estepa, and A. Desetta, eds. 1996. *Out with It: Gay and Straight Teens Write About Homosexuality*. New York: Youth Communications.

Kehoe, M. 1988. *Lesbians Over 60 Speak for Themselves*. New York: Harrington Park Press.

Kessler, B. 1997. QL: Texas foster parent and adoption policy. *Dallas Morning News*, November 11, p. 11.

Kid's Talk. 1998 *Kid's Talk Newsletter*, November/December. New York: Lesbian and Gay Community Services Center.

Kimmel, D. C. and B. E. Sang. 1995. Lesbians and gay men in midlife. In A. R. D'Augelli and C. J. Patterson, eds., *Gay, Lesbian, and Bisexual Identities Over the Lifespan*, pp. 190–214. Oxford: Oxford University Press.

Kinney, J., D. Haapala, C. Booth, and S. Leavitt. 1991. *Keeping Families Together: The Homebuilders Model*. Hawthorne, N.Y.: Aldine de Gruyter.

Kinney, J. M., C. Booth, and D. A. Haapala. 1991. *Keeping Families Together: The Homebuilders Model*. Hawthorne, N.Y.: Aldine de Gruyter.

Kleber, D. J., R. J. Howell, and H. Tibbits-Kleber. 1986. The impact of homosexuality in child custody cases: A review of the literature. *Bulletin of American Academy Psychiatry and Law* 14: 81–87.

Kolko, D. 1987. Treatment of child sexual abuse: Programs, progress, and prospects. *Journal of Family Violence* 2: 303–318.

Korbin, J. E . 1987. Child abuse and neglect: The cultural context. In R. Helfer and R. Kempe, eds., *The Battered Child*, pp. 23–41. 4th ed. Chicago: University of Chicago Press.

Korbin, J. E. 1994. Sociocultural factors in child maltreatment. In G. B. Melton and F. D. Barry, eds, *Protecting Children from Abuse and Neglect*, pp. 131–181. New York: Guildford Press.

Kournay, R. F. 1987. Suicide among homosexual adolescents. *Journal of Homosexuality* 13(4): 111–117.

Kruks, G. 1991. Gay and lesbian homeless/street youth: Special issues and concerns. *Journal of Adolescent Health* 12(7): 515–518.

Kurdek, L. A., ed. 1994. Social services for gay and lesbian couples. *Journal of Gay and Lesbian Social Services* [Special Issue] 1(2).

Kurdek, L. A. 1995. Lesbian and gay couples. In A. R. D'Augelli and C. J. Patterson, eds., *Gay, Lesbian, and Bisexual Identities Over the Lifespan*, pp. 243–261. Oxford: Oxford University Press.

Kurtz, D. P., A. Hick-Coolick, S. V. Jarvis, and G. L. Kurtz. 1996. Assessment of abuse in runaway and homeless youth. *Child and Youth Care Forum* 25(3): 183–194.

Kus, R. J., ed. 1995. Addition and recovery in gay and lesbian persons. *Journal of Gay and Lesbian Social Services* [Special Issue] 2(1).

Laird, J. 1979. An ecological approach to child welfare: Issues of family identity and continuity. In C. B. Germain, ed.. *Social Work Practice: People and Environments*, pp. 174–209. New York: Columbia University Press.

Laird, J. 1983. Lesbian and gay families. In F. Walsh, ed., *Normal Family Processes*, pp. 282–328. 4th ed. New York: Guilford Press.

Laird, J. 1996a. Invisible ties: Lesbians and their families of origin. In J. Laird and R.-J. Green, eds., *Lesbians and Gays in Couples and Families: A Handbook for Therapists*, pp. 89–122. San Francisco: Jossey-Bass.

Laird, J. 1996b. Family-centered practice with lesbian and gay families. *Families in Society: The Journal of Contemporary Human Services* 77: 559–572.

Laird, J. 1999. *Lesbians and Lesbian Families; Reflections on Theory and Practice*. New York: Columbia University Press.

Laird, J. and R.-J. Green, eds. 1996. *Lesbians and Gays in Couples and Families: A Handbook for Therapists*. San Francisco: Jossey-Bass.

Laird, J. and A. Hartman, eds. 1985. *A Handbook of Child Welfare: Context, Knowledge, and Practice.* New York: Free Press.

Lambda (Lambda Legal Defense and Education Fund). 1996. *Lesbians and Gay Men Seeking Custody and Visitation: An Overview of the State of the Law.* New York: Lambda.

Lambda. 1997. *Lesbian and Gay Parenting: A Fact Sheet,* September 28. New York: Lambda.

Larson, P. C. 1982. Gay male relationships. In W. Paul, J. D. Weinrich, J. C. Gonsiorek, and M. E. Hotvedt, eds., *Homosexuality: Social, Psychological, and Biological Issues,* pp. 219–232. Beverly Hills, Calif.: Sage.

Levine, C. O. 1978. Social work with transsexuals. *Social Casework* 59(3): 167–174.

Levy, E. F. 1992. Strengthening the coping resources of lesbian families. *Families in Society: The Journal of Contemporary Human Services* 73(1): 23–31.

Lewis, K. G. 1980. Children of lesbians: Their point of view. *Social Work* 25(3): 198–203.

Lewis, L. A. 1984. The coming-out process for lesbians: Integrating a stable identity. *Social Work* 29(5): 464–469.

Lindsey, D. 1994. *The Welfare of Children.* New York: Oxford University Press.

Lindsey, D. and S. A. Kirk. 1992. Note on research: The role of social work journals in the development of a knowledge base for the profession. *Social Service Review* 66: 295–310.

Lloyd, G. A. 1992. Contextual and clinical issues in providing services to gay men. In H. Land, ed., *AIDS: A Complete Guide to Psychosocial Intervention,* pp. 91–105. Milwaukee: Family Services of America.

Lloyd, G. A. and M. A. Kuszelewicz, eds. 1995. HIV disease: Lesbians, gays, and the social services. *Journal of Gay and Lesbian Social Services* [Special Issue] 2(3/4).

Loewenstein, S. F. 1980. Understanding lesbian women. *Social Casework* 61(1): 29–38.

Loiacano, D. 1993. Gay identity issues among black Americans: Racism, homophobia, and the need for validation. In L. D. Garnets and D. G. Kimmel, eds., *Psychological Perspectives on Lesbian and Gay Male Experiences,* pp. 364–375. New York: Columbia University Press.

Lopez, D. J. and G. S. Getzel. 1984. Helping gay AIDS patients in crisis. *Social Casework* 65(7): 387–394.

Loppnow, D. M. 1985. Adolescents on their own. In J. Laird and A. Hartman, eds., *A Handbook of Child Welfare : Context, Knowledge, and Practice,* pp. 514–532. New York: Free Press.

Lorde, A. 1984. *Sister Outsider.* Freedom, Calif.: Crossing Press.

Lui, P. and C. S. Chan. 1996. Lesbian, gay, and bisexual Asian-Americans and their families. In J. Laird and R.-J. Green, eds., *Lesbians and Gays in Couples and Families: A Handbook for Therapists*, pp. 137–152. San Francisco: Jossey-Bass.

Lukes, C. A. and H. Lands. 1990. Biculturality and homosexuality. *Social Work* 35(2): 155–161.

Luna, G. C. 1991. Street youth: Adaptation and survival in the AIDS decade. *Journal of Adolescent Health* 12(7): 511–514.

Maas, H. S. and R. E. Engler. 1959. *Children in Need of Parents*. New York: Columbia University Press.

MacEachron, A. E. 1996. Potential use of single-system design for evaluating affirmative psychotherapy with lesbian women and gay men. In C. Tully, ed., *Lesbian Social Services: Research Issues*, pp. 19–28. New York: Haworth Press.

MacPike, L., ed. 1989. *There's Something I've Been Meaning to Tell You.* Tallahassee: Naiad Press.

Mallon, G. P. 1992. Gay and no place to go: Serving the needs of gay and lesbian youth in out-of-home care settings. *Child Welfare* 71(6): 547–557.

Mallon, G. P. 1994a. Counseling strategies with gay and lesbian youth. In T. De Crescenzo, ed., *Helping Gay and Lesbian Youth: New Policies, New Programs, New Practices*, pp. 75–91. New York: Haworth Press.

Mallon, G. P. 1994b. We Don't Exactly Get the Welcome Wagon: The Experience of Gay and Lesbian Adolescents in New York City's Child Welfare System. Ph.D. dissertation, City University of New York.

Mallon, G. P. 1997a. Basic premises, guiding principles, and competent practices for a youth development approach to working with gay and lesbian youths in out-of home care. *Child Welfare* 77(1): 61–78.

Mallon, G. P. 1997b. Entering into collaborative search for meaning with gay and lesbian youths in out-of-home care: An empowerment-based model for training child welfare professionals. *Child and Adolescent Social Work Journal* 14(6): 427–444.

Mallon, G. P. 1997c. Toward a competent child welfare service delivery system for gay and lesbian adolescents and their families. *Journal of Multicultural Social Work* 4(3/4): 177–194.

Mallon, G. P. 1998a. After care, then where? Evaluating outcomes of an independent living program. *Child Welfare* 77(1): 61–78.

Mallon, G. P., ed. 1998b. *Foundations of Social Work Practice with Lesbian and Gay Persons*. New York: Haworth Press.

Mallon, G. P. 1998c. Gay, lesbian, and bisexual childhood and adolescent development: An ecological perspective. In G. Appleby and J. Anastas, eds., *Not Just a Passing Phase: Social Work with Gay, Lesbian, and Bisexual Persons*, pp. 115–144. New York: Columbia University Press.

Mallon, G. P. 1998d. Knowledge for practice with gay and lesbian persons. In G. P. Mallon, ed., *Foundations for Social Work Practice with Gay and Lesbian Persons*, pp. 1—30. New York: Haworth Press.

Mallon, G. P. 1998e. Social work practice with gay and lesbian persons within families. In G. P. Mallon, ed., *Foundations of Social Work Practice with Gay and Lesbian Persons*, pp. 145–181. New York: Haworth Press.

Mallon, G. P. 1998f. *We Don't Exactly Get the Welcome Wagon: The Experience of Gay and Lesbian Adolescents in Child Welfare Systems*. New York: Columbia University Press.

Mallon, G. P. (in review). Coverage of gay and lesbian issues in four social work journals, 1965–1996. *Families in Society: The Journal of Contemporary Human Services*.

Mallon, G. P. (in review). Tacit knowledge of a gay or lesbian child's identity by parents. *Families in Society: The Journal of Contemporary Human Services*.

Maluccio, A. N., E. Fein, and K. A. Olmstead. 1986. *Permanency Planning for Children: Concepts and Methods*. New York: Tavistock.

Malyon, A. K. 1981. The homosexual adolescent: Developmental issues and social bias. *Child Welfare League of America* 60(5): 321–330.

Marisol, A. v. Rudolph W. Guiliani et al., 929, F. Supp.662 (S.D.N.Y. 1996).

Markowitz, L. 1991a. Homosexuality: Are we still in the dark? *The Family Therapy Networker* 2: 27–35.

Markowitz, L. 1991b. You can go home again. *The Family Therapy Networker* 2: 55–60.

Martin, A. 1991. Power of empathic relationships: Bereavement therapy with a lesbian widow. In C. Silverstein, ed., *Gays, Lesbians, and Their Therapists*, pp. 172–186. New York: Norton.

Martin. A. 1993. *The Lesbian and Gay Parenting Handbook: Creating and Raising Our Families*. New York: Harper Perennial.

Martin, A. D. 1982. Learning to hide: The socialization of the gay adolescent. In S. C. Feinstein, J. G. Looney, A. Schartzberg, and A. Sorosky, eds., *Adolescent Psychiatry: Developmental and Clinical Studies*, vol. 10, pp. 52–65. Chicago: University of Chicago Press.

Martin, E. P. and J. M. Martin. 1995. *Social Work and the Black Experience*. Washington, D.C.: NASW Press.

McCandlish, B. M. 1985. Therapeutic issues with lesbian couples. In J. C. Gonsiorek, ed., *A Guide to Psychotherapy with Gay and Lesbian Clients*, pp. 71–78. New York: Harrington Park Press.

McCroskey, J. and W. Meezan. 1997. *Family Preservation and Family Functioning*. Washington, D.C.: CWLA Press.

McCurdy, K. and D. Daro. 1994. Child maltreatment: A national survey of reports and fatalities. *Journal of Interpersonal Violence* 9: 75–93.

McFarland. E. 1998. Foster care ban still sought for gays but not singles. *Arkansas Democratic Gazette*, August 26, p. 1B.

McGowan, B. G. 1988. Advocacy. *Encyclopedia of Social Work*, 18th ed., 1:89–95. Silver Spring, Md.: NASW Press.

McGowan, B. G. and W. Meezan, eds. 1983. *Child Welfare: Current Dilemmas, Future Directions*. Itasca, Ill.: Peacock.

McIntosh, P. 1989. White privilege: Unpacking the invisible knapsack. *Peace and Freedom*, 10–12.

McMahon, A. and P. Allen-Meares. 1992. Is social work racist? A content analysis of recent literature. *Social Work* 37: 533- 538.

McPhatter, A. R. 1991. Assessment revisited: A comprehensive model for assessing family dynamics. *Families in Society: The Journal of Contemporary Humsn Services* 72: 11–22.

McPherson, D. 1993. Gay Parenting Couples: Parenting Arrangements, Arrangement Satisfaction, and Relationship Satisfaction. Doctoral dissertation, Pacific Graduate School of Psychology.

McWhirter, D. P. and A. M. Mattison. 1984. *The Male Couple: How Relationships Develop*. Englewood Cliffs, N.J.: Prentice-Hall.

Melton, G. B. and F. D. Barry, eds. 1994. *Protecting Children from Abuse and Neglect*. New York: Guildford Press.

Metropolitan Community Church. 1990. *Homosexuality Not a Sin, Not a Sickness: What the Bibile Does and Does Not Say*. Los Angeles: MCC.

Meyer, C. 1983. Responsibility in publishing. *Social Work* 28(1): 3.

Minihan, A. 1980. Reaching and writing to improve practice. *Social Work* 25: 3, 14.

Miranda, D. 1996. I hated myself. In P. Kay, A. Estepa, and A. Desetta, eds. *Out with It: Gay and Straight Teens Write About Homosexuality*, pp. 34–39. New York: Youth Communications.

Mitchell, V. 1996. Two moms: Contribution of the planned lesbian family and the deconstruction of gendered parenting. In J. Laird and R.-J. Green, eds., *Lesbians and Gays in Couples and Families: A Handbook for Therapists*, pp. 343–357. San Francisco: Jossey-Bass.

Monette, P. 1992. *Becoming a Man: Half a Life Story.* New York: Harcourt Brace Jovanovich.

Morales, E. S. 1989. Ethnic minority families and minority gays and lesbians. *Marriage and Family Review* 14: 217–239.

Morrow, D. F. 1993. Social work with gay and lesbian adolescents. *Social Work* 38(6): 655–660.

Morton, D. R. 1983. Strategies in probation: Treating gay offenders. *Social Casework* 63(6): 33–38.

Moses, A. E. and R. D. Hawkins. 1982. *Counseling Lesbian Women and Gay Men.* St. Louis: Mosby.

Muzio, C. 1993. Lesbian co-parenting: On being/being the invisible (m)other. *Smith College Studies in Social Work* 63(3): 215–229.

Muzio, C. 1996. Lesbians choosing children: Creating families, creating narratives. In J. Laird and R.-J. Green, eds., *Lesbians and Gays in Couples and Families: A Handbook for Therapists*, pp. 358–369. San Francisco: Jossey-Bass.

NAIC (National Adoption Information Clearinghouse). n.d. *Working with Lesbian and Gay Parents.* Washington, D.C.: NAIC.

NASW (National Associiation of Social Workers. 1994a. Lesbian and gay issues. In NASW, eds., *Social Work Speaks*, pp. 162–165. Washington, D.C.: NASW Press.

NASW. 1994b. *NASW Code of Ethics.* Washington, D.C.: NASW Press.

NCPCA (National Committee for the Prevention of Child Abuse). 1991. *The Results of the 1990 Annual Fifty-State Survey.* Chicago: NCPCA.

NCPCA. 1993. *The results of the 1992 Annual Fifty-State Survey.* Chicago: NCPCA.

National Statistics on Runaway and Homeless Youth. 1998. *Frontline: National Runaway Switchboard Newsletter*, p. 1. Washington, D.C.: National Runaway Switchboard.

Needham, R. 1977. Casework intervention with a homosexual adolescent. *Social Casework* 58(7): 387–394.

Nelson, K. E. 1994. Family-based services for families and children at risk of out-of-home placement. In R. Barth, J. D. Berrick, and N. Gilbert, eds., *Child Welfare Research Review*, vol. 1, pp. 83–108. New York: Columbia University Press.

Nelson, N. 1997. *When Gay and Lesbian People Adopt.* Seattle: Northwest Adoption Exchange.

Newman, B. S. 1989. Including curriculum content on lesbian and gay issues. *Journal of Social Work Education* 25(3): 202–211.

News State by State. 1999. News State by State: New Hampshire. *San Francisco Frontier*, January 14, p. 9.

Newton, D. E. 1978. Homosexual behavior and child molestation: A review of the evidence. *Adolescence* 13(49): 29–43.

O'Brien, C. A., R. Travers, and L. Bell. 1993. *No Safe Bed: Lesbian, Gay, and Bisexual Youth in Residential Services*. Toronto: Central Toronto Youth Services.

Olds, D. L. and C. R. Henderson Jr. 1989. The prevention of maltreatment. In D. Cicchetti and V. Carlson, eds., *Child Maltreatment*, pp. 722–763. Cambridge, UK: Cambridge University Press.

Owen, W. F. 1985. Medical problems of the homosexual adolescent. *Journal of Adolescent Health Care* 6(4): 278–285.

Parents and Friends of Lesbians and Gays, *see* PFLAG.

Paroski, P. H. 1987. Health care delivery and the concerns of gay and lesbian adolescents. *Journal of Adolescent Health Care* 8(2): 188–192.

Parr, R. G. and L. E. Jones. 1996. Point/counterpoint: Should CSWE allow social work programs in religious institutions an exemption from the accreditation nondiscrimination standard related to sexual orientation? *Journal of Social Work Education* 32(3): 297–313.

Patterson, C. J. 1992. Children of gay and lesbian parents. *Child Development* 63: 1025–1042.

Patterson, C. J. 1994. Lesbian and gay couples considering parenthood: An agenda for research, service, and advocacy. In L. A. Kurdek, ed., *Social Services for Gay and Lesbian Couples*, pp. 33–56. New York: Harrington Park Press.

Patterson, C. J. 1995. Lesbian mothers, gay fathers, and their children. In A. R. D'Augelli and C. J. Patterson, eds., *Lesbian, Gay, and Bisexual Identities Over the Lifespan: Psychological Perspectives*, pp. 262–290. New York: Oxford University Press.

Patterson, C. J. 1996. Lesbian mothers and their children: Findings from the Bay area families study. In J. Laird and R.-J. Green, eds., *Lesbians and Gays in Couples and Families: A Handbook for Therapists*, pp. 420–438. San Francisco: Jossey-Bass.

Pecora, P. J., J. K. Whittaker, A. N. Maluccio, and R. D. Plotnick. 1992. *The Child Welfare Challenge: Policy, Practice, and Research*. Hawthorne, N.Y.: Aldine de Gruyter.

Peguese, M. 1999. Personal correspondence, February 4.

Pelton, L. H. 1991. Beyond permanency planning: Restructuring the public child welfare system." *Social Work* 36: 337–344.

Pelton, L. H. 1994. The role of material factors in child abuse and neglect. In G. B. Melton and F. D. Barry, eds., *Protecting Children from Abuse and Neglect*, pp. 131–181. New York: Guildford Press.

Peplau, L. A. 1993. Lesbian and gay relationships. In L. D. Garnets and D. Kimmel, eds., *Psychological Perspectives on Lesbian and Gay Male Experiences*, pp. 395–419. New York: Columbia University Press.

Peplau, L. A. and H. Amaro. 1982. Understanding lesbian relationships. In W. Paul, J. D. Weinrich, J. C. Gonsiorek, and M. E. Hotvedt, eds., *Homosexuality: Social, Psychological, and Biological Issues*, pp. 233–248. Beverly Hills, Calif.: Sage.

Peterson, K. J., ed. 1996. Health care for lesbians and gay men: Confronting homophobia and heterosexism. *Journal of Gay and Lesbian Social Services* 5(1).

PFLAG (Parents and Friends of Lesbians and Gays). 1990. *Why Is My Child Gay?* Washington, D.C.: PFLAG.

PFLAG. 1997. *Beyond the Bible: Parents, Families, and Friends Talk About Religion and Homosexuality*. Washington, D.C.: PFLAG.

Pharr, S. 1988. *Homophobia: A Weapon of Sexism*. Little Rock: Chardon Press.

Phillips, S., C. McMillen, J. Sparks, and M. Ueberle. 1997. Concrete strategies for sensitizing youth-serving agencies to the needs of gay, lesbian, and other sexual minority youths. *Child Welfare* 76(3): 393—409.

Pierce, W. 1992. Adoption and other permanency considerations. *Children and Youth Services Review* 14(1/2): 61–66.

Pies, C. 1985. *Considering Parenthood: A Workbook for Lesbians*. San Francisco: Spinsters/Aunt Lute.

Pies, C. 1990. Lesbians and the choice to parent. In F. W. Bozett and M. B. Sussman, eds., *Homosexuality and Family Relations*, pp. 138–150. New York: Harrington Park Press.

Pilkington, N. W. and A. R. D'Augelli. 1995. Victimization of lesbian, gay, and bisexual youth in community settings. *Journal of Community Psychology* 23(1): 33–56.

Polikoff, N. 1986. Lesbian mothers, lesbian families: Legal obstacles, legal challenges. *Review of Law and Social Change* 14(4): 907–914.

Pollack, J. S. 1995. *Lesbian and Gay Families: Redefining Parenting in America*. New York: Franklin Watts.

Potter, S. J. and T. E. Darty. 1981. Social work and the invisible minority: An exploration of lesbianism. *Social Work* 26(3): 187–192.

Price, D. 1999. Gay students are learning to fight back. *New Orleans Times-Picayune*, January 19, p. B7.

Quam, J., ed. 1997. *Social Services for Older Gay Men and Lesbians.* New York: Haworth Press.

Rabin, J., K. Keefe, and M. Burton. 1986. Enhancing services for sexual minority clients: A community mental health approach. *Social Work* 31(4): 294–298.

Raymond, D. 1992. "In the best interest of the child": Thoughts on homophobia and parenting. In W. Blumenfeld, ed., *Homophobia: How We All Pay the Price*, pp. 113–130. Boston: Beacon Press.

Reid, J. 1973. *The Best Little Boy in the World.* New York: Ballantine Books.

Reiter, L. 1989. Sexual orientation, sexual identity, and the question of choice. *Clinical Social Work Journal* 17(2): 138—150.

Reiter, L. 1991. Developmental origins of antihomosexual prejudice in heterosexual men and women. *Clinical Social Work Journal* 19(2): 163–175.

Remafedi, G. 1987a. Adolescent homosexuality: Psychosocial and medical implications. *Pediatrics* 79: 331–337.

Remafedi, G. 1987b. Male homosexuality: The adolescent's perspective. *Pediatrics* 79: 326–330.

Renzetti, C. M. and C. H. Miley, eds. 1996. Violence in gay and lesbian domestic partnerships. *Journal of Gay and Lesbian Social Services* [Special Issue], 4(1).

Ricketts, W. 1991. *Lesbians and Gay Men as Foster Parents.* Portland: University of Southern Maine.

Ricketts, W. and R. A. Achtenberg. 1987. The adoptive and foster gay and lesbian parent. In F. W. Bozett, ed., *Gay and Lesbian Parents*, pp. 89–111. New York: Praeger Press.

Ricketts, W. and R. A. Achtenberg. 1990. Adoption and foster parenting for lesbians and gay men: Creating new traditions in family. *Marriage and Family Review* 14(3/4): 83–118.

Riley, C. 1988. American kinship: A lesbian account. *Feminist Issues* 8: 75–94.

Rivera, R. R. 1987. Legal issues in gay and lesbian parenting. In F. W. Bozett, ed., *Gay and Lesbian Parents*, pp. 199–230. Westport, Conn.: Praeger.

Rivers, I. 1997. Violence against lesbian and gay youth and its impact. In M. Schneider, ed., *Pride and Prejudice: Working with Gay, Lesbian, and Bisexual Youth*, pp. 31–48. Toronto: Central Toronto Youth Services.

Roberston, L. 1996. All clear over surrogate baby. *Glasgow Herald*, September 3, p. 1.

Robertson, M. J. 1989. *Homeless Youth in Hollywood: Patterns of Alcohol Abuse.* Washington, D.C.: National Institute on Alcoholism and Alcohol Abuse.

Robinson, B., L. H. Walters, and P. Steen. 1989. Response to parents learning that their child is homosexual and their concerns over AIDS: A national study. *Journal of Homosexuality* 18: 41–62.

Roe. 228 Va 722, 726–27, 324 S.E.2d 691, 693 (1985).

Rofes, E. R. 1983. *I Thought People Like That Killed Themselves*. San Francisco: Grey Fox Press.

Rose, S. J. and W. Meezan. 1996. Variations in perceptions of child neglect. *Child Welfare* 75(2): 139–160.

Rosenberg, T. 1998. Helping them make it through the night. *New York Times*, July 12, p. A23.

Rothberg, B. and D. L. Weinstein. 1996. A primer on lesbian and gay families. In M. Shernoff, ed., *Human Services for Gay People: Clinical and Community Practice*, pp. 55–68. New York: Harrington Park Press.

Rotheram-Borus, M. J., M. Rosario, and C. Koopman. 1991. Minority youths at high risk: Gay males and runaways. In M. E. Colten and S. Gore, eds., *Adolescent Stress: Causes and Consequences*, pp. 181–200. New York: Aldine De Gruyter.

Rothman, B. 1996. Lesbian motherhood—before it was fashionable. *In the Family: A Magazine for Lesbians, Gays, Bisexuals, and Their Relations* 2(1): 20.

Runaway and homeless youth: Frequently asked questions. (n.d.). *Runaway and homeless youth: Frequently asked questions*. [W W W document]. URL: http://www.acf.dhhs.gov/programs/fybs/faq. html.

Ryan, C. and D. Futterman. 1998. *Lesbian and Gay Youth: Care and Counseling*. New York: Columbia University Press.

Rycus, J. S. and R. C. Hughes. 1998. *Field Guide to Child Welfare*. Washington, D.C.: CWLA.

Saffron, L. 1997. *What About the Children? Sons and Daughters of Lesbian and Gay Parents Talk About Their Lives*. London: Cassell.

Sang, B. E. 1993. Existential issues of midlife lesbians. In L. D. Garnets and D. G. Kimmel, eds., *Psychological Perspectives on Lesbian and Gay Male Experiences*, pp. 500–516. New York: Columbia University Press.

Saperstein, S. 1981. Lesbian and gay adolescents: The need for family support. *Catalyst* 3/4(12): 61–69.

Savage, J. J. 1998. Family-centered services for children. In C. Crosson-Tower, ed., *Exploring Child Welfare: A Practice Perspective*, pp. 195–222. Boston: Allyn and Bacon.

Savin-Williams, R. C. 1989. Gay and lesbian adolescents. *Marriage and Family Review* 14(3/4); 197–216.

Savin-Williams, R. C. 1994. Verbal and physical abuse as stressors in the lives of lesbian, gay male, and bisexual youths: Associations with school problems, running away, substance abuse, prostitution, suicide. *Journal of Consulting and Clinical Practice* 62: 261–269.

Savin-Willliams, R. C. 1995. Lesbian, gay male, and bisexual adolescents. In A. R. D'Augelli and C. J. Patterson, eds., *Lesbian, Gay, and Bisexual Identities Over the Lifespan: Psychological Perspectives*, pp. 165–189. New York: Oxford University Press.

Savin-Williams, R. C. 1998. *And Then I Became Gay*. New York: Routledge.

Savin-Williams, R. C. and R. G. Rodriguez. 1993. A developmental clinical perspective on lesbian, gay male, and bisexual youth. In T. P. Gullotta, G. R. Adams, and R. Montemayor, eds., *Adolescent Sexuality*, Advances in Adolescent Development series, vol. 5, pp. 77–101. Newbury Park, Calif.: Sage.

Sbordone, A. J. 1993. Gay Men Choosing Fatherhood. Ph.D dissertation, City University of New York.

Schneider, M. 1988. *Often Invisible: Counselling Gay and Lesbian Youth*. Toronto: Toronto Central Youth Services.

Schneider, M. 1989. Sappho was a right-on adolescent. In G. Herdt, ed., *Gay and Lesbian Youth*, pp. 111–130. New York: Haworth Press.

Schneider, M. 1998. *Pride and Prejudice: Working with Lesbian, Gay, and Bisexual Youth*. Toronto: Central Toronto Youth Services.

Schneider, M. and B. Tremble. 1985. Gay or straight? Working with the confused adolescent. *Journal of Homosexuality* 4(1/2): 71–82.

Schoenberg, R., R. Goldberg, and D. Shore, eds. 1985. *With Compassion Towards Some: Homosexuality and Social Work in America*. New York: Harrington Park Press.

Scott, W. and M. Shernoff, eds. 1988. *The Sourcebook on Lesbian and Gay Health Care*. Washington, D.C.: National Lesbian/Gay Health Foundation.

Seattle Commission on Children and Youth. 1988. *Report on Gay and Lesbian Youth in Seattle*. Seattle: SCCY.

Sgroi, S. M. 1982. *The Handbook of Clinical Intervention in Child Sexual Abuse*. New York: Free Press.

Shernoff, M. 1984. Family therapy for lesbian and gay clients. *Social Work* 29(4): 393–396.

Shaffer, D. and C. Caton. 1984. *Runaway and Homeless Youth in New York City*. A Report to the Ittleson Foundation, New York City, Division of Child Psychiatry, New York State Psychiatric Institute and Columbia University College of Physicians and Surgeons.

Shernoff, M. 1991. Eight years of working with people with HIV: Impact upon a therapist. In C. Silverstein, ed., *Gays, Lesbians, and Their Therapists*, pp. 227–239). New York: Norton.

Shernoff, M. 1995. Male couples and their relationship styles. *Journal of Gay and Lesbian Social Services* 2(2): 43–57.

Shernoff, M. 1996a. The last journey. *Family Therapy Networker* 3: 35–41.

Shernoff, M., ed. 1996b. *Human Services for Gay People: Clinical and Community Practice*. New York: Haworth Press.

Shernoff, M. 1996c. Gay men choosing to be fathers. In M. Shernoff, ed., *Human Services for Gay People: Clinical and Community Practice*, pp. 41–54. New York: Harrington Park Press.

Siegel, L. (1994). Cultural difference and their impact on practice in child welfare. *Journal of Multicultural Social Work* 3(3): 87–96.

Simon. B. L. 1987. *Never Married Women*. Philadelphia: Temple University Press.

Simon, B. L. 1994. *The Empowerment Tradition in American Social Work: A History*. New York: Columbia University Press.

Simoni, J. M. 1996. Confronting heterosexism in the teaching of psychology. *Teaching of Psychology* 23(4): 220–226.

Slater, S. 1995. *The Lesbian Family Life Cycle*. New York: Free Press.

Smith, S. L. 1993. *Family Preservation Services: State Legislative Initiatives*. Washington, D.C.: National Conference of State Legislatures.

Smothers, R. 1997. Court lets two gay men jointly adopt child. *New York Times*, October 23, p. B5.

Smothers, R. 1997. Accord lets gay couples adopt jointly. *New York Times*, December 18, p. B4.

Smothers, R. 1998. Church blesses union of 2 men in adoption case. *New York Times*, June 22, p. B5.

Solot, D. 1998. *Guidelines for Adoption Workers: Writing Lesbian, Gay, Bisexual, and Transgender Homestudies for Special Needs Adoptions*. Springfield, Va.: Adoption Resource Exchange for Single Parents.

Sophie, J. 1985. A critical examination of stage theories of lesbian identity development. *Journal of Homosexuality*, 12(3/4): 39–51.

Steele, B. 1987. Psychodynamic factors in child abuse. In R. E. Helfer and R. S. Kempe, eds., *The Battered Child*. 4th ed. Chicago: University of Chicago Press.

Stehno, S. 1982. Differential treatment of minority children in service systems. *Social Work* 27: 39–45.

Stehno, S. 1990. The elusive continuum of child welfare services: Implications for minority children and youth. *Child Welfare* 69: 551–562.

Stein, T. J. 1984. The Child Abuse Prevention and Treatment Act. *Social Service Review* 58: 22–31.

Stein, T. J. 1991. *Child Welfare and the Law.* New York: Longman.

Stein, T. J. 1996. Child custody and visitation: The rights of lesbian and gay parents. *Social Service Review* (September) 70: 437–450.

Stein, T. J. 1998. *Child Welfare and the Law.* Rev. ed. Washington, D.C.: CWLA Press.

Steinhorn, A. 1979. Lesbian adolescents in residential treatment. *Social Casework: The Journal of Contemporary Social Work* 60: 494–498.

St. Pierre, T. 1999. *Gay and Lesbian Adoption: State of the Issue.* Washington, D.C.: Human Rights Campaign.

Straus, M., R. Gelles, and S. Steinmertz. 1980. *Behind Closed Doors: Violence in the American Family.* New York: Anchor.

Street outreach program. n.d. *Street outreach program.* [W W W document]. URL: http://www.acf.dhhs.gov/programs/fybs/faq. html.

Strommen, E. F. 1989. "You're a what?" Family member reactions to the disclosure of homosexuality. *Journal of Homosexuality* 18(1/2): 37–58.

Sue, D. W., P. Arrendondo, and R. J. McDavis. 1992. Multicultural counseling competencies and standards: A call to the profession. *Journal of Multicultural Counseling* 20: 64–88.

Sue, S. W. and D. Sue. 1990. *Counseling the Culturally Different: Theory and Practice.* 2nd ed. New York: Wiley.

Sullivan, A., ed. 1995. *Issues in Gay and Lesbian Adoption: Proceedings of the Fourth Annual Pierce-Warwick Adoption Symposium.* Washington, D.C.: CWLA Press.

Sullivan, G., ed. 1995. Gays and lesbians in Asia and the Pacific: Social and human services. *Journal of Gay and lesbian Social Services* [Special Issue] 2(2).

Sullivan, T. 1994. Obstacles to effective child welfare service with gay and lesbian youths. *Child Welfare* 73(4): 291–304.

Sullivan, T. and M. Schneider. 1987. Development and identity issues in adolescent homosexuality. *Child and Adolescent Social Work* 4(1): 13–24.

Sutter, K. 1995. *Daily Effects of Heterosexual Privilege.* Tulsa: National Resource Center for Youth Services.

Switzer, D. K. 1996. *Coming Out as Parents.* Louisville: Westminster John Knox Press.

Szymanski, K. 1997. New Jersey couples win adoption rights. *New York Blade,* December 19, p. A1.

Tafoya, T. 1992. Native gay and lesbian issues: The two-spirited. In B. Berzon, ed., *Positively Gay,* pp. 253–262. Berkeley, Calif.: Celestial Arts.

Tammy, 416 Mass. 205, 619 N.E. 2d 315 (1993).

Tanner, A. 1996. Minister says foster children belong with "natural" families. *Edmonton Journal*, August 16, p. 2.

Tasker, F. L. and S. Golombok. 1997. *Growing Up in a Lesbian Family: Effects on Child Development*. New York: Guilford Press.

Taylor, N. 1994. Gay and lesbian youth: Challenging the policy of denial. In T. De Crescenzo, ed., *Helping Gay and Lesbian Youth: New Policies, New Programs, New Practices*, pp. 39–73. New York: Haworth Press.

Thompson, R. A. 1995. *Preventing Child Maltreatment Through Social Support: A Critical Analysis*. Thousand Oaks, Calif.: Sage.

Tievsky, D. L. 1988. Homosexual clients and homophobic social workers. *Journal of Independent Social Work* 2(3): 51–62.

Tracy, E. M. 1991. Defining the target population for family preservation services: Some conceptual issues. In K. Wells and D. Biegal, eds., *Family Preservation Services: Research and Evaluation*, pp. 138–158. Newbury Park, Calif.: Sage.

Tracy, E. M., D. A. Haapala, J. Kinney, and P. Pecora. 1991. Intensive family preservation services: A strategic response to families in crisis. In E. M. Tracy, D. A. Haapala, J. Kinney, and P. Pecora, eds., *Intensive Family Preservation Services: An Instructional Sourcebook*, pp. 1–14. Cleveland: Mandel School of Applied Social Sciences.

Transitional living program for homeless youth. n.d. *Transitional Living Program for Homeless Youth*. [W W W document]. URL: http:// www.acf.dhhs.gov/programs/fybs/faq. html.

Troiden, R. R. 1979. Becoming homosexual: A model of gay identity acquisition. *Psychiatry* 42: 362–373.

Troiden, R. R. 1988. *Gay and Lesbian Identity: A Sociological Analysis*. Dix Hills.

Troiden, R. R. 1989. The formation of homosexual identities. In G. Herdt, ed., *Gay and Lesbian Youth*, pp. 43–74. New York: Harrington Park Press.

Tuerk, C. 1995. A son with gentle ways: A therapist-mother's journey. *In The Family: A Magazine for Lesbians, Gays, Bisexuals, and Their Relations* (October) 1(1): 18–22.

Tully, C., ed. 1996. *Lesbian Social Services: Research Issues*. New York: Harrington Park Press.

Tully, C. and J. C. Albro. 1979. Homosexuality: A social worker's imbroglio. *Journal of Sociology and Social Welfare* 6(2): 154–167.

U.S. Dept. of Health and Human Services. 1998. The street outreach forum: Youth Development in action. *FYSB update*, May, pp. 5–9.

Valenzuela, W. 1996. A school where I can be myself. In P. Kay, A. Estepa, and A. Desetta, eds., *Out with It: Gay and Straight Teens Write About Homosexuality*, pp. 45–46. New York: Youth Communications.

Van Voorhis, R. and L. McClain. 1997. Accepting a lesbian mother. *Families in Society: Journal of Contemporary Human Services*, pp. 642–650.

Verhovek, S. H. 1997. Homosexual foster parent sets off a debate in Texas. *New York Times*, November 30, p. A20.

Victim Services/Traveler's Aid. 1991. *Streetwork Project Study*. New York: Victim Services.

Videka-Sherman, L. 1991. Child abuse and neglect. In A. Gitterman, ed., *Handbook of Social Work Practice with Vulnerable Populations*. New York: Columbia University Press.

Wadley, C. 1996a. Kicked out because she was a lesbian. In P. Kay, A. Estepa, and A. Desetta, eds., *Out with It: Gay and Straight Teens Write About Homosexuality*, pp. 58–60. New York: Youth Communications.

Wadley, C. 1996b. Shunned, insulted, threatened. In P. Kay, A. Estepa, and A. Desetta, eds., *Out with It: Gay and Straight Teens Write About Homosexuality*, pp. 57–60. New York: Youth Communications.

Walters, K. L. 1998. Negotiating conflicts in allegiances among lesbian and gays of color: Reconciling divided selves and communities. In G. P. Mallon, ed., *Foundations of Social Work Practice with Lesbian and Gay Persons*, pp. 47–76. New York: Haworth Press.

Webber, M. 1991. *Street Kids: The Tragedy of Canada's Runaways*. Toronto: University of Toronto Press.

Weissbourd, B. and S. L. Kagan. 1989. Family support programs: Catalysts for change. *American Journal of Orthopsychiatry* 59(1): 20–30.

Weithorn, L. A. and S. B. Campbell. 1982. The competency of children and adolescents to make informed decisions. *Child Development* 53: 1579–1589.

Wells, K. and D. A. Biegal, eds. 1991. *Family Preservation Services: Research and Evaluation*. Newbury Park, Calif.: Sage.

West, C. 1994. *Race Matters*. New York: Vintage.

Weston, K. 1991. *Families We Choose: Gay and Lesbian Kinship*. New York: Columbia University Press.

Whittaker, J. K. 1991. Understanding intensive family preservation services in the context of the total service continuum. In E. M. Tracy, D. A. Haapala, J. Kinney, and P. Pecora, eds., *Intensive Family Preservation Services: An Instructional Sourcebook*, pp. 143–156. Cleveland: Mandel School of Applied Social Sciences.

Whittaker, J. K., J. M. Kinney, E. Tracy, and C. Booth, eds. 1990. *Reaching High Risk Families: Intensive Family Preservation Services*. Hawthorne, N.Y.: Aldine de Gruyter.

Wicks, L. K. 1978. Transsexualism: A social work approach. *Health and Social Work* 2(1): 179–193.

Wilder v. Sugarman, 385 F. Supp. 1013 (S.D.N.Y. 1974) sub nom *Wilder v. Bernstein*, 499 F. Supp. 980 (S.D.N.Y. 1980).

Williams, M. 1997. Texas state employee challenges lesbian foster parents. *Athens Daily News*, December 24, p. 1.

Williams, W. 1986. *The Spirit and the Flesh: Sexual Diversity in American Indian Culture*. Boston: Beacon Press.

Williams, W. 1993. Persistence and change in the Berdache tradition among contemporary Lakota Indians. In L. D. Garnets and D. G. Kimmel, eds., *Psychological Perspectives on Lesbian and Gay Male Experiences*, pp. 339–347. New York: Columbia University Press.

Wisniewski, J. J. and B. G. Toomey. 1987. Are social workers homophobic? *Social Work* 32(5): 454–455.

Wolin, S. J. and S. Wolin. 1993. *The Resilient Self: How Survivors of Troubled Families Rise Above Adversity*. New York: Villard Books.

Woodman, N. J., C. T. Tully, and C. C. Barranti. 1996. Research in lesbian communities: Ethical dilemmas. In C. Tully, ed., *Lesbian Social Services: Research Issues*, pp. 57–66. New York: Haworth Press.

Woodman, N. J., ed. 1992. *Lesbian and Gay Lifestyles: A Guide for Counseling and Education*. New York: Irvington.

Wyers, N. 1987. Homosexuality in the family: Lesbian and gay spouses. *Social Work* 32(2): 143–149.

Zide, M. R. and A. L. Cherry. 1992. A typology of runaway youths: An empirically based definition. *Child and Adolescent Social Work* 9(2): 155–168.

Index

Able-Peterson, T., 66, 129, 131, 138

Abuse, 4, 26, 47, 57, 58, 59, 60, 61, 62, 82, 131, 148; emotional, 67 68–70, 128; physical, 61, 66–68, 128; sexual, 61, 67 70–71, 128; see also Neglect; Violence

Achtenberg, R., x, 23, 84, 100, 122, 149

ACLU (American Civil Liberties Union), 82, 87, 93

Adelman, H. S., 90

Administration for Children's Services (ACS), 127

Adoption and foster parenting: custody and visitation, 80–83, 93; financial incentives, 103; gay and lesbian parents, 80, 83, 85, 87, 93–108; gay men and, 98, 100; inclusiveness, 102–4; legal issues, 83–87; organizational bias against, 101–2, 104; policy development with gays and lesbians, 104–8; second-parent adoption, 80, 85, 86–87, 88, 91; shortage of parents and, 85; see also Foster care

Adoption and Safe Families Act of 1997 (ASFA), 9, 84, 94, 102, 103, 108

Adoption Assistance and Child Welfare Act of 1980 (AACWA), 9, 57

Adoption Resource Exchange for Single Parents, 105, 106

Advocacy, 25, 59, 149

Agency-operated boarding homes (AOBHs), 149

Ahn, H. N., 57, 76

AIDS, see HIV/AIDS

Allport, G., 19, 20

Alternative insemination, 87, 90, 100

Alyson, S., 53

American Civil Liberties Union (ACLU), 82, 87 93

Anastas, J., 22, 50

AOBHs (Agency-operated boarding homes), 149

Appleby, G., 22, 50

Archambault, F. X., 66, 128

ASFA, see Adoption and Safe Families Act

Assessment, 8, 30–31, 56, 147

"Baby M," 88

Baker, J. M., 43, 53, 65, 66

Baker, P. 102

Barthel, J., 37

Bawer, B., 36

Bell, L., 16, 80, 109, 128

Benkov, L., 23, 94, 101

Berger, R. M., 2, 16, 19, 22, 23
Berkman, C. S., 17, 22
Bernfeld, R., 88, 100
Bernstein, B. E., 23
Bernstein, N., 85, 89
Bias, 15, 50, 66, 80, 95, 143; cultural, 13; gender, 68; heterocentric, 21; organizational, 101–2, 104
Bibliotherapy, 53
Bigner, J., 23, 94
Billingsley, A., 13
Birnbaum, H. J., 83, 96
Bisexuals and bisexuality, 2, 87
Blade, The, 129
Bledsoe case, 96
"Board proposes banning gays from foster care" (IMPACT), 95
Boerner, H., 85, 89
Booth, C., 50, 55
Borhek, M. V., 53, 148
Bottoms, Sharon, 81
Brown, S. M., 37, 50, 66, 77, 128
Bucy, J., 66, 129, 138
Burnout, 32
Bush, George W. (governor), 84

Cain, R., 2, 18
Campbell, S. B., 90
Cantwell, 65
Cardarelli, A. P., 71
CAS (Children's Aid Society), 80, 125
CASMT (Children's Aid Society of Metropolitan Toronto), 15
Cass, V. C., 22, 40
Cates, J. A., 23, 134
Caton, C., 129, 136
Chafetz, J. S., 22, 98
Chan, C., 22, 23, 42
Cherry, A. L., 66, 129
Chestang, L., 26

Child Abuse and Neglect Act of 1974, 60
Child care workers, see Child welfare practitioners
Child maltreatment, 61, 63, 71, 76; see also Abuse; Neglect; Violence
Children of Lesbian and Gay Parents Everywhere (COLAGE), 54
Children's Aid Society (CAS), 80, 125
Child Welfare Administration (CWA), 16
Child Welfare Administration of New York City/Council of Family and Child Caring Agencies, 125
Child Welfare League of America, see CWLA
Child welfare system, see Child welfare practice and services
Child welfare practice and services: best interest of the child, 57, 60, 81, 82, 85, 93, 96, 97; competent practice with gays and lesbians, 13–14, 16, 18–21, 23–27, 33–34, 77, 126, 145, 147–51; creating safe environments, 119–23; crisis, 37, 50, 52; "hard-to-place children," 85; legal issues, 79, 91; minors' rights to participate in, 90-91; policy development for gay and lesbian adoption and foster parenting, 104–8; professional development, 14, 19; safety and protection issue, 57, 59, 60–61, 63, 66–72, 74–77, 91, 103; specialized, 123–26; and street kids, 137–39; see also Family
Child welfare practitioners, 16, 17, 68, 110, 143; risk assessment, 74–77; professional development, 14, 19; training of, 77, 95, 121, 122, 123, 124, 144; see also Social workers

Child Welfare Review Board (Arkansas), 2, 84

Chipungu, S. ., 13

Civil rights, of gays and lesbians, 13, 79, 80, 144

Class action lawsuits, 85, 146

Classism, 25

Cognitive strategies, 55

Cohen, N. A., 10, 58

Coleman, E., 22, 40, 134

Coming out, 40–41; abusive response to, 47; acceptance, 41, 43; child or adolescence and, 44, 46, 65; parent or spouse and, 47, 49; religious factors, 41–42; *see also* Disclosure

Communication skills, 55

Communities, 24, 55, 56, empowerment, 25

Competence, 23–27; cultural, 15, 21, 147; defined, 20; gay and lesbian practice with, 20, 33-34, 77; model of practice, 15; *see also* Child welfare practice and services; Gay and Lesbian Affirming Competence Model of Practice

Comstock, G. D., 119

Constant, A. v. Paul C. A., 82

Council on Social Work Education (CSWE), 16, 18; accreditation standards, 16

Counseling, 38, 39, 47; *see also* Therapy

"Courtesy stigma," 52

Crosson-Tower, C., 10, 57, 61, 70

Cross-orientation interaction, 20, 31

Crossroads Market, 54

CSWE, *see* Council on Social Work Education

"Cultural guides," 29

Culture, 28, 31

Custody and visitation, 80–83, 93; moral issues, 82, 83; "nexus approach," 82; state, 89

CWA (Child Welfare Administration), 16

CWLA (Child Welfare League of America), 15, 16, 125; adoption standards of, 97; Standards of Excellence for Family Foster Care, 97

Daro, D., 57, 58

Darty, T. E., 23

D'Augelli, A. R., 11, 65, 69

De Crescenzo, T., x, 1, 11, 17, 22, 23

De Monteflores, C., 40

Desetta, A., 53

de Vine, J. L., 23

Dew, R. F., 53, 148

Diagnostic and Statistical Manual of Mental Disorders (DSM), 10, 17

Different, perception of, 5, 57, 63

Different Light, A, 54

Diller, J. V., 15, 19, 20, 32

Direct instruction, 53–54

Disclosure, 35, 36, 40, 43–44, 47, 49, 62; cultural factors, 42; emotional factors and, 42–43; parental reactions to, 66, 69–70, 109, 129; *see also* Coming out

Discrimination, 1, 2, 25, 31, 146; institutional, 1, 59, 121; sexual orientation, 16

Diversity, 16, 26; cultural, 21; sexual, 18, 29, 125

Donor insemination, 88

Drop-in centers, 139

DSM (*Diagnostic and Statistical Manual of Mental Disorders*), 10, 17

Due, L., 53
Due Process clause, 89
Dulaney, D. D., 19, 22, 23
Dunlap, D. W., 82, 96

Edna McConnell Clark Foundation, 37
Education, 16, 17, 18, 19, 28, 56, 148; sexual orientation content in curriculum, 16, 17, 18, 67-68; *see also* Child welfare practitioners, training of; Social workers, training of
Elovitz, M. E., 82, 96
Engler, R. E., 103, 116, 118
Environments: developing safety in, 119–23; hostile, 27, 127, 131
Equality, 28, 29, 32, 91

Fairchild, B., 53, 148
Family: adaptations, 64; biological, 57; "created," 36, 101; ecological approach to, 36; family-centered services, 37, 50; functioning, 26; homosexuality as threat to, 36; preservation services, 37, 49, 50—56, 61, 148; reunification, 27, 122, 140, 148; siblings, 68; stability, threats to, 37; street kids, 133; structure, 26; support services, 37, 49, 56; systems, 15, 36, 39, 56, 148; values, 93; *see also* Intervention
Family and Youth Services Bureau, 140
Family foster homes, 111–12, 122
Family Tree, 105
Fanshel, D., 103, 116
Faria, G., x, 21, 56
Faubourg Marigny Book Store, 54
Fein, E., 10, 103

Festinger, T., 103
Focal Point, 15
Forrester, E. G., 23, 125
Foster care: by gays or lesbians, 2, 84, 85, 93–108, 149; legal issues, 84–87, 89; abuse in, 4, 80, 89, 118; *see also* Adoption and foster parenting
Fourteenth Amendment, 89–90, 91
Fraser, M., 10, 49
Freiberg, P., 84, 94
Freud, A., 88
Freud, S., 21
Futterman, D., 23, 64, 90

Galluccio, Michael, 87
Garbarino, J., 57, 58
Gay and Lesbian Adolescent Services (GLASS), 80, 102
Gay and Lesbian Affirming Competence Model of Practice, 8, 15, 19, 20–27, 33–34, 144, 150; basic knowledge, 20, 21–27; illuminated awareness, 20, 27–29; professional amalgamation, 20, 30–31
Gays and lesbians: adaptations by families, 64, 69; adoption and foster parenting, 80, 93, 94, 96, 97, 98, 100, 101–2, 107; children and adolescent placements, 86; civil rights, 13, 79, 80, 144; consent issues for minors, 90; coping strategies, 26, 50; equal treatment, 79; family laws and, 80, 93; hostility toward, 2; identity, 26, 35, 65, 113; identity, hiding of, 113, 115; isolation of, 53, 116; parenting, 80, 94–96, 98, 100, 105; perceptions of, 25, 63, 65; protective services, 77; siblings of, 68; *see also* Sexual orientation
Gender Identity Disorder, 3, 4, 5, 8

Gender neutral language, 120
Gender-nonconforming behavior, 57, 115
Gender roles, 2, 101
Germain, C. B., 16, 56, 148
Getzel, G. S., 23
Gilgun, J. F., 71
Giovanni's Room, 54
Giovannoni, J. M., 13
Gitterman, A., 16, 56, 148
Glad Day Bookshop, 54
GLASS (Gay and Lesbian Adolescent Services), 80, 102
Gochros, H., 16, 17, 18, 22, 23, 54
Goffman, E., 52
Goldberg, R., 18, 22
Golden, R., 10, 58
Goldstein, J. A., 58, 81, 85, 88
Golombok, S., 96
Gomes-Schwartz, B., 71
Gramick, J., 1, 17, 22
Green, A. A., 84, 94
Green, J. W., 29
Green, R. J., 23
Green Chimneys Children's Services, 80, 115
Griffin, C., 53, 148
Groninger, T., 84, 101
Groth, A. N., 83, 94, 96
Group homes, 110–11, 122, 149
Guardian, testamentary, 88
Guggenheim, M., 79
Gustavsson, N. S., 10, 58

Haapala, D., 10, 49, 50, 55
Hall, M., 23, 98
Harassment, verbal, 118–19, 130
Hare, J., 26
Hartman, A., 10, 17, 23, 35, 37, 50, 60, 93, 94, 100

Harvard Law Review, The, 83
Hayward, N., 53, 148
Henderson, C. R., 23, 58
Herek, G. M., 83, 96, 119
Heron, A., 53
Hershberger, S. L., 11, 65, 69
Heterocentrism, 2, 3, 25, 28, 31, 76, 79, 81, 143, 146, 149; defined, 1
Heterosexism, 17, 18
Heterosexual privilege, 1, 3, 25
Heterosexuals and heterosexuality, 2, 28, 87
Hetrick, E., 11, 23, 40
Hidalgo, H., 16, 22
Hiding, see Gays and lesbians, identity
HIV/AIDS, 105, 134, 136
Holden-Galluccio, Jon, 87
Holdway, D. M., 131
Homebuilders model, 56, 148
Homeless youth, 66, 127, 149; adaptation to life on the streets, 133–37; defined, 130; health issues, 128, 135–37; safety issues, 130–33; services for, 137–41, 149, 150; substance abuse, 135; survival sex, 134–35; typology of, 129–30; see also Runaways
Homophobia, 1, 17, 21, 149
Homosexuality, 2, 8, 10, 28 , 36, 52, 67, 82, 113, 121; see also Gays and lesbians
Hudson, W., 1
Huggins, J., 23, 125
Hughes, R. C., 58, 71, 74
Human Sexuality and Social Work (1972), 18
Humphreys, G. E., 16, 17
Hunter, J., 2, 11, 23, 42, 66, 81, 116, 134
Hutchison, E., 57, 61

Iasenza, S., 95
Icard, L., 22, 23
Identity, *see* Gays and lesbians
In Matter of Adoption of Evan, 86
In Matter of Jacob, 86
Integration, 123
Internet, resources for gays and
    lesbians, 53, 54, 55, 100, 102
Intervention, 8, 27, 30, 31, 32, 40, 44,
    50, 55, 56, 68, 147; risk assessment,
    70, 71–72, 74
Isolation, 53

Jacobsen, E. E., 23
Jacobson v. Jacobson, 82
Janus, M. D., 66, 128
Jenny, C. T., 83, 96
J.L.P.[H.] v. D.J.P., 82
Joel A. v.Guiliani, 85, 89, 91
Jones, L. E., 18, 98
*Joseph A. v. New Mexico Department
    of Social Services*, 85

Kaplan, L., 10, 49
Kelly, J. J., 19, 22, 23
Kessler, B., 84, 94
Kids' Talk 1998, 105
Kinney, J., 50, 51, 53, 55, 56, 148
Kournay, R. F., 136
Kruks, G., 66, 134
Kurdek, L. A., 23
Kus, R. J., 23

Laird, J., x, 10, 23, 26, 35, 37, 50, 56, 61,
    93, 94, 98, 147
Lambda, 82, 87, 88
Lambda Legal Defense and
    Education Fund, 82
Lambda Rising, 54
Lands, H., 18

*Lesbian and Gay Issues: A Resource
    Manual for Social Workers* (1985), 18
Lesbian and Gay Parenting Handbook,
    99
Lesbian and Gay Rights Project, 87
Lesbians, *see* Gays and lesbians;
    Homosexuality
Levy, E. F., 23, 26, 98
Lewis, K. G., 23, 98
Lewis, L. A., 22, 98
Life-course development theory,
    21–22
Lindsey, D., 10, 17
Lloyd, G. A., 23
Loewenstein, S. F., 23, 98
Lorde, A., 143
Lott, Senator Trent, 2
Lukes, C.A., 18
Luna, G. C., 66, 134

Maas, H. S., 103, 116, 118
MacEachron, A. E., 23, 31
MacPike, L., 54
Macro issues, 31
Mainstreaming, 123
Mallon, G. P., 2, 8, 11, 13, 14, 16, 17, 19,
    21, 22, 23, 25, 26, 36, 50, 57, 65, 66,
    71, 77, 80, 85, 89, 95, 97, 109, 113,
    118, 122, 123, 124, 126, 128, 130, 131,
    132, 149, 150
Maluccio, A. N., 10, 103
Malyon, A. K., 11, 40
MAPP (Model Approaches to
    Partnership in Parenting), 99, 102
Marisol v. Guiliani, 85
Markowitz, L., 23
Martin, A., 23, 88, 94, 99
Martin, A.D., 11, 23, 40, 113
"Massachusetts Adoption of Tammy,"
    86

Mattison, A. M., 23
McCandlish, B. M., 23
McGowan, B. G., 10, 25
McIntosh, P., 25
McPhatter, A. R., 20, 23, 32
McPherson, D., 98
McWhirter, D. P., 23
Media, 95, 143
Meezan, W., 37, 57, 61
Melton, G. B., 57, 58
Mental health, 69; see also Abuse,
    emotional; Neglect, emotional and
    psychological
Meyer, C., 17
Minority children, differential treat-
    ment of, 13
Model Approaches to Partnership in
    Parenting (MAPP), 99, 102
Modeling, 54–55
Molestation, 82, 83, 94, 96
Monette, P., 53
Money, 87
Morrow, D. F., 11, 23
Morton, D. R., 23
Moser, C., 23
Moses, A. E., 22
Muzio, C., 94, 98
Myths, 2, 28, 29, 46, 52, 53, 66; gay
    and lesbian parenting and, 93,
    94-96

NACAC (North American Council
    on Adoptable Children), 97
NAIC (National Adoption Informa-
    tion Clearinghouse), 105
NASW (National Association of
    Social Workers), 16
National Adoption Information
    Clearinghouse (NAIC), 105
National Association of Social

Workers (NASW), statement on
    Gay Issues, 16
National Network for Youth, 127
Needham, R., 11, 23
Neglect, 26, 57, 58, 59, 60, 61, 62, 148;
    emotional and psychological, 61,
    65, 131; see also Abuse; Violence
Neighborhoods, 24
Newman, B. S., 16, 17
Newton, D. E., 83, 94, 96
North American Council on Adopt-
    able Children (NACAC), 97
Northwest Adoption Exchange, 105

O'Brien, C. A., 16, 80, 109, 128
Olmstead, K. A., 10, 103
Oppression, 25, 42, 121
Orme, J. G., 52
Our World Too, 54
Out-of-home care, 14, 57, 109, 149;
    creating safe environments in,
    119–23; gay and lesbian adoles-
    cents in, 112–19; harassment and
    violence in, 118—19; multiple
    placements, 116, 117; see also
    Group homes; Family foster
    homes
Owen, W., 136

Parents and Friends of Lesbians and
    Gays (PFLAG), 42, 53, 148
Parents and parenting: biological, 80,
    81, 86; foster and adoptive parents,
    shortage of, 85; legal, 87; nongay,
    81, 86; "psychological parent"
    theory, 88; termination of rights,
    80, 81, 83; see also Adoption and
    foster parenting
Paroski, P.H., 136
Parr, R. G., 18

Patterson, C. J., 23, 82, 93, 96, 98

Pecora, P., 10, 49, 147

Pedophilia, 96

Peer outreach, 139

Peguese, M., 82

Pelton, L. H., 57, 61, 103

Permanency planning, 14, 112

Person:environment, 16

Person In Need Of Supervision
  (PINS), 60

Peterson, K. J., 16, 22, 23

PFLAG (Parents and Friends of
  Lesbians and Gays), 42, 53, 148

Pharr, S., 2, 22, 145

Pies, C., 94, 97, 98

Pilkington, N. W., 69

PINS (Person In Need Of Supervision), 60

P.L. 96-272, 57

P.L. 105-89, 94

Polikoff, N., 2, 81

Post Traumatic Stress Disorder
  (PTSD), 4, 5

Poverty, 61

Power hierarchies, 2

Poyer, K. L, 83, 96

Problem solving, 55–56

Procreation, 87—89, 91

Professional amalgamation, 19, 31–32;
  training, 50, 56, 77; see also Child
  welfare practitioners; Social
  workers

Prostitution, 134

Psychology, 18

PTSD (Post Traumatic Stress Disorder), 4, 5

Quigley-Rick, M., 90

Racism, 13, 20, 25, 42

Raymond, D., 2, 41, 81, 85

Reiter, L., 1, 22, 68

Remafedi, G., 11, 24, 129, 136

Residential Treatment Center (RTC),
  3

Resources, 24, 53, 55, 105; on the
  internet, 53, 54, 55, 100, 102

Ricketts, W. A., x, 1, 2, 23, 84, 100, 122,
  149

Rivers, I., 24, 66, 70, 141

Roe v. Roe, 82

Roesler, T. A., 83, 96

Rofes, E. R., 136

Rose, S. J., 57, 61

Rotheram-Borus, M. J., 135

RTC (Residential Treatment Center),
  3

Runaways, 66, 127; adaptation to
  life on the streets, 133-37; defined,
  129; health issues, 127–28, 135–37;
  safety issues, 130–33; services for,
  137–41; substance abuse, 135;
  survival sex, 134–35; typology
  of, 129–30; see also Homeless
  youth

Ryan, C., 23, 64, 90

Rycus, J. S., 58, 71, 74

Savin-Williams, R. C., 11, 23, 42, 53, 66

Sbordone, A. J., 98

Schaecher, R., 11, 23, 42, 116, 134

Schneider, M., 11, 23

Schoenberg, R., 18, 22

Schultz, S. J., 18, 40

Seattle Commission 1988, 118, 127

Segal, E.A., 10, 58

Segregation, 123

Self-awareness, 85

Self-worth, 69

Sex trade industry, 134

Sexual: behavior, 7; identity, 8; intercourse, 87

Sexual orientation, 2, 7, 8, 9, 15-16, 22, 24, 29, 32, 62, 69, 120; and child welfare professionals, 14-16, 18-19, 20, 22, 24, 29; counseling for, 38, 39, 47; family-centered services, 37, 40, 49, 50-56; in residential treatment centers, 3; discrimination, 16; legal issues, 79-90, 93, 150; *see also* Gays and lesbians

Shelters, 140

Sheppard, Matthew, 2

Shernoff, M., 23, 95, 98

Shinn, E., 103, 116

Shore, D., 18, 22

Siegel, L., 13, 15

SILPs (Supervised Independent Living Programs), 149

Simon, B. L., 22, 25

Simoni, J. M., 18

Slater, S., 23

Smothers, R., 87, 93

Social control, 2

Socialization, 28

Social networks, 36

Social workers, training of, 16-17, 18, 50, 56; *see also* Child welfare practitioners; Professional amalgamation

Sodomy statutes, 82, 83, 96

Solot, D., 105, 106

Steele, B., 61, 62, 63

Stein, T. J., x, 10, 13, 60, 79, 85, 89

Steinhorn, A., x, 13

Stereotypes, 2, 4, 28, 52, 53, 66, 91, 93, 115, 151

Stewart B. McKinney Act, 129

Stigma, 3, 24, 36, 42, 52, 64, 82, 96, 122, 143; "courtesy," 52

Straight Spouses Network, 54

Street kids, 130; *see also* Homeless youth; Runaways

Streetwork Project, 129

Strommen, E. F., 23, 53, 148

Substance abuse, 135

Suicide, 24, 136

Sullivan, A., 25, 84, 104, 105

Sullivan, T., x, 11, 80, 151

Supervised Independent Living Programs (SILPs), 149

Surrogacy, 87, 88–89, 90, 100

Sutter, K., 25

Switzer, D. K., 53

System kids, 130

Szymanski, K., 87, 93

Tasker, F. L., 96

Therapy, 47, 148; *see also* Counseling

Thompson, R. A., 57, 61

Tibbits-Kleber, H., 81

Toomey, B. G., 17, 22

Tracy, E. M., 49, 50

Training, *see* Professionals; Child welfare practitioners, training of; Education; Social workers, training of

Transitional Living Programs (TLPs), 140

Transsexuality, 121

Transvestism, 121

Travers, R., 16, 80, 109, 128

Tremble, B., 11

Troiden, R. R., 22, 40

Trust, 30, 32, 52

Tuerk, C., 53

Tully, C., 22, 23, 98

United States Supreme Court, 89

Value clarification, 55

Verhovek, S. H., 82, 96

Victim Services/Traveler's Aid, 118, 129

Violence, 24, 26, 51, 57, 59, 66, 118-19, 130, 148; *see also* Abuse; Neglect

Visitation, *see* Custody and visitation

Walters, K. L., 42

Weil, M., 37, 50, 77

West, J., 20, 98

Weston, K., 36

Whitehead, Mary Beth, 88

White skin privilege, 25

Whittaker, J. K., 37

Wicks, L. K., 22

Wilder v. Sugarman, 85

Williams, M., 82, 96

Williams, W., 22

Wirth, A. G., 53, 148

Wirth, M. J., 148

Wisniewski, J. J., 17, 22

With Compassion Towards Some: Homosexuality and Social Work in America (1985), 18

Woodman, N. J., 16, 22, 23

World Wide Web sites, 53–54, 100, 102; *see also* Internet

Zide, M. R., 66, 129

Zinberg, G., 17, 22